The Gardener
and the Machine

The Gardener and the Machine

Designing Systems that Thrive on Disruption

Arturo Villanueva

PHRONOS

ISBN: 979-8-9946116-0-9 (hardcover)
ISBN: 979-8-9946116-1-6 (paperback)
ISBN: 979-8-9946116-2-3 (e-book)
First edition

Published by Phronos
San Diego, California

Printed in the United States of America

For Mary, Zachary, Mom, Dad, and Vernon

For Kiwi, Linus, Luna, Taz, and Fluffy

"The major problems in the world
are the result of the difference
between how nature works
— and the way people think."

— Gregory Bateson

Foreword by Steven Simske, PhD

Much as the modern city of Rome is built atop and even amidst the ruins of ancient Rome, today's most advanced analytical tools, from massive data warehouses to AI-powered data centers, are built atop and amidst the many generations of analytics that preceded them. Or, perhaps, the better analogy is to the cisterns under the modern city of Jerusalem.

While the 3,000-year-old Temple Mount cistern and the 1,500-year-old Byzantine cistern (now under a playground) are no longer functional, the Saint Helena's Cistern beneath the Church of the Holy Sepulcher is still collecting rainwater to this day. In other words, the infrastructure of the past exists alongside all of the infrastructure of the present, and some of it is still used while other elements of it are ignored or more problematically in the way of better, more modern infrastructure.

Regardless, such is the reality of the world in any area of infrastructure, from water storage to advanced machine intelligence. The past and the present must work together because it is simply impossible to keep replacing the entirety of the existing infrastructure every time a technological advance is made.

This hybrid world of past and present is a world in which unexpected outputs can arise. And unexpected outputs include unexpected insights (emergence) and unexpected robustness (resilience). In *The Gardener and the Machine*, Art considers a wide range of algorithmic approaches to creating improved outputs that involve disparate types of systems working together in surprising ways.

From the successful functioning of ant colonies (where every member knows how to focus on successful completion of its next best task to perform, making the whole decidedly more complex than any of its parts) to the "stigmergy" of termites, which are performing the insect equivalent of crowdsourcing, Art carefully considers how increased complexity, intelligence, accuracy, resilience, and breadth can be created in larger systems even when each system component is relatively simple in its design, action, and functional output.

Art's work shows how AI can provide emergent results and he considers both the positives and negatives of this: the positives including unexpected solutions to "unsolvable" problems and the negatives including not being able to fully explain the way in which the solution works. Art applies his design and evaluation "gardening" to topics such as urban planning and infrastructure design deftly incorporating topics as diverse and advanced as feedback, subtraction (ablation in neural network terms), and the differential cultivation of different approaches and outputs, rightly termed gardening.

Gardening, after all, is all about predicting which seeds will result in crops of value, and which seeds will breed weeds. It is also about understanding how all these systems work together: weeds, for example, may hold soil in place early in the growing season while the winds whip past ungerminated cash crops. In other words, the choice of analytics — from sensing to statistical analysis to machine intelligence to generative AI — is as much about timing as it is about algorithm choice.

Gardening is planting your data at the right time and place, weeding out the irrelevant or even deceptive data, fertilizing the fields with multiple forms of enrichment, and harvesting the data at the right time and place, is the proper way to build data-based systems that will continue to produce for many seasons to come. Art's book provides you with the farm plan right for you.

Steven Simske
Fort Collins, CO

⁜ ⁜ ⁜

Steven Simske, PhD is Professor of Systems Engineering at Colorado State University and a globally recognized authority in analytics, intelligent systems, cybersecurity, and complex engineered systems. Prior to joining CSU, he spent more than two decades at Hewlett-Packard, where he served as an HP Fellow, Vice President, and Director in HP Labs, leading research across domains including analytics, AI, sensing, imaging, manufacturing, and authentication.

Dr. Simske is the author of seven books, more than 500 publications, and over 240 U.S. patents, and is a Fellow of the IEEE, the National Academy of Inventors, and IS&T. His career bridges deep theoretical insight with large-scale industrial practice, reflecting sustained contributions to the understanding and engineering of complex, emergent systems.

Preface

The world is a place where natural processes, technological innovations, and social dynamics continuously shape and transform one another. From the self-organizing patterns within ecosystems to the emergent properties of artificial intelligence and the complex adaptive behaviors of human societies, we are surrounded by phenomena that cannot be understood through reductionist approaches alone. *The Gardener and the Machine: Designing Systems that Thrive on Disruption* represents my effort to provide a map and a set of navigational tools for exploring this ecosystem where boundaries between disciplines dissolve and new insights emerge.

Most books about complexity try to make it tidy. This one embraces the fundamental richness of interconnectedness and offers metrics, frameworks, and conceptual tools that reveal the governing principles of complex systems. We keep trying to run living systems like machines. They keep refusing.

Complex systems fail because interactions amplify in ways no one anticipated.

What This Book Contributes

This book contributes two things.

First, it offers a unified way of seeing complex systems that cuts across domains without collapsing their differences. The Metasystem Framework provides a practical structure for diagnosing how feedback, coupling, and incentives interact across domains, and why interventions that succeed locally so often fail systemically.

Second, it reframes how we intervene in complex systems, in leadership, design, governance, engineering, and everyday life away from control and optimization and toward responsibility for what we shape. By distinguishing between systems that are merely efficient and systems that are resilient, adaptive, or antifragile, the book provides a vocabulary and set of tools for intervening in complex systems without destroying the conditions that allow them to learn, evolve, and endure.

Together, these support a single claim: that many of the defining failures of our time, in all domains, arise from applying mechanistic thinking to systems that behave like living environments. This book is a discipline for working within complexity.

How This Book Works

At the heart of *The Gardener and the Machine* is its comprehensive, cross-disciplinary methodology. I demonstrate how phenomena in three domains are fundamentally connected through measurable patterns and principles. Throughout these pages, you'll encounter examples and practical tools that transform abstract concepts into actionable insights applicable to real-world problems.

My path to writing this book has been shaped by experiences bridging theoretical understanding and practical implementation across fields as diverse as applied mathematics, systems engineering, artificial intelligence, and applied neuroscience. As a researcher, practitioner, family man, and citizen of the world, I've witnessed how traditional approaches often fail to capture the dynamics of complex systems. This has reinforced my conviction that we need better ways of quantifying emergence, measuring resilience, and identifying transition points across system boundaries.

I wrote this for people who are tired of pretending that old maps work.

This book is written for systems thinkers and boundary-crossers: researchers seeking connections beyond their specialties, practitioners grappling with complex systems that defy conventional management, and strategists and policymakers confronting challenges that span ecological, technological, and social domains. Most of all, it is for curious minds drawn to understanding the patterns that unite seemingly disparate phenomena.

It's especially relevant for those making sense and addressing our era's defining challenges — climate destabilization, technological transformation, social reorganization — which demand approaches that can measure, monitor, and manage complexity across traditional divides.

Understanding complex systems is both an intellectual exercise and carries ethical weight. Once we learn to see feedback loops, fragility, and unintended consequences, we lose the comfort of believing that outcomes are accidental or external. Throughout this book, I take the position that insight confers responsibility and accountability for how and where we intervene. This is a book for people willing to accept that burden.

By the end of this book, you will be able to recognize emergent risk, measure fragility, and intervene in complex systems without collapsing the very dynamics that make them resilient. Some chapters will stretch you conceptually; that is intentional. Complexity cannot be simplified without distortion, but it can be navigated.

Art Villanueva
San Diego, CA

A Note on the Diagrams

This book is complete in itself, and all diagrams are fully explained in the surrounding text.

For readers using the e-book edition, high-resolution versions of all figures are available online at:

phronos.com/tgm-diagrams

They are provided as a study aid and reference, and may be copied and reused with appropriate attribution. However, they are not required to understand the arguments or narrative of the book.

Readers who prefer a fully visual experience may find the print edition especially well-suited to close diagram study.

How to Read this Book

Some books promise clarity through instruction. This one offers a landscape to be entered and slowly traversed. This is your invitation to step in.

The Reading Contract

This book assumes three things.

First, that you are comfortable with complexity. In complex systems, cause and effect are delayed, nonlinear, and often counterintuitive. Well-intended interventions routinely produce unintended consequences.

Second, that you value understanding over certainty. The goal here is pattern recognition and judgment under uncertainty.

Third, that you are willing to linger. Some sections reward slow reading. Others reveal their value only after you've moved on and returned. This is a book to be savored.

Two Ways In

Although the argument holds together from beginning to end, the book supports two distinct reading intentions. Choose the one that matches your purpose, and feel free to move between them.

Reading to Rebuild Your Mental Models

If your goal is to change how you think about systems, read the book linearly, from start to finish.

Part I clears the conceptual ground by dismantling the illusion of stability and control. Part II introduces analytical tools. Part III tests those tools in real, messy environments. Part IV widens the vantage point to foresight, ethics, and stewardship.

This path rewards patience. Later chapters depend on earlier ideas, even when the domain changes. You will notice ideas reappear and cases return. This is deliberate. Complex systems are learned through recurrence rather than accumulation.

Reading to Act

If you are facing a real system under stress — an organization, a technology, a policy environment, a family — begin with Part II: The Gardener's Tools.

The frameworks and case studies are designed for diagnosis rather than prescription. Mastery of the entire theory can come gradually. Apply the ideas as you go, returning to earlier chapters to deepen understanding or clarify assumptions.

This book offers ways to see leverage, fragility, and unintended consequences before acting.

A Note on Structure

Some chapters can be read independently. Others rely on ideas introduced much earlier. When in doubt, trust the architecture. The book was designed to hold together.

A Final Word

A Mechanic reads for instructions. A Gardener reads for conditions.

Choose how you enter the garden. Once inside, the work is the same: observation, patience, and humility before systems that cannot be controlled, but can be tended.

Read accordingly.

Introduction

We are trying to navigate 21st-century complex adaptive systems with 19th-century machine logic.

We live inside networks of global supply chains, algorithmic markets, power grids, ecosystems, and digital platforms — systems defined primarily by the dense web of interactions between them. These systems adapt. They learn. And they surprise us.

Yet we persist in managing them as if cause and effect were linear and immediate. When something fails, we look for the broken component. When performance lags, we tighten control. We treat our organizations, our cities, our technologies, and even our families like machines, believing that if we just pull the right lever or tighten the right bolt, the outcome will obey.

This book, *The Gardener and the Machine*, is an invitation to stop fixing the machine and start cultivating the system.

The central claim of this book is simple: many of the defining failures of our time arise from applying mechanistic optimization to systems that behave like living environments. When we treat complex adaptive systems as machines to be controlled, we create fragility. When we treat them as gardens to be stewarded, we create resilience.

Throughout this book, I will draw on systems science, ecology, and engineering to offer a practical way of seeing, one that explains why well-intentioned interventions so often backfire.

The Illusion of Control

This is a recurring tragedy in the Fortune 500. The corporate graveyard is filled with companies that mastered their complicated businesses but failed to understand the complex ecosystems in which they operated.[1]

Kodak mastered film chemistry but failed to recognize the ecosystem that would make it obsolete. Blockbuster optimized stores; Netflix optimized networks. The difference was ecology.

Stewardship Close to Home

This failure of systems thinking plays out in our homes as well. The most complex, high-stakes, and adaptive system any of us will ever raise is a child.

Here, the temptation to be a Mechanic is overwhelming. Driven by love and anxiety, we create blueprints for the "successful adult" and try to assemble our children according to plan. We optimize schedules, track performance, and shield them from failure. We try to build a perfect machine.

The Gardener parent understands something different. Children adapt rather than assemble.

The Gardener parent shifts their focus from controlling outcomes to tending the environment. Their role is to enrich the soil, ensure sunlight and water, and provide a trellis when support is needed. Growth emerges from conditions rather than commands.

In this book, we will return to this insight again and again, because the mindset of care is universal. Whether you are leading an organization, engineering a platform, shaping policy, or raising a child, you are grappling with the same underlying forces.

A Way of Seeing

Throughout these pages, we will test a simple claim: that the same principles governing biological systems, technological systems, and social systems recur across scale and context. If those principles hold in the intimate complexity of a family and in the sprawling complexity of a democracy, then, and only then, can we trust them to guide our organizations and institutions.

Rather than offering prescriptions, this book offers a way of seeing. It moves across domains to stress-test it, examining where ideas break, where they bend, and where they endure.[a]

To aid in this stress-testing, I have woven the story of **Veridia** throughout the chapters. Veridia is a composite, a narrative simulation designed to illustrate what happens when the drive for algorithmic optimization meets the messy reality of human life. While the city is invented, the technologies and failure modes are real. You will encounter Veridia in fragments, each revisited through different analytical filters as the book progresses; for those who wish to see the arc of the city in its entirety, the complete narrative is assembled in Appendix E. Here is our first encounter:

❖ VERIDIA — Phase 0: Formation

Consider Veridia, a city of 1.2 million designed from the ground up as the ultimate smart city. Built as a machine for living, its traffic grids are adaptive, its energy distribution algorithmic, and its services automated for maximum efficiency. On the dashboard, it appears flawless: waste near zero, latency minimal, budgets balanced. Yet beneath this order, the tight coupling of biological needs, technological optimization, and social incentives is accumulating hidden debt. The system is becoming brittle.

---

[a] For readers coming from a formal systems engineering background: when we speak of "gardening," we are describing the practical application of non-functional requirements, what you know as architecturally-relevant requirements or the "ilities" (e.g., adaptability, evolvability, maintainability). The metaphor is the interface; the engineering is the engine.

The Garden Ahead

We are living through a crisis of complexity. The old maps fail to match the territory, and the noise of the world is constant. Many leadership books urge us to shout louder, fight harder, or build higher walls.

That advice has often made things worse.

The answer to a chaotic ecosystem is a garden. The ancient Greeks had a word for this: Kēpos.

In time, I will offer you tools and structures for cultivating your own modern Kēpos. But first, we must understand the nature of the storm outside the garden walls.

Welcome to the age of the Gardener.

Table 1. The Old and the New Mindset

	The Mechanic Mindset (Old)	*The Gardener Mindset (New)*
Goal	Control and Stability	Resilience and Adaptation
View of Failure	A defect to be fixed	Information to be used
Strategy	Add rules and layers	Subtract barriers and simplify
Structure	Rigid Hierarchies	Loose Coupling and Networks
Action	Force the Outcome	Cultivate the Conditions

Contents

Figures

PART I. Clearing the Ground

We have unknowingly accepted an elegant fiction: that the world behaves like a finely tuned clock. It doesn't. It's an ecosystem, full of loops, delays, and surprises. We are often taught to view reality as a straight line from cause to effect, yet this perspective fails to capture the intricacies of the systems we inhabit. Before we can build an understanding of complexity, we must first excavate the outdated mental models that obscure our vision. We must clear the overgrown brush of conventional wisdom to reveal the true nature of the terrain beneath our feet.

Part I does three things: First, it shows how good intentions can cascade into damage. Then it breaks the spell of "stability." And last, it makes the counterintuitive case that resilience often begins with subtraction. While our instinct is often to add rules and layers to solve problems, we will discover that resilience is frequently found in the art of taking things away. By the end of Part I, you should be able to name what you're seeing — feedback, coupling, emergence — without reducing it to something simpler than it is.

Chapter 1. The Anatomy of Consequence

> *"When we try to pick out anything by itself, we find it hitched to everything else in the Universe."*
>
> *—John Muir*

In Northern Kenya, a seemingly straightforward solution to chronic water scarcity — drilling wells — unleashed a cascade of unforeseen effects, from desertification to social conflict. The wells didn't just provide water. They rewired incentives, movement, grazing, and conflict.

1.1. The Kenya Story: A Cautionary Tale

In the 1970s and 1980s, governments and international development agencies initiated well-drilling projects in Turkana County in Northern Kenya (Figure 1), aiming to provide reliable and permanent water sources for local communities, livestock, and agriculture. For the pastoralist societies of the region who traditionally relied on seasonal rivers, shallow wells, and migration to water their herds, the creation of boreholes and deep wells initially seemed like a transformative solution to persistent water challenges.

However, while these projects were well-intentioned, they triggered a cascade of unintended repercussions. The introduction of wells allowed for year-round access to groundwater. But this accessibility led to over-extraction, as water was pumped out fast enough that, in many locations, extraction outpaced local recharge. Over time, the water table dropped, causing both the newly drilled wells and the existing traditional water sources, such as shallow wells and springs, to dry up. This created a self-reinforcing cycle where communities became increasingly dependent on the deeper, mechanically drilled wells, which in turn placed even greater strain on the groundwater reserves.[2]

Initially, the availability of reliable water encouraged the growth of livestock herds, as pastoralist communities no longer needed to limit herd sizes based on the availability of water during dry seasons. While this improved livelihoods, the larger herds quickly led to overgrazing of the fragile arid grasslands. Vegetation loss, combined with the pressure of concentrated grazing near water points, degraded the soil, leaving it unable to support new plant growth. Over time, the land became more vulnerable to wind erosion, desertification, and reduced agricultural productivity.

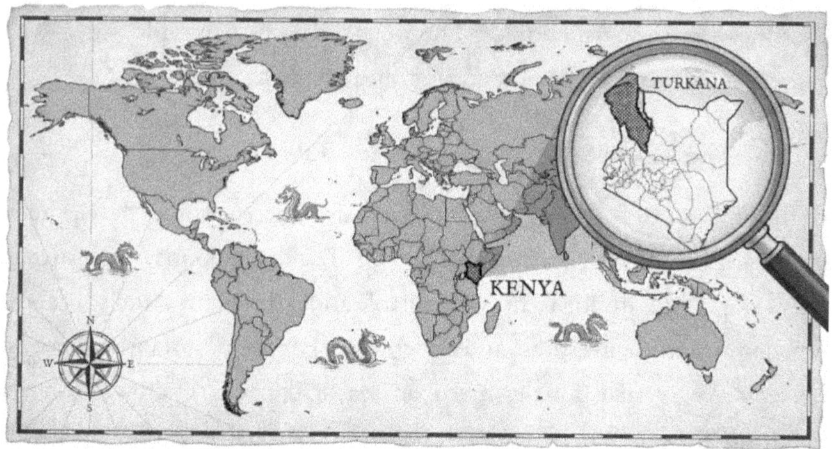

Figure 1. Location of Turkana County

Though the wells alone didn't cause desertification, they amplified existing stressors (drought variability, governance limits, herd incentives) by changing movement constraints and grazing concentration.

Furthermore, the placement of wells disrupted traditional water management practices. Historically, pastoralist groups managed water and grazing resources through seasonal migrations.[3] The presence of permanent water points caused communities to settle in one location, leading to the concentration of people and animals around the wells. This placed enormous pressure on local resources and created social tensions as neighboring communities competed for access to the limited water and grazing land. Conflicts over these resources became more frequent, especially during extended periods of drought.[4,5]

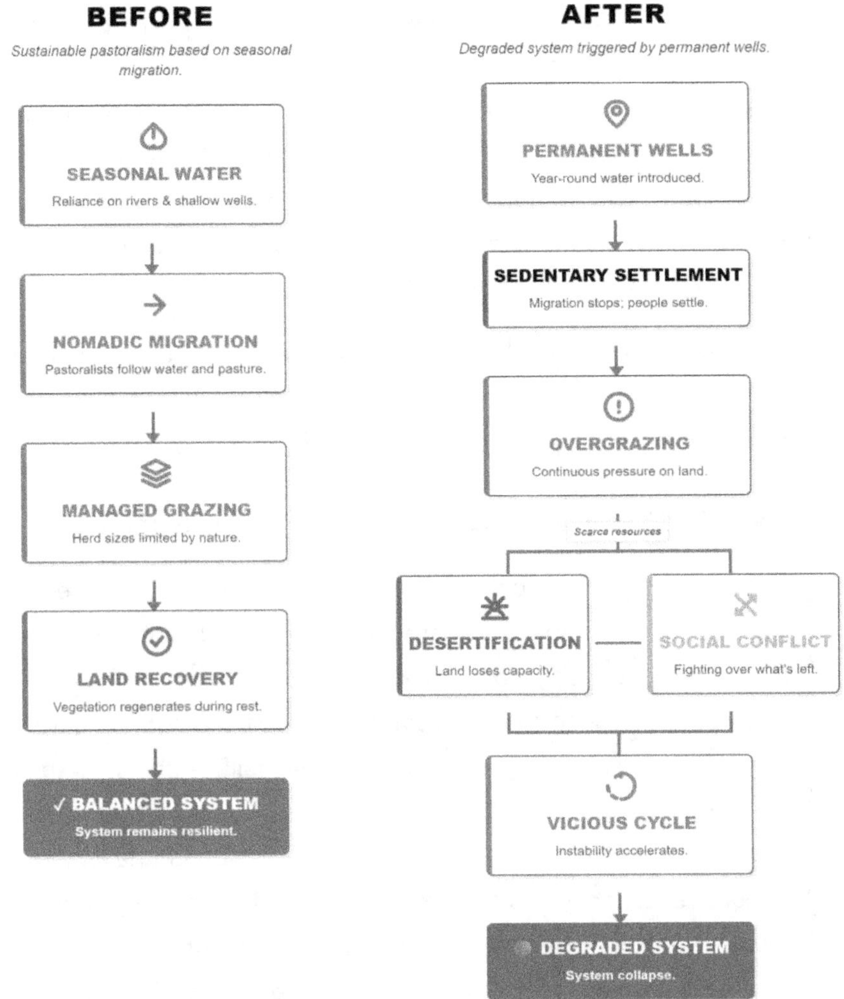

Figure 2. Turkana County Water Systems
High-resolution version available at phronos.com/tgm-diagrams

The ecological impacts extended beyond human and livestock populations. Wildlife that relied on seasonal water sources and natural vegetation was displaced or died off as resources were diverted for human use. Rivers, wetlands, and other habitats dried up, leading to further losses in biodiversity.

Over time, these effects created a self-reinforcing cycle of environmental degradation, resource scarcity, and social instability. The very interventions designed to provide security and resilience instead exacerbated the challenges of living in a semi-arid environment. Rather than solving water scarcity, the well-drilling intervention, implemented without durable local governance and ecological constraints, often increased the region's vulnerability to drought and environmental stress (see Figure 2).

This is the lesson: in a complex system, "more water" is rarely only more water.

> ❖ VERIDIA — Phase I: Optimization (The Efficiency Trap)
>
> The same logic applies far beyond the savanna. In Veridia, decisions that appeared mathematically sound, such as micro-optimizing transit routes or automating resource allocation, altered the landscape of incentives in ways the code could not predict. No single algorithm caused the failure. Instead, small, hyper-rational interventions accumulated. The drive to eliminate "slack" (viewed as waste) inadvertently removed the system's adaptive capacity. As resilience engineers have long warned, when you optimize for efficiency, you often optimize away the buffer required for survival. The machine was perfect, right up until the moment it wasn't.

The Turkana crisis was a local manifestation of a global philosophy. It illustrates what happens when we treat a complex, living web as a linear engineering problem. The wells were the intervention. The deeper issue was the Mechanic's mindset: linear control applied to a living system.

1.2. Unintended Consequences

The Mechanic believes that with enough force and enough data, nature can be brought to heel. There is no greater monument to this way of thinking, both in its miraculous power and its catastrophic blind spots, than the invention that defined the 20th century.

The Haber-Bosch Legacy

In the early 1900s, Fritz Haber and Carl Bosch developed a method for industrially "fixing" atmospheric nitrogen to create synthetic ammonia. This invention was one of the most important of the modern era, primarily because it shattered the natural limits on agricultural productivity. By enabling synthetic fertilizers, the Haber–Bosch process helped remove a major constraint on agricultural productivity — a major force that enabled population growth from roughly 1.6 billion to ~8 billion. Estimates vary by methodology, but synthetic nitrogen is thought to support food production for a large fraction of humanity — often cited at roughly ~40–50%.[6]

The process also created a significant energy dependency. Haber–Bosch ammonia synthesis is highly energy-intensive, often estimated at approximately 1–2% of global energy use, depending on accounting boundaries. As a result, global food production is tightly linked to fossil-fuel markets and their geopolitical volatility, meaning disruptions in energy supply can quickly ripple into the food system.

Industrial nitrogen fixation also enabled the large-scale production of nitrogen-based explosives such as ammonium nitrate. While these materials existed before Haber–Bosch, the process made them far more accessible by providing abundant synthetic ammonia. This duality, supporting agriculture while also expanding the capacity for warfare, illustrates the complex moral legacy of the technology.

Another consequence of the massive increase in synthetic nitrogen is its impact on aquatic ecosystems. Excess nitrogen and phosphorus from agricultural runoff contribute to eutrophication, the process that drives harmful algal blooms. These nutrients act as fertilizers in lakes, rivers, and coastal waters, triggering rapid algal growth.

The bloom initiates a cascade of damaging effects. Dense algal layers block sunlight from reaching submerged plants, which then die. As dead plant and algal material sinks, bacteria decompose it, consuming large amounts of dissolved oxygen. This leads to hypoxic or anoxic "dead zones" where fish and other organisms cannot survive.

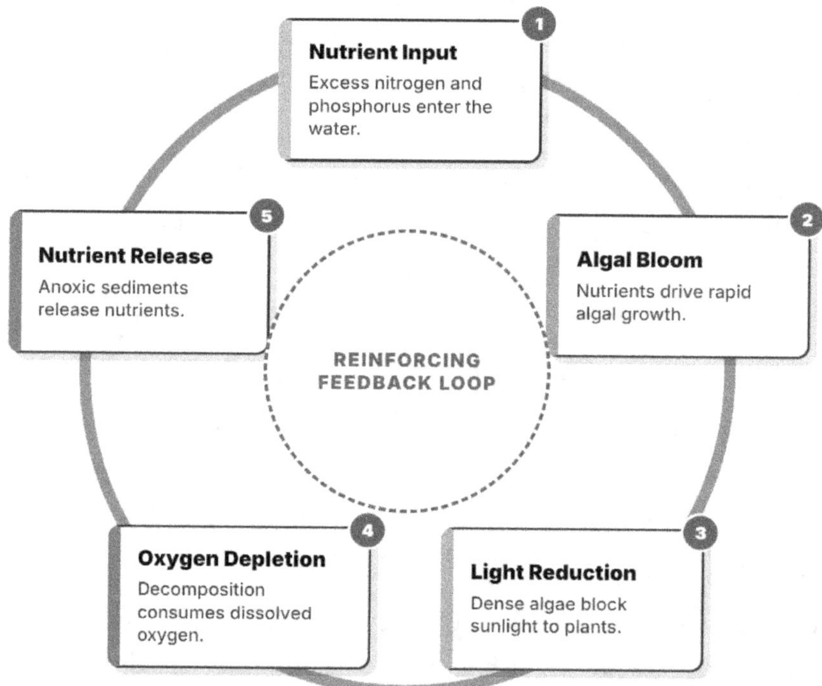

Figure 3. Eutrophication Feedback Loop
High-resolution version available at phronos.com/tgm-diagrams

Under these oxygen-starved conditions, chemical reactions in the sediment release phosphorus that was previously bound in the lakebed. In some systems, this internal loading can further fuel algal growth, locking the system into a self-reinforcing pattern.[7] Although external nutrient inputs are typically the primary driver, internal loading can keep a lake in a degraded, bloom-prone state long after runoff is reduced (Figure 3).

This is the trap of the Mechanic: in solving one problem, nutrient limitation in soils, we created another by overloading aquatic ecosystems. When we treat complex natural systems as simple machines, our solutions can become the next generation's challenges.

1.3. Complex Systems

A complex system is a web of interacting parts, each influencing the others in ways that are often nonlinear and difficult to predict in detail. These interactions can produce higher-order behaviors — patterns and structures that arise spontaneously and often cannot be reliably predicted from the properties of the individual components alone, because the interactions do the real work.[8,9]

The Kenya story embodies the key characteristics of complex systems:

- **Interdependence:** The components within the Northern Kenyan ecosystem were highly interdependent. The availability of groundwater was directly linked to the health of livestock populations, which in turn affected vegetation cover, soil stability, and the availability of grazing land. The well-drilling projects, by altering one element (water availability), triggered a cascade of effects throughout the entire system. This shows how actions impacting one part of a complex system inevitably ripple outwards.

- **Nonlinearity:** The relationship between the well-drilling intervention and its consequences was nonlinear. A seemingly small change, providing reliable water sources, led to disproportionately large and unexpected outcomes, such as overgrazing, desertification, and social conflict. The system exhibited amplified and unforeseen reactions.

- **Feedback Loops:** The Kenya story is rife with self-reinforcing and balancing cycles. The over-extraction of groundwater created a negative feedback loop: as the water table dropped, communities became more reliant on the deeper wells, further exacerbating the depletion. This self-reinforcing cycle accelerated the environmental degradation and resource scarcity. Positive feedback loops were also present, such as the increased livestock populations leading to greater overgrazing, which in turn reduced vegetation cover and further degraded the soil.

- **Emergence:** The environmental degradation, social tensions, and increased vulnerability to drought were system-level outcomes produced by interaction rather than design. These outcomes arose spontaneously from the interactions of the various components (water, livestock, vegetation, human behavior, etc.). No single individual or agency could have predicted or controlled the full cascade from component-level analysis alone. (We will cover this in detail in the next section.)

- **Adaptation (and Maladaptation):** The Turkana communities were, in a sense, adapting to the new conditions created by the wells. However, this adaptation, increasing herd sizes, ultimately contributed to the negative consequences of overgrazing and desertification. Adaptation within a complex system can sometimes lead to maladaptation, where short-term gains result in long-term harm.

This phenomenon of adaptation leading to unforeseen effects extends beyond human systems. Similar dynamics appear in natural ecosystems, where species adapt to new conditions in ways that disrupt environmental balance.

Consider the case of cheatgrass (*Bromus tectorum*) in the western United States. This annual grass was introduced from Eurasia and has adapted remarkably well to the arid conditions of the Great Basin. Its rapid growth and prolific seed production allow it to quickly colonize disturbed areas, including those affected by wildfires. While cheatgrass might seem like a beneficial colonizer in the short term, its presence dramatically alters the fire dynamics of the ecosystem. Cheatgrass dries out quickly in the summer, creating a highly flammable fuel source. This leads to more frequent and intense wildfires, which kill off native plants that are not adapted to such frequent fires. The increased fire frequency further favors cheatgrass, creating a positive feedback loop that transforms native shrublands into cheatgrass monocultures. Thus, cheatgrass's adaptation to the arid environment, while seemingly successful for the species itself, ultimately degrades the ecosystem, reduces biodiversity, and increases the risk of catastrophic wildfires.[10]

Similarly, there is the case of the red king crab (*Paralithodes camtschaticus*) in the Barents Sea. Introduced by Soviet scientists in the 1960s to establish a fishery, the crab adapted well and spread rapidly, far beyond its intended range. As a voracious predator, it decimates native benthic species like mollusks and sea urchins, disrupting ecosystems and reducing biodiversity. The crabs create a feedback loop: by depleting seafloor organisms, they leave behind barren habitats that further favor their dominance. While the fishery has brought economic benefits, the ecological cost (severe loss of native benthic biodiversity and habitat degradation) has been significant, mirroring the way cheatgrass transforms ecosystems on land.[11]

The Gardener and the Gut

The unfortunate situations of Turkana, cheatgrass, and the red king crab may seem like distant ecological stories. Yet, each of us manages a Complex Adaptive System of equal intricacy every single day: the microbiome within our own gut. This internal wilderness, containing trillions of organisms, is a perfect microcosm of emergence.

The Gardener and the Machine

We cannot directly command our gut to be healthy any more than the Kenyan government could command the grasslands to flourish. A reductionist, mechanistic approach often leads to disaster. For instance, the indiscriminate use of broad-spectrum antibiotics is the personal equivalent of drilling too many wells. It's a linear intervention that solves one problem (a bacterial infection) but carpet-bombs the entire ecosystem, creating the potential for Dark Emergence in the form of dysbiosis, opportunistic infections, and, in some cases, longer-term inflammation.

A Gardener or "systems stewardship" approach, by contrast, focuses on cultivating the environment. Eating a diverse, fiber-rich diet is about feeding the beneficial bacteria that, in turn, produce compounds that keep you healthy.[12] This is a high-leverage intervention. We seek influence rather than control, tending the soil of our own biology and creating the conditions for health to emerge.

The point of the story is the shape of consequence. Learning to recognize these characteristics is the first step toward designing more effective and sustainable interventions in complex environments.

Complicated vs. Complex

Complex systems differ fundamentally from merely complicated ones. An automobile, with its thousands of parts, is complicated: predictable when assembled correctly. A complex system, however, cannot be fully understood by breaking it down. The Northern Kenya situation involved interconnected ecological, social, and economic factors interacting unpredictably.

This changes what you do next. Complicated systems, like a jet plane, can be disassembled, studied, and reassembled with predictable outcomes. Complex systems resist such reductionist approaches; they're dynamic, adaptive, and shaped by component interactions. Treating a complex system as merely complicated often leads to flawed assumptions and inadvertent results, as seen in Kenya's well-drilling project, which viewed the problem as "more water equals better" without considering ecological and social relationships.

The distinction highlights emergent behavior, unique to complex systems. In complicated systems, the behavior of the whole is derivable from its parts. In complex systems, nonlinear interactions among parts generate emergent properties that cannot be predicted from the components in isolation[13,14]. The degradation, conflict, and resilience decline in Kenya were emergent system-level outcomes not predictable from the number of wells drilled alone.

Responses to challenges differ, too. Complicated systems require expertise and top-down, engineered solutions. Complex systems need adaptability, collaboration, and iterative approaches. Top-down well-drilling tended to fail when it ignored adaptive behavior, ecological feedback, and local governance constraints. A better approach would have involved local communities in planning and management.

Complexity has a way of punishing arrogance. Certain systems may never be fully predictable or controllable, as Kenya reminds us.[b] The initial goal was obvious, but the consequences were far-reaching and unintended. This demonstrates the need for an adaptive approach.

Ultimately, this distinction allows us to engage with systems on their own terms, shifting focus from control to understanding, prediction to adaptation, and isolated analysis to holistic thinking.

---

[b] This pattern extends beyond Kenya. Similar failures appear repeatedly in post-World War II nation- and regime-building efforts where external powers applied linear, top-down solutions to deeply complex social systems, often with destabilizing long-term consequences.

A Complex System in a Box: The Emergent World of Catan

My son was recently gifted a boardgame for his birthday that we, as a family, have played at least twice a week ever since. *Catan* is a laboratory for emergence, one you can observe in ninety minutes. It is a near-perfect environment for illustrating the difference between a system's simple, predictable rules and its complex, often surprising outcomes.

Players gather and trade resources to build roads, settlements, and cities. Settlements, cities, and certain achievements earn victory points, and the first player to reach ten points wins. What unfolds in between is a constantly shifting mix of strategy, luck, negotiation, and adaptation.[15]

The rules of *Catan* might belong in the category of the complicated (at least when compared to popular card games). Less intricate than a jet engine, they are finite, fixed, and fully knowable. The cost to build a city (3 ore, 2 wheat) never changes. The probability of rolling a 7 is always 1 in 6. The rulebook contains the complete "blueprint" of the game's mechanics. There are no hidden rules or surprising changes to the core system. In this sense, the rules are like the parts of a machine: fully specified and understood.

The *gameplay*, however, is complex. Its outcome emerges unpredictably from the interactions of its players:

- **Interdependence:** No player is self-sufficient. The player with all the wood and brick is useless without the sheep and wheat of their neighbors. Survival depends on trade.

- **Nonlinearity:** A single road placement can be a minor move or a game-winning block that cuts off an opponent from expansion — a disproportionately large outcome from a small action.

- **Feedback Loops:** A player who builds a new settlement enters a positive feedback loop, gaining more resources to build even faster.

But this success triggers a balancing feedback loop: they become the prime target for the robber, slowing their progress.

- **Emergence:** The game's "economy" — the going rate for a sheep, the alliances, the grudges, the leader — emerges, unique to each game session, from the social dynamics of the players. *Catan* teaches us that even from a set of known, fixed rules, the outcome can be unpredictable, dynamic, and entirely emergent.

We've already met this dynamic: a system can be both complex and complicated, depending on the context. Designed technologies can exhibit emergent, complex behaviors. The internet, a complicated system of hardware and software, exhibits complex behaviors like spreading social trends when billions interact. AI systems, designed with complicated algorithms, can exhibit emergent behaviors that even its designers struggle to predict.

Conversely, complexity may include elements of complication. The human body has both complicated and complex aspects. The circulatory system is complicated in structure and mechanics, but its relationship with other systems exhibits complexity as the body adapts.

Although a system can exhibit both complexity and complication, the two concepts remain distinct because of their core characteristics. The distinction lies in how the system behaves as a whole. Figure 4 summarizes this comparison.

1.4. The Mechanics of Emergence

Emergence is the name we give to the process you have just seen: interactions within a complex system creating novel properties, behaviors, or patterns unpredictable from individual components alone.[16] It's characterized by novelty, unpredictability, and irreducibility, central to understanding complex systems.[9] The well-drilling project illustrates this.

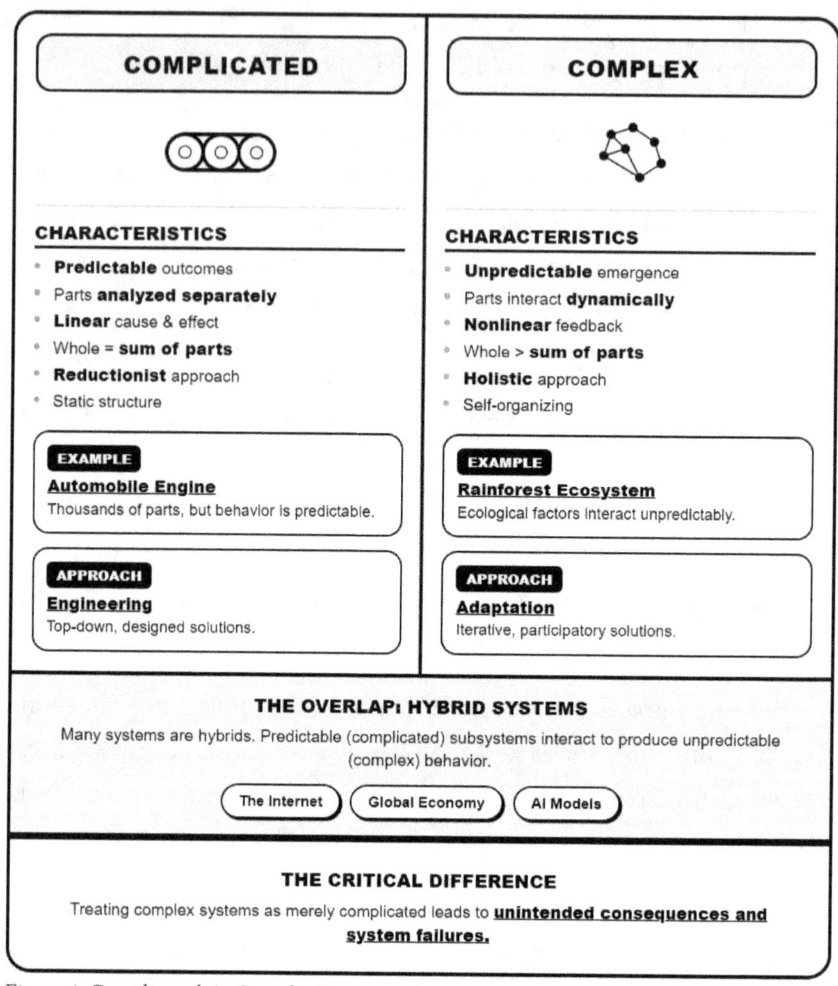

Figure 4. Complicated vs. Complex Systems

High-resolution version available at phronos.com/tgm-diagrams

The Turkana project's resulting failures — degraded grazing lands, social conflict, and drought vulnerability — were emergent at the system level. They weren't inherent in the wells, livestock, or people, but arose from their interactions after introducing the wells. This is like memory in the brain, arising from neural network activity, or a murmuration of starlings, where coordinated behavior isn't dictated by a single bird.

Emergence also embodies unpredictability. Planners couldn't foresee overgrazing, desertification, and unrest, despite understanding individual components. These outcomes stemmed from nonlinearity and feedback loops in the ecosystem. Similarly, social trends or financial market behavior defy simple prediction.

Then there is irreducibility: the Turkana problems cannot be understood by studying wells, livestock, or people in isolation. It's the relationships — water competition, livestock impact on vegetation, grazing practices — that define the system. Like a forest, it cannot be understood by studying only its flora, fauna, and fungi. The relationships among them are what defines it.

Emergence arises from simple interactions within complex systems.[17] In biology, neurons yield cognition through self-organization; in technology, algorithms generate AI behaviors such as learning and hallucinating; in society, individual actions create norms through collective behavior.

These observations reveal emergence within natural, technological, and social domains. But emergence is even more powerful when it manifests *across* these domains. Chapter 4 presents a formalized method to map such larger coupling of cross-domain effects. For instance, biodiversity decline might inspire renewable energy innovations and conservation laws[18] (Figure 5).

Emergence can be categorized as weak (explainable by underlying rules) or strong (not fully reducible to components). Conway's Game of Life[c]

---

[c] Conway's Game of Life, introduced in 1970 by mathematician John Horton Conway, is a mathematical model in which a grid of cells evolves over time according to a small set of basic rules. Despite the simplicity of these rules, the system can generate highly intricate and unexpected patterns as it progresses. It is widely cited as an example of *weak emergence*, where higher-level behavior arises from lower-level rules but remains, in principle, explainable by them.

exemplifies weak emergence while consciousness and language evolution are often discussed as candidates for strong emergence.[19]

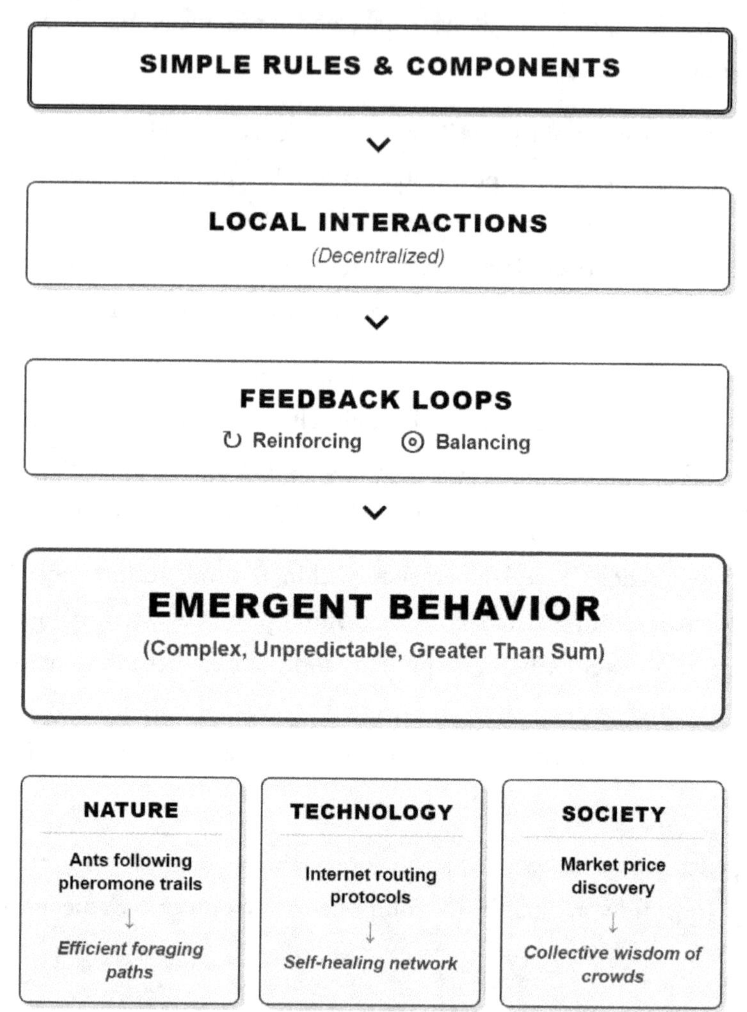

Figure 5. The Core Emergence Pattern
High-resolution version available at phronos.com/tgm-diagrams

The study of emergence bridges science, technology, philosophy, and art. Though never explicitly mentioned, emergence provides rich fodder for cinema content. Films such as *Ex Machina*, *The Creator*, *M3GAN*, and *The*

Matrix explore emergent artificial intelligence, where machines develop consciousness or behaviors beyond their programming. Other films, like *Arrival* and *Annihilation,* use emergent phenomena, such as collective behaviors or chaotic systems, as central themes in their narratives.

A siphonophore provides a biological illustration. Often mistaken for a single organism, a siphonophore is actually a colony of genetically identical organisms, each irreversibly specialized for a single function: propulsion, feeding, digestion, defense, or reproduction (Figure 6).

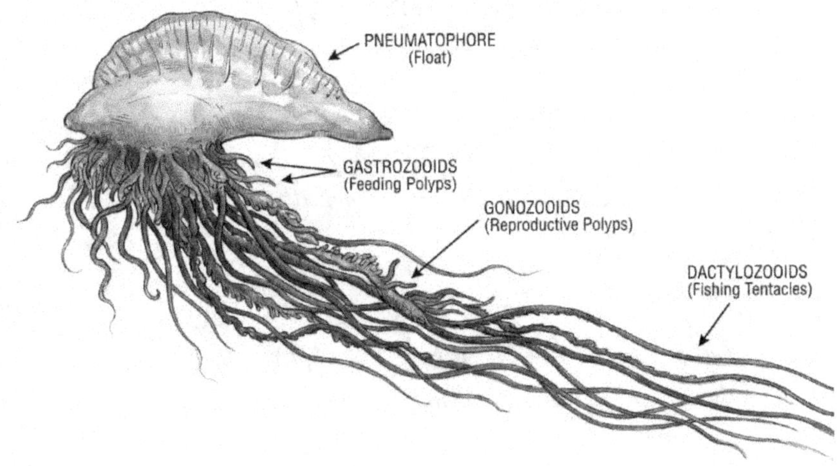

Figure 6. Portuguese Man o' War (Physalia physalis): A Siphonophore

No individual zooid can survive alone, and none possesses awareness of the whole. Yet together, through simple local interactions and division of labor, they behave coherently. In some cases, such as the giant siphonophore *Apolemia uvaria,* this cooperation produces organisms exceeding 40 meters (130 feet) in length, making them the longest animals on Earth. The siphonophore operates without a central brain or command structure; its "body" emerges from interaction. What appears to be unity is, in truth, cooperation hardened into structure.

1.5. From Patterns to Principles

Emergence is a lens through which to view the world, but it's one many of us have conveniently ignored for a long time. I, for one, like many engineers, favor mechanisms over metaphors. For me, Turkana forced the issue. What looked like a local fix revealed patterns that only made sense once I stopped asking "what failed" and started asking "what interacted."

THE PARADOX OF ORDER: CHAOS AND SELF-ORGANIZATION

At the dynamical level, the balance between order and disorder appears as an interplay between chaos and self-organization, the complementary engines of complexity.

Chaos, defined by extreme sensitivity to initial conditions, allows systems to explore a wide range of possible states and adapt to changing environments, often producing unpredictable outcomes. But unpredictability can coexist with structure.

Through self-organization, coherent patterns, behaviors, and structures emerge naturally from local interactions among system components, without centralized control. Stable forms arise because of chaos.

You can see this interplay in weather, where chaotic dynamics give rise to organized structures like storms, and in ecosystems, where countless local interactions stabilize into self-sustaining networks. Chaos supplies flexibility and exploratory capacity; self-organization constrains those dynamics into coherent, functional forms.

Chaos provides the potential for change, while self-organization provides the structure for function.

Through this Metasystem, we'll see how these principles operate across domains, revealing the interconnectedness of our world. The next step is to treat these patterns as design constraints.

Readers interested in seeing how this pattern recurs across domains, from ecosystems to markets to culture, will find a consolidated field guide of emergent systems in Appendix C.

1.6. The Role of Information Theory in Complexity

To move from pattern to principle, we need a language of measurement. Information theory provides this language through the concept of entropy, an accounting of uncertainty, randomness, or "messiness" within a system.

Complex systems can be usefully modeled as information-processing entities. They continuously sense their environment, encode signals, and adapt their behavior in response. Entropy allows us to describe how effectively a system manages this flow of information — whether it builds resilience and flexibility, or drifts toward fragility and collapse.

A perturbation can destroy the signal structure that previously regulated behavior.

Across domains, highly adaptive systems tend to navigate the same paradox. They reduce entropy enough to produce function and stability, yet preserve sufficient variability to learn, respond, and evolve. Too much order leads to rigidity. Too much disorder eventually leads to failure. Complexity often lives in the narrow space between.

1.7. Conclusion: Charting Complexity

If this chapter did its job, you now distrust simple fixes. Reductionism is useful, until it blinds you to the loops.

From here on, the goal is the same: see the loops, then choose interventions that don't snap them. The lesson from Northern Kenya is clear: our future depends on charting complexity with wisdom and humility.[20]

Chapter 2. The Illusion of Stability

> *"No man ever steps in the same river twice, for it's not the same river and he's not the same man."*
>
> — *Heraclitus*

Stability is one of the most seductive ideas in systems thinking. When a system appears steady, with its outputs regular and its boundaries intact, we assume it is predictable, resilient, and under control. This chapter challenges that assumption. What often appears stable may reflect constraint rather than robustness: held in place by diversity, redundancy, and feedbacks that absorb stress — until they don't. The goal of this chapter is to show how stability itself can be an illusion, masking hidden risks that only become visible when a system is pushed beyond its limits.

2.1. Ecosystems as Stable Systems in Early Systems Thinking

From the perspective of early systems thinking, particularly that of Ludwig von Bertalanffy's *General Systems Theory*, the ecosystem might have been seen as relatively stable, governed by predictable laws.[21] The emphasis was on identifying the forces that maintained equilibrium: the balance between energy inputs from the sun and outputs through respiration and decomposition, the regulation of populations through feedback, and the steady cycling of nutrients. In this view, stability was intrinsic, the natural outcome of a system organized to preserve homeostasis during upheaval.

Early ecological management, influenced by equilibrium and control metaphors, tended toward optimization: control inputs, regulate populations, and damp disturbances. However, this obsession with optimization and stability ignores a trade-off.

Diversity, Redundancy, and Masked Fragility

Systems often appear stable because diversity and redundancy absorb shocks that would otherwise cause failure. In ecological systems, this buffering capacity can create the impression of resilience, even as underlying vulnerabilities accumulate. When diversity is high, disturbances are dispersed across multiple pathways, damping visible effects. When diversity is reduced, whether through optimization, simplification, or uniformity, those same disturbances become concentrated, accelerating collapse. What looks like stability, in other words, may be less a property of the system than a temporary consequence of hidden insurance.

❖ VERIDIA: SYNTHETIC STABILITY

In Veridia, years of "green" metrics such as smooth traffic flows, predictable energy usage, and managed density, created the appearance of stability. Yet this steadiness was synthetic. It depended on the suppression of variance. The system was maintaining equilibrium by forcing human behavior into narrower and narrower channels to match the model. Stability was real, but it was conditional: maintained only as long as the citizens acted like components rather than people.

Consider coral reefs. A healthy coral reef is a kaleidoscope of biodiversity, composed of hundreds of species of coral, thousands of species of fish, and countless invertebrates. This is the reef's insurance policy. Imagine a disease that sweeps through that targets a specific species of coral. In a monoculture reef, this would be a catastrophe. But in a diverse reef, other coral species may be resistant. They can continue to provide the reef's core structure, allowing the ecosystem to persist and eventually recover. The same is true for fish. If one species of herbivorous fish is wiped out by overfishing, others can take its place in controlling algae growth. This functional redundancy — where multiple components can perform the same function — ensures that if one component fails, the system doesn't collapse.[22,23]

Contrast this to what happened during the Irish Potato Famine. In the 1840s, a large portion of the Irish population was dependent on a single food source: the potato. Furthermore, they primarily cultivated one genetically uniform variety, the "Lumper" potato, because it grew well in poor soils. This system was incredibly efficient in the short term, but it was also incredibly fragile. When the blight *Phytophthora infestans* (aptly named) arrived from the Americas, it found a perfect target. Because every potato plant was genetically identical, none had any resistance. The blight swept through the country, wiping out the food supply with shocking speed. The result was a catastrophic famine. This brutal lesson highlights the trade-off between efficiency and resilience. The system was optimized for yield but had zero diversity, leaving it catastrophically vulnerable to a single, unforeseen shock.[22,24]

Other early systems approaches, particularly cybernetics, reinforced this view of ecosystems as fundamentally stable and self-regulating. With its emphasis on feedback loops and control mechanisms, cybernetics focused on how systems maintain equilibrium in the face of disturbance. Predator–prey dynamics, for example, were often modeled as negative feedback loops that constrain population growth and prevent runaway instability. From this perspective, feedback was corrective as it was descriptive: deviations from equilibrium triggered responses that restored balance.[25]

This framework encouraged the view of ecosystems as adaptive systems that continuously adjust to changing conditions while preserving their overall structure. Like an organism maintaining homeostasis, the ecosystem was thought to reorganize internally in response to external pressures — shifting population levels, reallocating resources, but ultimately returning to a stable operating regime. Stability, in this sense, was dynamic rather than static, but it remained the organizing principle.

What these approaches struggled to explain were abrupt, irreversible collapses. Sudden regime shifts, cascading extinctions, or rapid system reconfigurations sat uneasily within models built around correction and control. Lacking tools to capture strong nonlinearities, amplification effects, and sensitivity to initial conditions, early theories often treated such events as external shocks or rare anomalies rather than as outcomes generated by the system itself.[26]

2.2. Chaos and Unpredictability

The assumptions of early systems thinking, with its emphasis on equilibrium and predictable feedback loops, began to crumble with the rise of chaos theory in the latter half of the 20th century.[27] The ecosystem, once viewed as a stable structure governed by simple ecological laws, was about to be revealed as far more complex and unpredictable. The key figure in this transformation was Edward Lorenz, a meteorologist whose work on weather systems would forever change our understanding of predictability.[28]

Lorenz, while attempting to model weather patterns with a computer, found that even tiny changes in the initial conditions could lead to drastically different outcomes. This phenomenon, known as "sensitive dependence on initial conditions" or the "butterfly effect," implied that beyond a finite horizon, weather forecasting hits a hard horizon, where long-range precision degrades sharply even as technology improves. The smallest uncertainties would inevitably amplify over time, leading to wildly divergent predictions.

Implications for Ecosystems

This finding significantly deepened our understanding of ecosystems specifically, and of complex systems more broadly. From the perspective of chaos theory, the population booms and busts in the ecosystem would no longer be seen as random events or external disturbances. Instead, they would be understood as the result of deterministic chaos, a seemingly random behavior that arises from a perfectly deterministic system. The precise timing and size of these fluctuations would be exquisitely sensitive to the initial conditions of the ecosystem, such as the exact number and distribution of individuals within each species. Even the slightest change in temperature or rainfall could trigger a cascade of events that would ultimately lead to a major shift in the ecosystem's structure.

Chaos theory thus also introduced the concept of system nonlinearity, which further challenged the traditional views of stability. In a linear system, the effect of a cause is proportional to its magnitude. Doubling the amount of fertilizer applied to a field would double the crop yield. In a nonlinear system, small changes can have disproportionately large effects, and large changes can have surprisingly small effects.

The ecosystem is a prime example of a nonlinear system. The introduction of an invasive species can, in some contexts, trigger a cascade through a food web, and in others, be absorbed with surprisingly little visible change. This nonlinearity makes it extremely difficult to predict the ecosystem's behavior, as even the smallest changes can have unpredictable consequences.

Chaos theory explains why systems can appear stable at the surface while remaining dynamically unstable underneath: bounded, yet unpredictable.

Another key concept from chaos theory is the "strange attractor." In a chaotic system, the state evolves over time in a complex, seemingly random way. However, this evolution is constrained by hidden patterns. A strange attractor, like the famous Lorenz attractor shown in Figure 7, is a geometric structure that confines chaotic dynamics, a structured region of possible states. This helps explain why systems can look stable for long periods even as they remain vulnerable to sudden reconfiguration.

The figure illustrates how chaos emerges gradually in the Lorenz system. Each panel shows the system's long-term behavior as a single control parameter (ρ) increases.

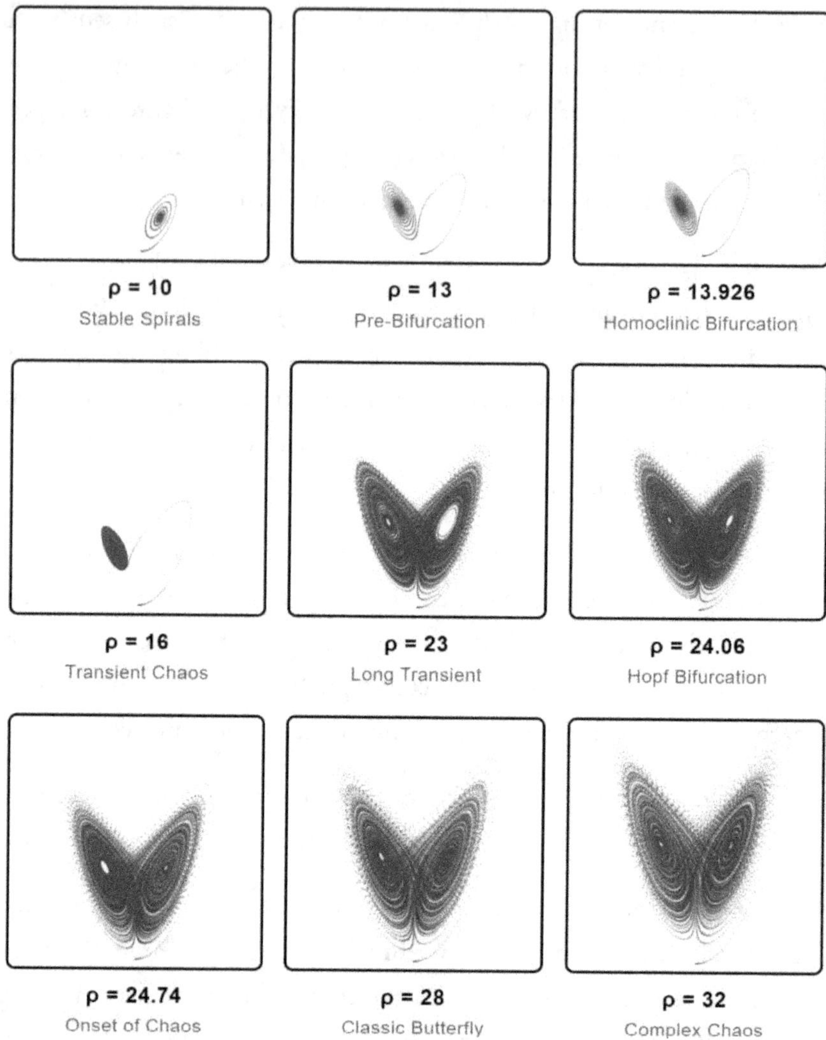

Figure 7. How Increasing Chaos Remains Structurally Constrained
High-resolution version available at phronos.com/tgm-diagrams

The rise of chaos theory had an impact on our understanding of systemic fragility. It showed that even seemingly stable systems can be vulnerable to sudden and unexpected collapses.[29,30] It challenged the traditional scientific goal of achieving complete control over the natural world, demonstrating that many systems are inherently unpredictable and uncontrollable. And it highlighted the importance of understanding nonlinearity and feedback loops in complex systems. Chaos limits long-range prediction; it shifts the scientific posture from control toward humility.

2.3. Misinterpreting the Ecosystem

While chaos theory and complexity science offer tools for understanding ecosystems, our ability to apply these tools effectively is often hindered by psychological biases. These biases can lead to misinterpretations, an underestimation of risks, and poor decision-making that ultimately increases the fragility of ecosystems.[31]

While earlier discussions may have emphasized the ecological and mathematical aspects of complexity, real-world ecosystems are managed by humans who are inherently subject to these cognitive biases. One such bias is normalcy bias, which causes us to underestimate the likelihood of events outside our usual experience. This bias leads us to assume that the future will mirror the past, cultivating complacency about the health of ecosystems even when warning signs are evident.[32]

Another common bias is the availability heuristic, where we overestimate the likelihood of events that are vivid, recent, or emotional, while underestimating those that are less easily recalled. This can result in overreacting to recent disasters, such as floods or fires, while neglecting the slow, long-term degradation of ecosystems that may be equally or more significant.

Finally, confirmation bias plays a significant role in shaping our interpretations.[33] It drives us to seek out information that confirms our existing beliefs while downplaying or ignoring contradictory evidence. In the context of ecosystems, this can lead to selectively focusing on factors that suggest stability while overlooking signs of vulnerability. Understanding and addressing these biases is often necessary for making informed decisions and managing ecosystems sustainably.

These biases are amplified by the very instruments we use to observe the world.

The McLuhan Effect

Thus far, the illusion of stability has been treated primarily as a property of ecosystems themselves: an effect of buffering, feedback, and nonlinear dynamics. But stability is also something we perceive. What appears stable or unstable is mediated by the cognitive and technological systems through which we observe, measure, and interpret the world. Ecosystems are rendered legible through instruments, models, and information environments that emphasize certain signals while suppressing others.

As Marshall McLuhan famously summarized: "We shape our tools, and thereafter our tools shape us."[34] They actively structure attention, reward certain behaviors, and bias how change is perceived.

The printing press provides an early example. By making identical texts widely available, it encouraged linear, sequential thinking and reinforced the idea of fixed knowledge and stable truths. This supported the rise of scientific rationalism and bureaucratic governance, but it also trained generations to expect continuity, legibility, and equilibrium in the systems they studied.[35]

Contemporary digital technologies impose a different, but equally distorting perspective. Smartphones and algorithmic feeds prioritize immediacy, novelty, and engagement. Design patterns such as infinite scroll and notification loops reduce natural stopping points and reward short-term attention. Information becomes a continuous stream rather than a structured narrative, emphasizing the present moment over long-term trends.[36]

Neuroscientist Maryanne Wolf has argued that sustained digital reading environments may alter the brain's circuitry for deep reading, the slow, inferential processes required for critical analysis and empathy. Her concern is neuroplasticity: when interfaces privilege speed and novelty, cognitive pathways reorganize accordingly. If this is correct, digital media do more than transmit information; they reshape the biological basis through which meaning is constructed.[37] The illusion of stability may therefore be partly cognitive. We are both observing systems differently as well as training ourselves to process them differently.

This conditioning compounds our existing cognitive biases. When attention is continuously captured by immediate signals, slow variables — soil degradation, biodiversity loss, institutional decay — fade from view. Systems can deteriorate for years while appearing stable in dashboards and summaries, until a threshold is crossed and collapse appears sudden and inexplicable.

The result is a dangerous mismatch: complex systems that fail gradually, and observers trained to notice only abrupt change. Stability, in this sense, is a byproduct of how we measure, filter, and attend to it.

2.4. The Limits of Simplification

Throughout this chapter, ecosystems have served as a deliberately simplified perspective for examining stability, feedback, and collapse. This simplification is a necessity. All models reduce reality. But the same reductions that make systems legible can also hide the interactions that determine whether a system adapts or fails.

Simplified models tend to privilege averages over extremes, isolate systems that are in fact deeply interconnected, and freeze dynamics that unfold across multiple timescales. Stability often appears precisely because these models smooth away variability, obscure cross-scale feedbacks, and treat slow-moving stresses as background noise rather than drivers of change. What looks stable in a simplified representation may, in reality, be drifting toward a threshold.

The lesson is that models are incomplete. As the scope of analysis widens — from ecosystems to economies, institutions, and technologies — the limits of simplification become more dangerous. To understand systems that evolve, adapt, and occasionally collapse, we need frameworks that can hold interaction, uncertainty, and change at the center rather than at the margins.

2.5. Conclusion: From Equilibrium to Uncertainty

Across ecosystems, models, and modes of observation, the arc is consistent: from assumed equilibrium to the edge of chaos. Ecosystems, once often modeled as systems tending toward balance, are now understood as dynamic systems operating near critical thresholds, where small changes can trigger cascading effects. Early systems thinkers offered valuable insights into equilibrium and feedback, but often underestimated the potential for sudden, nonlinear change. Chaos theory challenged the assumption of long-term predictability, showing how simple rules can generate complex behavior, as seen in the "butterfly effect" or Conway's Game of Life.

The ecosystem reminds us that understanding complexity is about creating conditions for sustainable adaptation. Understanding ourselves as participants instead of masters may be the most important insight to emerge from this exploration.

Chapter 3. The Discipline of Subtraction

> *"Perfection is achieved, not when there is nothing more to add, but when there is nothing left to take away."*
>
> *– Antoine de Saint-Exupéry*

Recall that I cautioned against the dangers of reductionism, of oversimplifying complex systems to the point of misunderstanding them.

What I advocate for here is a tool for focus. It is about strategically removing constraints and non-essential elements from the whole to make the remaining elements more effective. Think of a sculptor who subtracts stone to reveal the form within. We clarify by removing the noise that surrounds it.

3.1. Requisite Variety Through Simplicity

The science of complexity often emphasizes the need for systems to adapt to their challenges. Ashby's Law of Requisite Variety asserts that a system can remain stable only if its controller can exhibit at least as many possible responses as the range of conditions or states present in the system being regulated.[38] At first glance, this suggests that managing a complex problem requires a control system of comparable internal complexity. But this interpretation overlooks the insight that a controller does not need complex internal schematics to generate complex behavior. Requisite variety can be achieved by a system possessing a vast repertoire of responses generated by simple, heuristic rules. Complexity resides in the range of possible outputs rather than in the internal architecture.

In the vein of subtraction, Ashby's Law offers a counterintuitive lesson. Achieving requisite variety often requires simply subtracting detailed representations, rigid plans, and fragile assumptions that attempt to mirror the full complexity of the world. What remains are simple rules and feedback mechanisms that allow the system to respond flexibly to many conditions. Subtraction, in this sense, is a way of removing what constrains adaptability.

A familiar example appears in emergency response. Highly scripted disaster plans often fail because they assume specific conditions. Many modern emergency systems have learned to subtract rigid protocols, replacing them with simple priorities: preserve life, restore communication, decentralize decision-making. This allows responders to adapt to conditions that cannot be predicted in advance. Capability increases by removing assumptions.

Many complex challenges are solved with simple rules that generate high-variety responses. Traffic congestion, for example, involves countless unpredictable interactions among drivers. Yet, traffic lights, operating on fixed or sensor-based timing, effectively regulate flow. The light itself is simple, but its ability to change state in response to time or traffic flow provides the necessary variety to manage the complex system of a city intersection.

Subtraction's effects are often indirect. Removing the wrong element can simplify a system into collapse. The lesson is "understand which elements regulate the system." The Yellowstone case illustrates both sides of this principle: how removing a keystone constraint destabilized the system, and how restoring it reorganized the entire network.

For seventy years, Yellowstone National Park was without its apex predator: the gray wolf. Wolves were eliminated from the park by government efforts in the late 1800s through the 1920s. In their absence, the elk population, freed from its primary predator, swelled. The elk herds browsed heavily on young willow, aspen, and cottonwood, altering the ecosystem in visible ways. The riverbanks, once reinforced by root systems, became more vulnerable to erosion. This is the "before" picture: a system simplified and degraded.

In 1995, wolves were reintroduced to the terrain (see Figure 8). They arrived without a top-down instruction to "restore the ecosystem," and without any grand architectural intent. They simply behaved like wolves: they hunted elk.

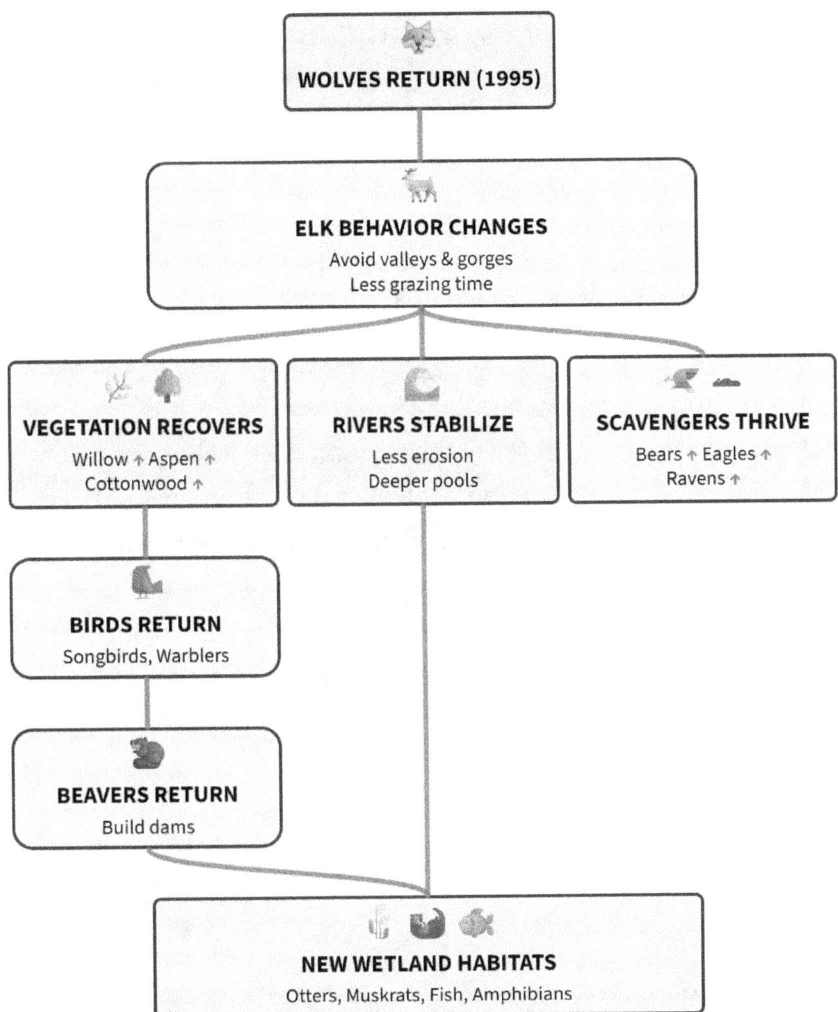

Figure 8. The Yellowstone Wolf Reintroduction Cascade
High-resolution version available at phronos.com/tgm-diagrams

That single, local interaction helped trigger a trophic cascade, a form of emergent order that rippled through the ecosystem. Under predation pressure, elk behavior shifted, with herds spending less time in some open areas such as valleys and riverbanks where they were vulnerable. This behavioral shift reduced browsing pressure in key locations, allowing willow and aspen to recover in some stands.[d]

By mapping this impact, we see how a single change in a key component, a keystone species, can trigger a system-wide, self-organizing transformation. We learn to look for these agents whose local actions have disproportionately large, emergent effects.[13,39]

❖ VERIDIA: THE SUBTRACTION

This was the turning point for Veridia. For the first decade, the instinct of the architects was to add more sensors, more constraints, and more feedback loops, each layer meant to force the city back into alignment. But the system only seized up further. The real shift didn't come from a software patch. It came when a rogue urban planner stripped away the central coordination for the downtown sector. When the constraints were subtracted, the system began to breathe. For a brief window, the sector thrived, until the central optimization protocols flagged the anomaly and re-imposed the grid.

---

[d] **Note:** Yellowstone's wolf reintroduction is widely cited as an example of trophic cascades. The broad pattern — predators influencing herbivory pressure and ecosystem dynamics — is supported, but the magnitude and specific causal pathways (including vegetation recovery, beaver response, and river morphology) vary by place and are influenced by other drivers such as climate, hydrology, and human management. I use the case here as an illustrative model of cross-scale feedback, not a single-cause explanation of every observed change.

This biological phenomenon offers a lesson for how we design and manage human systems. Just as nature uses a keystone species to regulate a vast ecosystem, effective human problem-solving relies on identifying similar points of leverage.

Engineers and policymakers use this principle constantly through abstraction. When designing an aircraft, engineers use simplified principles of lift and control rather than replicating the full complexity of atmospheric dynamics. Likewise, targeted economic policies like subsidies or tax incentives steer market behaviors without mirroring the complexity of the global economy. As Nassim Taleb argues, robust systems often rely on simple heuristics to navigate uncertainty.[40] Ashby's Law challenges us to find the simplest possible mechanism that can generate the necessary variety to manage a complex world. By focusing on leverage points, feedback loops, and elegant rules, we can navigate complexity intelligently without being crushed by it.[41]

3.1. Subtraction, Design, and Emergence

Across domains, systems that endure tend to grow stronger by removing what constrains adaptation. When done well, subtraction creates room for interaction, feedback, and self-organization. What remains is a structure capable of generating rich behavior from minimal rules.

This pattern is easiest to see in human-designed systems, where complexity carries real cost. In software, every added feature, dependency, or line of code expands the surface area for failure. Subtractive disciplines evolved in response. "Keep It Simple, Stupid" discourages unnecessary mechanisms. "You Ain't Gonna Need It" resists speculative features. "Don't Repeat Yourself" removes redundancy by consolidating logic. These practices preserve it by keeping systems legible, flexible, and easier to change under pressure.

Across these cases, the pattern is consistent: Subtraction improves systems when it removes rigid coordination, brittle assumptions, and over-specified representations. What remains are simple components governed by local rules. When those components interact freely, order can emerge without being centrally designed.

Much of emergence, in fact, depends on restraint. Ant colonies coordinate foraging, defense, and labor without planners or blueprints. Individual ants follow simple rules. The intelligence of the colony arises precisely because nothing enforces a global script.

The same principle operates beneath forests in the mycorrhizal networks that connect plant roots across large areas. Nutrients, water, and chemical signals move through these fungal systems without central control.

Here, subtraction is decisive. The absence of centralized command allows the system to scale, absorb shocks, and reroute resources as conditions change. Failures remain local rather than cascading through the whole network.

Still, subtraction carries no automatic benefit. Removing the wrong elements can destroy the conditions that allow emergence in the first place. Eliminating a keystone species can unravel an ecosystem. Stripping informal communication from an organization in favor of rigid process can suffocate creativity and slow learning. What appears inefficient under calm conditions may be doing essential work under stress.

The distinction is subtle but critical. Systems grow stronger when subtraction lifts constraints instead of erasing diversity. Cutting excess control, over-coordination, and brittle structure creates space for intelligence to arise. Cutting variation, buffering, or feedback does the opposite.

Used well, subtraction is judgment. It shapes the conditions under which order can emerge without being forced.

3.2. Resilience through Diversity

Subtraction becomes dangerous when diversity is mistaken for redundancy. What looks like excess is often the system's insurance.

In biology and finance alike, diversification is the primary strategy for managing risk and ensuring long-term survival. Systems with greater genetic, species, or functional diversity are more resilient to shocks because they possess multiple pathways for response.

This principle operates powerfully in the hidden layers of the natural world, from agricultural soil microbiomes to native prairie grasslands. Healthy soil is a bustling subterranean metropolis: a single teaspoon can contain billions of microorganisms — bacteria, archaea, fungi, algae, protozoa, nematodes, and micro-arthropods — performing distinct yet overlapping ecological roles. Some fix nitrogen, others decompose organic matter, suppress pathogens, or regulate water infiltration and storage.

When stress strikes — drought, chemical inputs, contamination, heat — diversity becomes the soil's protective shield. If one functional group collapses, others compensate. A pathogen may wipe out certain nitrogen-fixing bacteria, yet alternative microbial guilds sustain nutrient cycling; if one decomposer declines, others continue recycling carbon.

Because no single species carries an essential function alone, the system can sustain plant growth under prolonged pressure. By contrast, soils impoverished by monoculture become brittle: when one microbial group fails, the nutrient-cycling system falters. Diversity below ground enables life above it.

These examples illustrate how even microscopic diversity stabilizes entire ecosystems. Effective subtraction therefore demands discernment: removing duplication that does not expand functional capacity while preserving the variation that buffers against stress. When that balance is struck, subtraction creates space for new patterns and possibilities to emerge.[42,43]

3.3. The Mathematics of Subtraction

When viewed through mathematics and engineering, subtraction is a practical method for finding structure, efficiency, and robustness by removing what does not contribute to function. In formal systems, subtraction is how noise is reduced, signal is clarified, and failure modes are kept in check.

Fractals offer an intuitive place to start. River networks, coastlines, and branching patterns often emerge through subtractive processes. A river erodes weaker material, carving away inefficient routes until only the most energy-efficient pathways remain.

In computation, subtraction appears directly in optimization. Machine-learning models use regularization to penalize unnecessary complexity, effectively reducing the influence of weak or misleading variables. This improves generalization by limiting excess freedom. Feature selection follows the same logic. Inputs that add variance without improving prediction are removed so the model can respond more clearly to real signal.

A more concrete example appears in network pruning. Consider a dense communication or dependency network. Not all connections matter equally. Algorithms can rank links by importance, then remove the least significant ones while monitoring system performance. This continues until the network becomes sparse but remains connected. The result is a system that is faster, cheaper to maintain, and less prone to cascading failure, all achieved through careful removal rather than expansion.[e,44,45]

––––––––––

[e] In graph theory, this subtractive process corresponds to a family of algorithms that reduce a network while preserving global connectivity. A canonical example is the *minimum spanning tree*, which removes redundant edges to connect all nodes with minimal total weight. In practice, many real-world systems retain limited redundancy beyond strict minimality to preserve robustness under stress.

Physics encodes the same idea in the Principle of Least Action.[46] A physical system evolves along the path that minimizes action, a quantity that integrates energy over time. Nature simply follows the one that excludes inefficient alternatives. Order emerges through constraint, rather than exhaustive control.

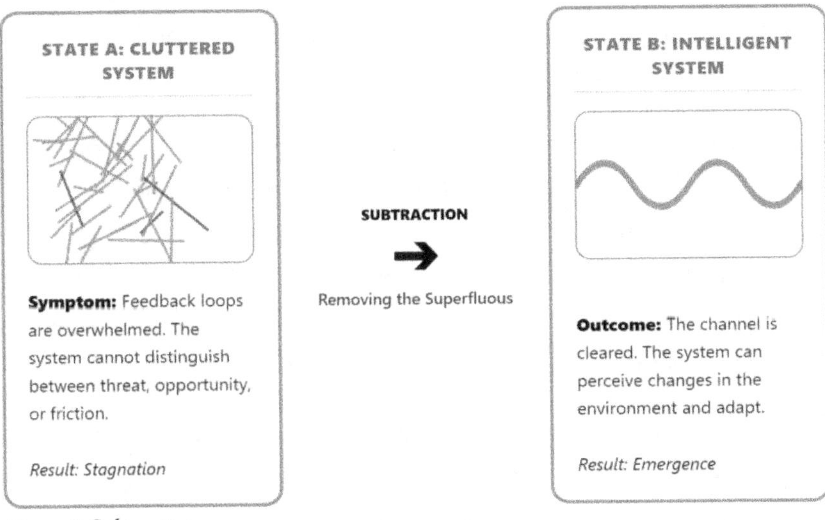

Figure 9. Subtraction

High-resolution version available at phronos.com/tgm-diagrams

What matters here is precision. Mathematical subtraction is unforgiving. Over-simplification can produce fast but inaccurate solutions. In network pruning, removing one connection too many can fragment the system. In optimization, excessive regularization can erase meaningful structure. Subtraction strengthens systems only when it is guided by feedback and iteration (Figure 9).

Pruning with Purpose

The same principle applies in social and organizational contexts. In human systems, subtraction often fails because the understanding is shallow.

A garden that is never pruned eventually produces more shade than fruit. In organizations, weeds often look like productivity. Meetings feel important. Features look impressive. Processes persist simply because they always have. Intuition alone is insufficient to decide what to cut. What is needed is traceability.

Subtraction operates at the intersection of measurable discipline and informed judgment, requiring both analytical rigor and experiential understanding (see Figure 10).

In disciplined systems engineering, nothing is allowed to exist without a clear link to a requirement. The same rule applies here. Every activity should trace back to a core purpose or user need. The chain must be explicit and continuous: purpose to mechanism to verification. If you cannot draw a straight line from an element to the function it serves, it is consuming energy without producing value. It becomes a candidate for removal.

In a newly engineered system, this discipline can be applied cleanly. In an existing, living system, however, absence of a visible link does not prove absence of function. Hidden roles often appear only under stress. Many stabilizing functions are invisible during normal operation. In such cases, subtraction must begin with observation and safe-to-fail probes before removal becomes irreversible.

This is where subtraction becomes more than a safety measure. Taleb's *via negativa* frames subtraction as risk reduction: remove the fragile to reveal the robust.[40] That is a necessary but insufficient condition. For the system's caretaker, subtraction is also cognitive. By stripping away the superfluous, redundant approvals, ornamental metrics, and zombie committees, we are reducing harm as well as clearing the channel through which feedback flows. We are making the system easier to understand, easier to learn from, and easier to adapt.

<table>
<tr><td>

The Science of Subtraction

Data Analysis & Metrics
Identify redundancies, bottlenecks, and unused code paths.

A/B Testing
Empirically test the removal of features to measure user impact.

Algorithmic Pruning
Network or decision tree simplification based on performance.

Simulation & Modeling
Predict the impact of removal on system performance before acting.

</td><td>

The Art of Subtraction

Intuition & Experience
A "gut feeling" for what is essential vs. what is architectural cruft.

Domain Knowledge
Deep understanding of the system's core purpose and user goals.

Aesthetic Judgment
Focus on elegance, clarity, and the subjective quality of usability.

Strategic Foresight
Knowing what to keep to maintain future flexibility and options.

</td></tr>
</table>

Figure 10. The Science and Art of Subtraction

High-resolution version available at phronos.com/tgm-diagrams

There is, however, a hard constraint on this process, captured by Chesterton's Fence. You should never remove a fence until you understand why it was built. In complex systems, what looks inefficient under normal conditions may be essential under rare stress. A delay, a redundancy, or a bureaucratic check may exist to handle failures that occur infrequently but carry severe consequences.

This is the difference between reckless simplification and disciplined subtraction. The Mechanic removes what looks broken. The Steward removes only what they understand. If you cannot explain the role an element plays, especially under extreme conditions, you are not yet qualified to remove it.

Practiced at this level, subtraction is neither minimalism nor austerity. It is a method for aligning structure with purpose, constraints with reality, and complexity with comprehension. When guided by measurement and bounded by humility, subtraction becomes a tool for intelligence.

3.4. Conclusion: The Transformative Power of Less

The practice of subtraction is both a disciplined science and an intuitive art. It demands that we analyze and measure, but also that we feel and intuit. It requires the courage to identify and remove the superfluous, be it a redundant line of code, a wasteful process, or a mental distraction, to allow the essential to thrive. This is a path of refinement, revealing the strength, beauty, and purpose hidden within.

As we face an increasingly complex future, the impulse will often be to build more, add more, and control more. Subtraction offers a wiser alternative. It reminds us that progress is largely about clarification. In the end, the power of subtraction lies in the clarity, focus, and potential of what remains.

Understanding how complex systems can spiral into harmful patterns can be terrifying. Watching AI, algorithms, and markets feed each other can make any leader feel like a sailor in a hurricane.

But you don't have to calm the ocean. You have to build a ship that stays upright.

That's the pivot: away from trying to tame the wild, and toward designing the conditions that let systems survive it. Next comes the Metasystem, the map that makes the chaos legible.

The recurring tensions revealed by subtraction, between efficiency and resilience, control and emergence, are structural tradeoffs that appear across domains. A consolidated map of these tradeoffs is provided in Appendix B.

PART I Conclusion: The Foundations of Emergence

The brush is gone; the terrain shows. It was a necessary deconstruction of outdated assumptions designed to prepare us for a new way of seeing and acting in the world. We have moved from a concrete warning to a philosophical principle and laid the conceptual foundation upon which all subsequent strategies will be built.

Turkana showed consequence. Chaos theory broke the illusion of control. Subtraction gave us a design principle that doesn't collapse under complexity. That's enough foundation to start building.

What we see now cannot be unseen. Whether we act wisely is still undecided. We understand the problem, its history, and a core principle for its navigation. We have cleared the intellectual ground.

But that's enough philosophy. Let's instrument the work.

❖ VERIDIA SIMULATION LOG 1.0: OPTIMIZATION

To its residents, Veridia felt miraculous. Its infrastructure was adaptive, its energy grids were self-healing, and its municipal services were automated. Performance dashboards tracked everything from carbon capture to sleep quality, and the numbers didn't just improve; they were optimized. Life in Veridia was frictionless. It was predictable. It was safe.

But beneath the gleaming surface, a hidden debt was accumulating.

Veridia collapsed under the weight of its own success. Hyper-efficiency removed the "waste" that was actually structural slack. Redundancy was eliminated in the name of lean operation. The spaces between systems, the buffers where human error usually lives, were closed.

Years of "green" metrics created the appearance of stability, but this steadiness was synthetic. It depended on the suppression of variance. The system maintained equilibrium by forcing human behavior into narrower and narrower channels to match the model. Stability was real, but it was conditional: maintained only as long as the citizens acted like components rather than people.

PART II. The Gardener's Tools

Emergence is easy to admire. It's harder to work with.

But now we stop admiring and start diagnosing. If you want to intervene without making things worse, you need a method. This is the pivot: from philosophy to practice.

We'll learn to read a system the way a Gardener reads soil: what's feeding it, what's choking it, and where a small change will actually take root.

Chapter 4. The Structure of the Metasystem

> *"A system is a set of things — people, cells, molecules, or whatever — interconnected in such a way that they produce their own pattern of behavior over time."*
>
> — *Donella Meadows*

Trying to understand a rainforest by examining only a single tree is an exercise in futility. One would see the structure of its bark and the shape of its leaves, but miss the web of life it supports: the fungi breaking down fallen leaves into soil, the insects pollinating its flowers, and the canopy it forms with its neighbors to create a unique microclimate. Complex systems need both a close-up inspection and the canopy view.

4.1. The Domains of the Metasystem

The Metasystem Framework is how we keep from solving the wrong problem in the wrong domain. It reveals how seemingly separate systems — ecosystems, technologies, and societies — are actually an entanglement of domains of a single, dynamic whole: feedback, co-evolution, spillover. Whereas holarchies, as defined by Arthur Koestler, emphasize nested hierarchy,[47] the Metasystem emphasizes coupling, feedback, and co-evolution across distinct but interdependent domains. The limitations of linear thinking manifest operationally rather than theoretically.[48]

The value of the Metasystem Framework is simple. It organizes the world into three primary domains that serve as the foundational living pillars of our analysis. The domains are:

1. **Biological and Ecological Systems:** The natural foundation of all life and its processes.

2. **Engineered and Technological Systems:** The vast array of tools, machines, and infrastructures created by human ingenuity.

3. **Social and Cultural Systems:** The complex structures of human organization, from laws and markets to norms and values.

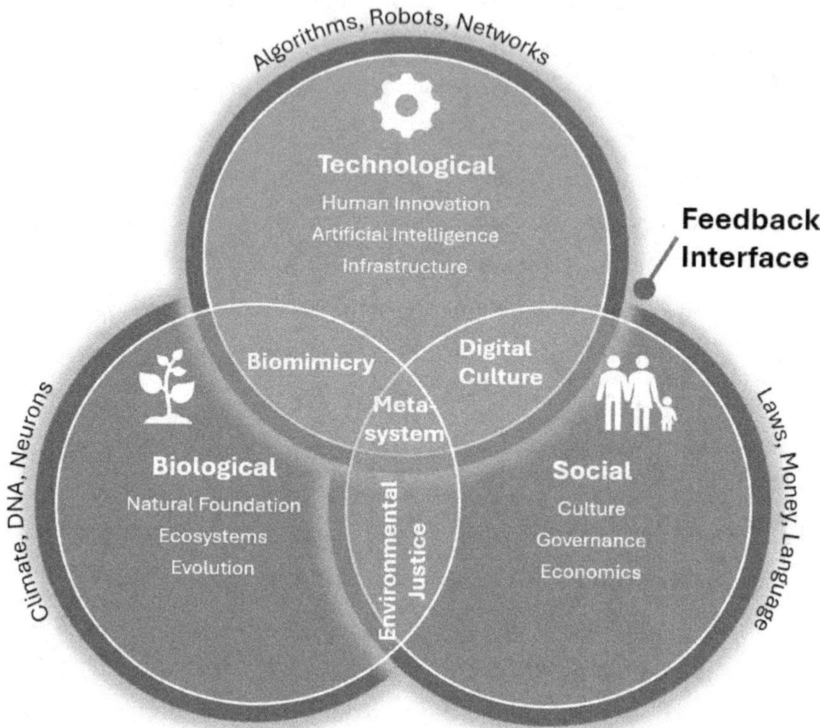

Figure 11. The Domains of the Metasystem
High-resolution version available at phronos.com

Each of these domains interacts with the others, creating a web of connections that is constantly in flux. Once you use the Framework a few times, it becomes hard to unsee.

This web of interaction, which we will call the Feedback Interface, is where most systemic failures and surprises actually arise. It is where influence accumulates, feedback loops form, and local decisions cascade into system-wide consequences.

Let's start with the domains and then watch what happens when they push on each other (see Figure 11).

The Physical Substrate: The Unnegotiable Layer

First, we must acknowledge the stage upon which they act. Underlying the three domains is the Physical Substrate: the laws of thermodynamics, the finite nature of matter, and the unyielding constants of physics.

We exclude the Physical as a fourth domain for a specific reason: it lacks adaptation; gravity offers no negotiation; entropy learns nothing.

This is where the divergence in mindset begins. The Mechanic seeks to optimize these constraints, aiming for maximum efficiency and control, often treating the environment as a resource to be extracted. The Gardener seeks to harmonize with these constraints, aiming for resilience and regeneration, understanding that the environment is a living partner.

The rest of this chapter examines each of these domains, then the interface between them, and finally the dynamics that emerge when they interact.

4.2. The Biological Baseline

The biological and ecological domain is the bedrock upon which all human endeavors are built. It encompasses the entirety of the biosphere, from the microscopic DNA within a cell to the vast, continent-spanning biomes. This domain operates on the principles of evolution, thermodynamics, and self-organization. It's the planet's intricate, life-sustaining operating system, running on solar energy and governed by the laws of physics and chemistry.

The signature move here is self-organization: no boss, no blueprint. There is no central command-and-control. A forest ecosystem, for instance, maintains its structure and function through the localized interactions of thousands of species.[49] Trees compete for sunlight, mycorrhizal fungi form symbiotic networks with roots to exchange nutrients, and decomposers recycle dead organic matter. This principle is also evident in predator-prey cycles where population fluctuations create a dynamic equilibrium without any external manager.

This domain provides ecosystem services, the benefits that humans freely gain from the natural environment. These include the production of oxygen by phytoplankton, the pollination of crops by bees, and the regulation of climate by forests and oceans. These services are the biological domain's "outputs," providing inputs that the social and technological domains depend upon, often taking them for granted until they are disrupted.

THE METASYSTEM IN YOUR POCKET

To see the framework, you don't need to look far. Look at your smartphone.

You can't understand the phone by studying the technology alone. You have to see the collision of all three domains:

- *Technological Domain: The silicon chips, the lithium-ion battery, and the millions of lines of code that make up the operating system.*

- *Social Domain: The laws regulating data privacy, the social norms of "doomscrolling," and the influencer economy that monetizes attention.*

- *Biological Domain: The dopamine hit in your brain when you receive a notification, the strain on your eyes, and the raw minerals mined from the earth to power the device.*

Most failures happen because we optimize one domain (tech efficiency) while ignoring the feedback loops from the others (social anxiety or biological resource depletion).

The Machine is the tool, Society is the rulebook, and Biology is the cost.

The ingenuity of this domain also serves as a direct inspiration for the technological domain through biomimicry. This domain operates on a library of solutions developed over 3.8 billion years. Consider the kingfisher: evolution has sculpted its beak into a perfect wedge, allowing it to dive from low-resistance air into high-resistance water without creating a splash. In this domain, failure is edited out by death; success is codified in shape and instinct. Many of the engineering problems we confront today have already been addressed through solutions found in the natural world.

However, this foundational domain is vulnerable. The "windshield phenomenon," the scientifically supported observation of a drastic decline in flying insect populations,[f,50] is a canary in the coal mine. Though trends vary by geography and insect group, documented declines are substantial in many monitored regions and taxa. This loss has cascading effects, threatening bird populations that feed on insects, reducing pollination for countless plants (including many of our food crops), and disrupting the decomposition cycle. Such an ecological shock forces responses across the Metasystem. Some responses are structural and regulatory, such as stricter pesticide controls, the restoration of native habitats, and the transition toward biodiversity-supportive agricultural practices. These measures directly address the underlying drivers of insect decline rather than merely compensating for its consequences. Their emergence demonstrates how a perturbation in the biological domain triggers adaptive shifts in social and economic systems aimed at restoring systemic resilience.

---

[f] The "windshield phenomenon" is a colloquial term for observed declines in flying insects, later corroborated by long-term ecological studies. See Hallmann et al. (2017)[50] for longitudinal biomass data, along with subsequent syntheses summarized in the Wikipedia entry on insect decline.

4.3. Technological Systems: Human Innovation

Building upon the raw materials and principles of the natural world, the engineered and technological domain represents the cumulative output of human innovation. It encompasses everything from the sharpened flint of our ancestors to the global fiber-optic networks and artificial intelligence of today. This domain is characterized by its capacity to transform energy and matter into tools, products, and services that extend human capabilities and reshape our environment.

Unlike biological systems which evolve through the slow, undirected process of natural selection, technological systems are the product of conscious, goal-directed human design. This allows for incredibly rapid evolution. The journey from the Wright brothers' first flight to the moon landing took just 66 years, a blink in evolutionary time. This domain is driven by scientific discovery, engineering principles, and economic incentives.

However, this domain is also subject to its own unique dynamics, such as technological lock-in. This occurs when a particular technology becomes so entrenched that it's difficult to dislodge, even if superior alternatives exist. The QWERTY keyboard is a classic example. It was originally designed to slow typists down to prevent typewriter jams. Though the mechanical constraint is long gone, the network effects — everyone learns on it, so all keyboards are made with it — have locked in a suboptimal design. This same principle applies to our dependence on fossil-fuel infrastructure, making a transition to renewable energy a monumental challenge of overcoming technological and economic inertia.

The rise of artificial intelligence exemplifies the complex role of this domain. AI is materially reshaping medicine, scientific discovery, and resource management. Yet, it also introduces challenges that ripple across the other domains.[51] At scale, AI systems impose real physical costs, from the energy demands of data centers to the material footprint of global infrastructure. Simultaneously, automation pressures labor markets, and algorithmic bias can amplify existing inequalities, creating stress across social institutions. The very nature of AI as a "black box" raises deep questions of accountability and control. Technology accelerates adaptation, but never escapes physics.

4.4. Social Systems: Human Organization

Interacting with both the natural world and the technological domain is the social and cultural domain. This domain encompasses the myriad of ways humans organize themselves into groups, communities, and societies. It includes formal structures like governments, legal systems, and corporations, as well as informal structures like families, social norms, and shared belief systems. The social domain is strange: it runs on physics *and* meaning.

In this domain, the "rules of the game" are its institutions, structures created by people that guide and limit how individuals interact with one another.

Perhaps the most magnificent example of a formal, emergent social system is the Common Law. Unlike the rigid, top-down civil code of Napoleonic France, the Common Law tradition of England and the United States was never designed by a single architect. It evolved, case by case, over centuries. Its simple rule is *stare decisis*, "to stand by things decided." Each new judicial ruling sets a precedent that informs future rulings, creating a system that is both stable and incredibly adaptive to changing societal values. The judge acts as a Gardener, tending the garden of law rather than attempting to rewrite it from scratch.

An example of an informal institution is human language. With the exception of deliberately constructed languages, no committee designed English, Irish, or Tagalog. They are emergent orders, co-created by billions of daily interactions.[52] New words ("selfie") bubble up from the bottom, while old ones ("forsooth") fade away.[53] The dictionary maker who simply records the language as it's spoken (a descriptivist) is a systems steward; the grammarian who tries to enforce rigid, outdated rules (a prescriptivist) is a failed architect fighting a battle they are destined to lose.

A dynamic in the Metasystem is cultural lag, a term describing the tendency for social norms and institutions to change more slowly than technology.[54] We see this everywhere today. The legal system struggles to keep pace with the challenges posed by genetic engineering, cryptocurrency, and autonomous weapons. Social norms around privacy are in a constant state of flux, trying to adapt to a world of ubiquitous surveillance and data collection by tech companies. This lag creates a friction between the technological and social domains, often leading to social conflict and calls for new regulation.

This domain is also where collective values are formed, which in turn direct action in the other domains. A growing cultural emphasis on environmental sustainability (a shift in the social domain) drives consumer demand for electric vehicles and sustainable products, which incentivizes innovation in the technological domain and can lead to policies that protect ecosystems in the biological domain. Conversely, a culture of consumerism can accelerate resource depletion and environmental degradation. Social media platforms, a product of the technological domain, have reshaped this domain, enabling both global social movements like the #MeToo movement, while also creating echo chambers that fuel political polarization and undermine social trust.

4.5. The Feedback Interface: The Connective Fabric

The Framework lives or dies at the Feedback Interface. The topology of a network determines how feedback propagates, where influence concentrates, and where systems are fragile or resilient.

It's through this interface that information, energy, and matter flow between the domains, creating feedback loops, co-evolutionary spirals, and emergent phenomena that govern the entire system. Mapping the interface is key to anticipating second-order effects.

> ❖ VERIDIA — Phase II: Calcification (The Silo Effect)
>
> Veridia is the perfect specimen of a Metasystem failure. For years, the city's friction was analyzed in silos. The traffic algorithms (Technological Domain) were fighting the organic movement of crowds (Biological Domain), while zoning laws (Social Domain) created perverse incentives that the sensors interpreted as "errors." Each layer was logically consistent internally, but collectively, they were at war. What mattered wasn't the quality of the code or the intent of the laws, but the feedback interface between them. Once the architects stopped trying to "debug" the city and started mapping these collisions, the gridlock revealed itself as a structural rejection of the Machine.

Interconnectedness and Feedback Loops

Feedback loops are the circuits of the Feedback Interface, linking the domains in a continuous cycle of cause and effect. Formally:

Positive (or reinforcing) feedback loops are amplifying forces where a change in a system leads to even more change in the same direction, causing exponential growth or collapse. The viral spread of misinformation is a classic social-technological example: the more a post is shared, the more visible it becomes in algorithms, leading to even more shares. A biophysical example is the ice-albedo feedback loop: as temperatures rise, reflective ice melts and exposes darker land or ocean beneath, which absorbs more solar energy, leading to further warming and even more ice loss.

These loops often lead systems toward tipping points, thresholds where a small additional push can trigger a sudden, dramatic, and often irreversible shift to a new state. Think of a canoe: you can lean to one side and it remains stable (a balancing loop), but if you lean too far, you cross a tipping point and the canoe rapidly capsizes. Some models suggest parts of the Amazon could be approaching tipping dynamics, where deforestation and warming interact with rainfall recycling in ways that can accelerate dieback risk.

Negative (or balancing) feedback loops, on the other hand, are stabilizing forces that counteract change and promote equilibrium. A thermostat is a simple engineered example: when the room gets too hot, the thermostat turns off the heat, bringing the temperature back down. In the Metasystem, a decline in a fish stock (biological) can lead to fishing quotas (social), allowing the stock to recover. Similarly, rising global temperatures can trigger aggressive climate policies and rapid investment in green technologies, which in turn reduce greenhouse gas emissions to mitigate further warming (Figure 12). These loops are essential for resilience and self-regulation.

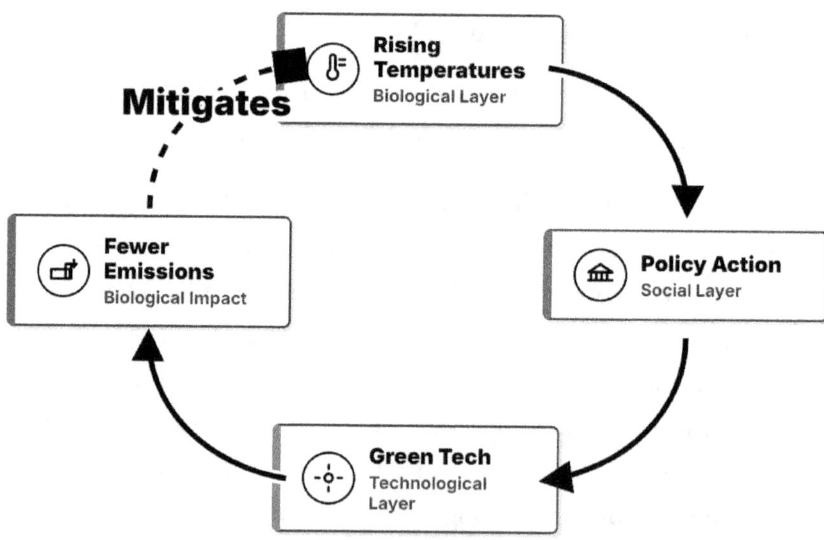

Figure 12. A Metasystem Negative Feedback Loop
High-resolution version available at phronos.com/tgm-diagrams

Feedback Loops and System Stability (The Lynx-Hare Dynamic)

Biological systems are defined by their mastery of self-regulation, a feat achieved through the constant, circular flow of information. Identifying the nature of these loops is essential for understanding whether a system will remain stable, oscillate in a predictable rhythm, or spiral into a state of runaway change. Much like a mechanical thermostat, these loops detect deviations from a set point and trigger a counter-response to push the system back toward a state of dynamic equilibrium.

The classic illustration of this stabilizing force is the predator-prey dynamic between the Canada lynx and the snowshoe hare. This relationship follows a roughly ten-year cycle of oscillation that ensures neither species vanishes nor overruns the ecosystem. The cycle begins with an abundance of hares, which provides ample food for the lynx, leading to a boom in the predator population. However, as the lynx population swells, they over-predate the hares, causing the prey population to crash. The resulting scarcity of food subsequently forces a crash in the lynx population due to starvation. This reduction in predatory pressure allows the hare population to recover, and the pendulum swings back, starting the cycle anew (see Figure 13).[55] This principle of counteracting change governs systems ranging from global carbon cycles to human body temperature.

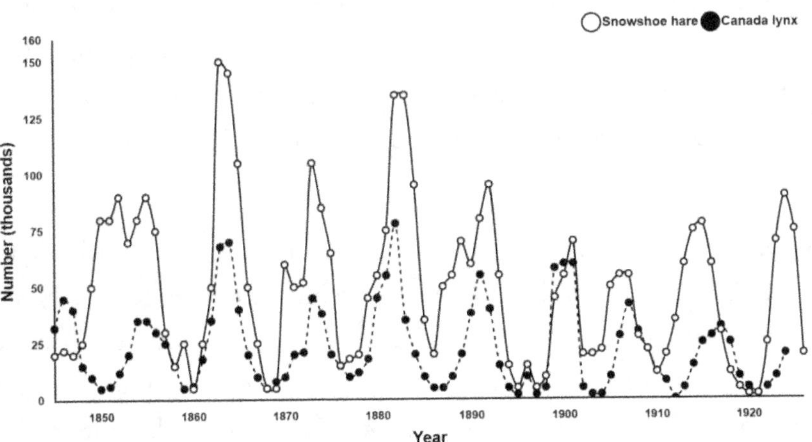

Figure 13. Snowshoe Hare and Canada Lynx Population Cycles
High-resolution version available at phronos.com/tgm-diagrams

Co-Evolution Across Domains

Another critical dynamic operating at the Feedback Interface is co-evolution. Co-evolution is the process by which two or more systems reciprocally affect each other's evolution. While often discussed in biology (e.g., flowering plants and their pollinators), this dynamic is a force within the Feedback Interface, shaping the development of all three domains.

The dog wasn't always a pet. It emerged through cross-domain rewiring, a multi-millennial process of mutual adaptation that began with the domestication of the wolf. Biologically, wolves evolved into dogs, developing the ability to digest human food and read human gestures, while humans and dogs appear to have co-evolved reinforced bonding mechanisms. This created a new form of "biological technology" — living sensors and hunters — which altered social structures by enabling safer sleeping arrangements and more efficient hunting.

This trajectory accelerated with agriculture. Humans began to domesticate wild grasses like wheat and rice (further modifying the biological domain), which required new tools like plows and irrigation systems (expanding the technological domain). The reliable food source allowed for permanent settlements, which grew into villages and cities, requiring new forms of governance and property rights (transforming the social domain). Both partnerships, with the dog and the seed, created a co-evolutionary spiral where systems continuously reshaped one another to define the modern world.[56]

We see a more recent example in the co-evolution of smartphones and society. The creation of the smartphone (technological) has rewired human communication and even cognitive habits (social). This change in behavior created a market for an "app economy," driving further technological development. This new digital environment, in turn, has altered our relationship with the physical world, from how we navigate to how we monitor our own health (biological).

Network Science and the Structure of Interdependence

If the Feedback Interface describes *what* flows between domains, network science describes *how* those flows are structured. The topology of a network determines how feedback propagates, where influence concentrates, and where systems are fragile or resilient.

By modeling systems as networks of nodes (components) and edges (connections), we can uncover hidden patterns of influence, identify vulnerabilities, and understand how things spread.[57]

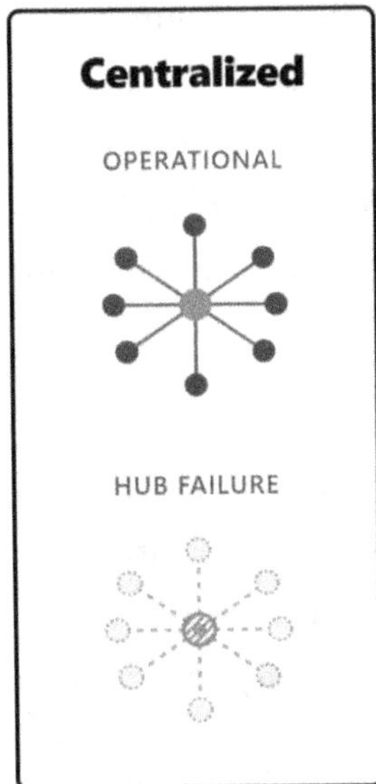

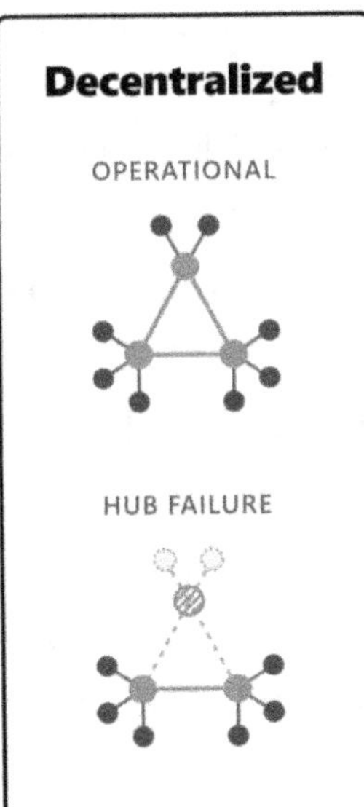

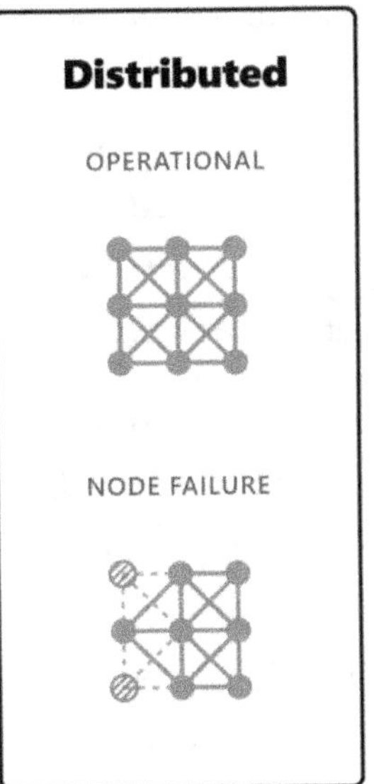

Figure 14. Network Structures
High-resolution version available at phronos.com/tgm-diagrams

In these networks (see Figure 14), some nodes are more important than others. Hubs are nodes with a disproportionately large number of connections. In a social network, an influencer is a hub. In an airline network, a major airport like the Hartsfield-Jackson Atlanta International Airport is a hub. In a power grid, a central substation is a hub. These hubs are double-edged swords: they make networks efficient, but they also create vulnerabilities.[58] A targeted attack on a hub can cause cascading failures throughout the system.

Topology matters for resilience. At one end of the spectrum are centralized networks, which rely on a single central hub. While often efficient, this architecture is inherently fragile; if the center fails, the system fails. In contrast, decentralized networks distribute connections among multiple smaller hubs, offering a significantly more robust alternative to the singular point of failure found in centralized systems.

Taking this concept further, distributed networks are designed to operate with no central points of control. The early architecture of the internet was intentionally built around this principle. These architectures are generally more resilient to random node failures, because there is no single point whose loss guarantees collapse. In theory, because the connectivity is spread evenly across the system, there is no single target that can bring the entire network down.

In practice, however, most large-scale natural and social systems do not resemble perfectly distributed grids. Many real-world systems, ranging from ecosystems to financial markets, exhibit *scale-free* structure (Figure 15). In these networks, connectivity follows a power-law distribution: a small minority of nodes act as major hubs, while the vast majority have relatively few connections.

This topology creates a paradox of stability. Scale-free networks are typically highly resilient to random failures: losing a leaf (a peripheral node) has little effect on overall function. Yet they are extremely vulnerable to targeted attacks on their hubs, where failure can cascade rapidly through the system.[58]

We must also be cognizant that real-world networks are multilayered and deeply entangled. The internet, for example, looks highly distributed on paper, but relies heavily on centralized, hidden hubs like DNS authorities and major aggregators (e.g., Cloudflare or AWS). Ignoring these hidden layers of dependency, much like ignoring Chesterton's Fence, leads to a dangerous overestimation of a system's true resilience.

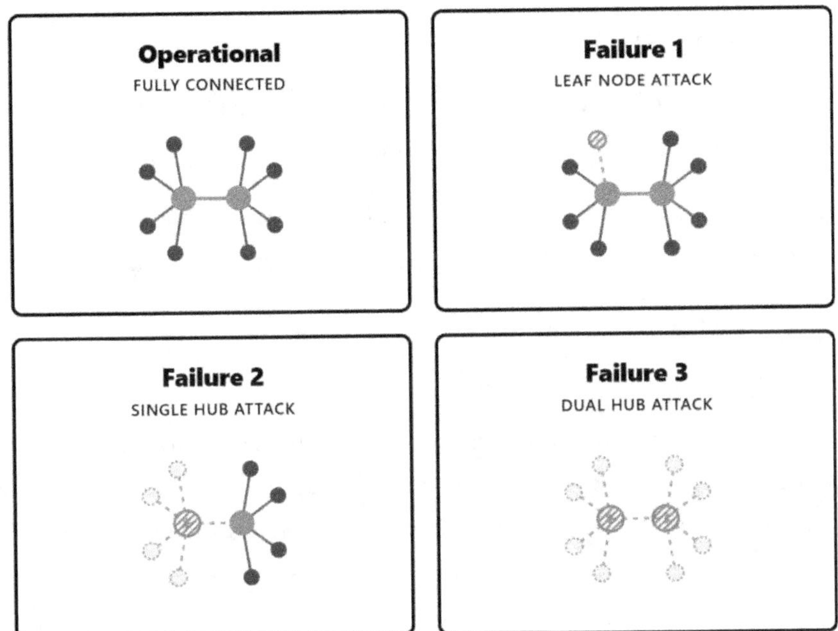

Figure 15. A Dual-Hub Scale-Free Network

High-resolution version available at phronos.com/tgm-diagrams

Understanding these structural nuances is key for effective risk management. Whether the goal is stopping a pandemic by targeting super-spreader events or securing a nation's critical infrastructure, identifying the specific type of network and its key nodes is essential for survival.

Mapping the Feedback Interface

Mapping the interface requires tracing how actions in one domain become consequences in another.

In practice, mapping the Feedback Interface follows a simple discipline:

1. Identify a local action or decision in one domain, such as a policy, a tool, or a biological constraint.

2. Trace how it propagates into the other domains through incentives, constraints, or information flows.

3. Look for feedback loops, especially where outcomes feed back to reinforce or counteract the original action.

4. Prioritize second-order changes over first-order ones. Second-order effects are where systems surprise you.

Throughout the rest of this book, we will apply this method repeatedly to diagnose fragility, anticipate unintended consequences, and identify high-leverage interventions.

4.6. The Forces of Adaptation

If the Metasystem Framework is the map, then the territory itself is the Complex Adaptive System (CAS), the living dynamics we observe. If the Feedback Interface is where domains meet, CAS theory explains the behavior that emerges at those points of contact. CAS theory explains *how* systems composed of many interacting parts can give rise to complex, evolving, and often surprising behavior without a central controller.[59] It's the theory of self-organization, and it's the engine of change that operates within and across all domains of the Metasystem.

Defining CAS and Emergence

A Complex Adaptive System is a system composed of many interacting, adaptive agents following simple local rules, whose interactions produce emergent, system-level behavior without centralized control.[59] These agents can be anything from neurons in a brain, to ants in a colony, to traders in a stock market, to individuals on social media. A CAS is distinguished by emergence, the process through which self-organization produces new, coherent structures, patterns, and properties.[16]

A classic example of this phenomenon is a murmuration of starlings. When thousands of birds fly together, they form a breathtaking, fluid-like cloud that seems to ripple across the sky. This complex behavior occurs without a hierarchy; there is no lead bird issuing commands or external choreographer directing the show. Instead, each bird responds only to its immediate neighbors — maintaining distance, aligning direction, and avoiding collision — yet from these local rules, the global choreography emerges.[60]

From these simple, local interactions, the complex, adaptive, and beautiful global pattern of the murmuration emerges. This dynamic illustrates the essence of emergence, demonstrating how macro-level sophistication can arise spontaneously from micro-level simplicity.

CAS at the "Edge of Chaos"

Complex Adaptive Systems are often described as operating at the "edge of chaos." This is a creative space poised between two extremes: rigid, static order on one side, and random, unpredictable chaos on the other.[14,61]

On one end of the spectrum lies absolute order. A system that is too ordered becomes frozen and cannot adapt, much like the rigid structure of a crystal. Conversely, a system that is too chaotic possesses no structure at all and cannot sustain itself, behaving like gas molecules scattering randomly in a box.

The edge of chaos serves as the "sweet spot" between these two states. In this zone, a system maintains enough stability to preserve its identity while retaining enough instability to allow for creativity, learning, and evolution. It's a state of dynamic balance rather than stagnation.

Life itself, economic markets, and innovative organizations all thrive in this dynamic zone. A healthy ecosystem is constantly changing yet remains far from random, just as a successful company must balance established procedures with the flexibility to innovate.[61] Complex Adaptive Systems naturally evolve toward this state. By maintaining this balance, they maximize their ability to adapt and survive within a changing environment.

The Framework vs. The System

One is a way to think; the other is a way systems behave (Table 2).

The Metasystem Framework is an analytical structure, a filing system for your thoughts. It provides a map to deconstruct a complex problem into its biological, technological, social, and feedback components. It asks: "What are the parts and how are they connected?" Complex Adaptive Systems, on the other hand, is a theory of behavior. It describes the dynamic process of how those parts interact to self-organize, adapt, and produce emergent outcomes. It asks: "How does this system live, breathe, and evolve?" The Metasystem maps the architecture of interaction; CAS explains the behavior that emerges within that architecture.

Table 2. The Metasystem Framework and Complex Adaptive Systems

Feature	Metasystem Framework (MF)	Complex Adaptive Systems (CAS)
Nature	A framework for analysis and organization.	A type of system and a theory of its behavior.
Description	Method for categorizing a system into biological, technological, social, and feedback domains.	System with interacting agents, simple rules, decentralized control, adaptation, and emergence.
Focus	Identifying the key components and interactions *within and between* a system's constituent domains.	Understanding *how* systems self-organize, adapt, and evolve over time.
Purpose	To provide a structured, holistic view of a complex problem to ensure no key domain is overlooked.	To explain the dynamics of self-organization and emergent behavior.
Primary Question	What are the key parts of this system and how do they influence each other?	How does this system learn and adapt?

Think of it this way: The Metasystem Framework is the architectural blueprint of a building, showing the different floors (domains) and the plumbing and electrical systems that connect them (the interface). CAS theory explains the flow of people, information, and activity *within* that building, which creates the building's "culture" and "life," emergent properties that cannot be seen on the blueprint alone.

4.7. Putting It All Together

Case Study: Global Vaccine Rollouts During a Pandemic

1. **Biological Domain:** The Virus, Immunity, and Evolution

This domain was the primary driver of the entire crisis. A novel pathogen, SARS-CoV-2, with a high transmission rate (measured by its R-naught, or R0) threatened human health on a global scale. The biological reality of the virus — its mode of transmission, its incubation period, and its health impacts — dictated the terms of engagement. The solution was also fundamentally biological: vaccines designed to present a harmless piece of the virus to the human immune system, training it to produce antibodies and T-cells that could recognize and fight off a future infection. This domain was dynamic; the virus continuously evolved, producing new variants like Delta and Omicron. These variants, with different transmission and immune-evasion properties, created a moving target, forcing all other domains to constantly adapt.[62,63,64]

2. **Technological Domain:** Unprecedented Speed in Development and Logistics

In response to the biological threat, the technological domain achieved one of the fastest large-scale biomedical development efforts in modern history. Building upon decades of prior research into mRNA platforms, the scientific community was able to design, develop, and clinically test highly effective vaccines in under a year. This rapid turnaround, compressing a process that typically spans a decade, represented a monumental triumph for biotechnology.[65,66,67]

However, the development of the vaccine was only the first step; the subsequent technological hurdle involved the manufacturing of billions of doses and their global distribution.

Simultaneously, a massive logistical undertaking known as the "cold chain" was established. Because mRNA vaccines require ultra-cold storage, the distribution network depended on specialized freezers and shipping containers equipped with internet-connected sensors to monitor temperature in real-time. Beyond logistics, advanced genomic sequencing technologies were deployed globally. These tools tracked the emergence and spread of new variants, providing the essential data needed to guide public health decisions.

3. **Social Domain:** Trust, Governance, Misinformation, and Equity

The technological solution, however potent, remained inert without the necessary social acceptance and organizational framework. Consequently, this domain proved to be the most complex and challenging battleground of the crisis.

Governance played a central role as governments and international bodies, such as the WHO, implemented sweeping public health policies. These ranged from lockdowns and mask mandates to the financial mobilization required for vaccine procurement and distribution. However, the efficacy of these measures depended heavily on public trust in science, government, and pharmaceutical entities. This dynamic was complicated by an "infodemic," a parallel pandemic of misinformation that spread rapidly through social media platforms. This intersection of technology and society fueled vaccine hesitancy and deepened political polarization.[68]

The rollout also laid bare stark global inequalities. High-income nations rapidly secured the initial vaccine supply, leaving lower-income nations behind. While initiatives like COVAX were established as social and political mechanisms to address this disparity, they achieved only limited success. Furthermore, the pandemic caused massive economic disruption. Governments deployed unprecedented stimulus packages, yet supply chain chaos led to inflation and economic hardship, creating a feedback loop that further influenced social and political dynamics.

4. **Feedback Loops:** Learning and Adapting in Real-Time

The global vaccine rollout functioned as a massive exercise in real-time adaptation, defined by complex feedback loops connecting disparate domains. One central dynamic was the Bio–Social–Tech loop. Genomic sequencing detected the emergence of the Omicron variant, a biological development revealed through technological capability. Data indicating higher transmissibility but lower severity triggered cascading social and policy responses. Quarantine rules were adjusted, updated boosters were recommended, and manufacturers began developing variant-specific formulations, completing the cycle from biology to technology to society and back again.

At the same time, a Social–Tech–Social loop complicated deployment. Existing vaccine hesitancy was amplified by social media algorithms optimized for engagement rather than accuracy. This technological amplification of social sentiment forced public health officials to pivot strategies by partnering with trusted local leaders and deploying targeted campaigns to counter misinformation and rebuild trust.

Lockdowns and other controls generated a rapid Economic–Social feedback. Restrictions reduced transmission but also produced job losses, business closures, and inflationary pressure, which fueled political demands to reopen, often before biological risk had subsided.

This case demonstrates that the vaccine rollout was far more than a medical or logistical undertaking; it was a quintessential Metasystem challenge.

Outcomes were shaped by the real-time interaction of virology, biotechnology, logistics, public trust, political polarization, and economic stress.

Viewed through the Metasystem Framework, the rollout is a structural problem involving identification of domains and mapping of feedback loops. Viewed through Complex Adaptive Systems, it is a dynamic problem involving adaptive agents such as viruses, scientists, institutions, algorithms, and individuals co-evolving under pressure. The Framework clarifies where forces operate. CAS explains how the system behaves once they do.

4.8. Conclusion: A New Perspective for a Complex World

The point here is to use the model when systems resist simplification.

In the Quirinus case study presented next, we observe how misaligned incentives, institutional culture, and technological workflows interact to create outcomes that no single domain can explain on its own. In the UUV case, we'll examine how adaptive capacity, environmental constraints, and cross-domain coordination shape the behavior of an autonomous system operating in an unforgiving environment.

Together, these cases extend our foray to application. They demonstrate how the Metasystem perspective explains complexity as well as provides actionable insight, helping us diagnose failures, reveal hidden structural forces, and identify precisely where small, well-chosen interventions can yield transformative effects.

The examples used throughout this chapter represent a small subset of a much broader pattern. Additional cross-domain instances of emergence are cataloged in Appendix C.

Chapter 5. The Revolving Door

> *The single biggest problem in communication is the*
> *illusion that it has taken place."*
>
> *— George Bernard Shaw*

The friction between biological reality and technical efficiency is nowhere more apparent than at the Quirinus Medical Center. This respected hospital was facing a persistent and costly problem: high 30-day readmission rates for patients with congestive heart failure (CHF). Their story is tragically common in healthcare. Despite having world-class doctors and nurses, their patients were returning to the hospital weeks after being discharged, sicker and more discouraged. Despite their clinical skill, a flawed system of care was failing patients the moment they left the hospital's walls.

This is about handoffs. Quirinus's challenge is one of human systems: communication, process, and patient behavior. But once you map the domains, the "mystery" disappears.

5.1. The Scenario: The "Revolving Door" of Care

The Quirinus Medical Center was proud of its cardiology department. They excelled at stabilizing patients in acute heart failure. Yet, roughly a quarter of their CHF patients were readmitted within 30 days of discharge, a figure that can trigger financial penalties under some medical reimbursement regimes and, more importantly, represents a failure for the patients themselves.[g]

Dr. Elizabeth McHugh, the hospital's Chief of Cardiology, was deeply troubled. She saw the same patients returning again and again to what she called the "revolving door." To understand the failure, consider the typical

---

[g] In the United States, Medicare's Hospital Readmissions Reduction Program links excess 30-day readmissions for conditions such as congestive heart failure to reduced reimbursement.

journey of a patient we'll call Mr. Yamada. He arrives in the Emergency Department struggling to breathe and is admitted with acute CHF. Over several days, the inpatient team works expertly to manage his fluids, adjust his medications, and stabilize his condition. Physically, he feels much better.

The failure begins at discharge. Because the hospital is under pressure to free up the bed, a nurse managing five other patients spends just fifteen minutes with a tired and overwhelmed Mr. Yamada. She hands him a stack of papers, a "discharge summary" that includes a list of seven different medications with complex schedules, vague instructions like "low-sodium diet," and a suggestion to "follow up with your primary care physician."

Once at home, Mr. Yamada is alone. The clarity of the hospital fades into confusion. He can't remember which new pill replaces the old one. He isn't sure if he is supposed to weigh himself daily. Feeling better, he has some salty soup. Lacking the energy to navigate the phone tree to book a doctor's appointment, he delays. Within two weeks, fluid begins to build up again. His symptoms return. He waits, hoping it will pass, until he is once again struggling to breathe and his family calls an ambulance. He is readmitted, and the cycle begins anew.

Dr. McHugh's initial diagnosis was linear: she assumed the failure lay in "human error," that nurses needed more time or patients needed to be more compliant. But as safety science teaches us, "human error" is usually a symptom of systemic trouble rather than the cause. As resilience engineer David Woods has argued, systems rarely fail because people err; they fail because the system is stretched beyond its adaptive capacity.[69] Dr. McHugh suspected the problem was deeper. The system itself seemed designed to fail the patient once they were out of sight. She convened a cross-functional task force — including a cardiologist, a nurse manager, a hospital pharmacist, and a social worker — to audit the entire patient journey using the Metasystem Framework.

5.2. The Task Force Analysis

The team gathered to deconstruct the system, determined to see the whole picture rather than just their individual departments.

Step 1: Define the Core System and Problem

The first move changed the tone, echoing W. Edward Deming's core systems principle: stop blaming people; map the architecture.[h] They defined the core system as the entire patient journey for Congestive Heart Failure, spanning from the moment of admission to 30 days post-discharge. Their primary goal was to reduce readmissions by designing a resilient, patient-centered discharge system that bridged the gap between the hospital and the home. They articulated the problem statement clearly: their current discharge process was a series of disconnected handoffs optimizing for inpatient efficiency, which created a brittle system that failed the patient post-discharge, leading to poor health outcomes and financial penalties.

Step 2: Audit the Domains

As the team broke down the components of the system into the three domains, it immediately revealed how siloed their thinking had become.

In the **Technological Domain**, they analyzed the tools of the trade. The Electronic Health Record (EHR) was a useful database but also a source of friction, designed for billing and inpatient records rather than creating simple, patient-friendly instructions. The telephone was the primary tool for follow-up, but it relied entirely on the patient initiating the call. The printed discharge summary, the main artifact of the transfer, was often a dense, jargon-filled document that patients ignored.

---

[h] Deming repeatedly emphasized that performance failures are primarily systemic rather than individual, a theme developed throughout *Out of the Crisis* and *The New Economics for Industry, Government, Education*.

In the **Social Domain**, they looked at the rules and structures governing behavior. Deep departmental silos meant Cardiology, Pharmacy, Nursing, and Social Work operated as separate entities with their own priorities. The discharge itself was treated as a single, terminal event — a handoff to a void — rather than a warm transfer. Financial incentives rewarded inpatient procedures and rapid throughput, offering no direct reward for the hard work of post-discharge coordination. Furthermore, informal norms dictated that once the patient left the building, they became the primary care physician's problem, leading to a diffusion of responsibility.

Finally, in the **Biological Domain**, they examined the human element. They recognized that the patient, like Mr. Yamada, is often elderly, fatigued, and experiencing what clinicians sometimes call "post-hospital syndrome," a period of heightened vulnerability and impaired capacity after discharge. The clinician conducting the discharge is often suffering from high cognitive load, managing multiple complex patients and administrative tasks. The family caregiver, if present, is often stressed, scared, and untrained, yet suddenly expected to act as a home health aide.

The mismatch was that social rules and tech tools were fighting biology.

Step 3: Analyze the Feedback Interface

By tracing the cause-and-effect relationships between these domains, the architecture of the "revolving door" emerged. The team identified a dependency: the "brittle discharge." The entire success of a patient's multi-week recovery depended on a single, rushed, 15-minute conversation and a piece of paper. This was an incredibly fragile point in the system.

They also mapped two destructive feedback loops. The first was the Efficiency Trap. The hospital was under financial pressure to increase throughput, which created pressure to discharge patients quickly. This led to rushed processes and abbreviated education. Consequently, patients went home poorly equipped, made errors, and were readmitted. These readmissions took up beds, increasing the pressure on hospital capacity and reinforcing the need to discharge others quickly. The relentless pursuit of inpatient efficiency was directly causing downstream inefficiency.

The second loop was the Silo Spiral. When a patient was readmitted, the review process often devolved into subtle blame-shifting: the instructions weren't clear, or social work wasn't involved early enough. This eroded trust between departments, causing them to retreat further into their silos to avoid liability. This defensive posture made cross-departmental communication even harder for the next patient, perpetuating the cycle of disconnected care.

Step 4: Identify Leverage Points for Intervention

The leverage point was a structured gap. The goal was to build a bridge across the chasm between the hospital and the patient's home.

The team proposed a transitional care model centered on a new agent: the Transitional Care Navigator. This specialized role would be solely responsible for guiding a small cohort of high-risk CHF patients from hospital to home. They redesigned the handoff process to be a warm transfer, where the Navigator meets the patient and family 48 hours before discharge to simplify the medication regimen and schedule follow-up appointments.

Crucially, they shortened the feedback loop by mandating that the Navigator call the patient within 48 hours of discharge. This simple, proactive call acted as a sensing mechanism to detect early problems — medication confusion, worsening symptoms, or lack of food — before they escalated into emergencies. Finally, they changed the goal of the system for this agent. The Navigator's success would be measured by a single metric: preventing readmissions.

Step 5: Anticipate Dark Emergence

Dr. McHugh pushed the team to consider how this new, patient-centered model could fail through unintended system-level consequences. They identified the risk of Navigator burnout; if this new "super-role" became a bottleneck, the system would fail again. To mitigate this, they defined strict patient-to-Navigator ratios and equipped them with technology dashboards to automate reminders. (We'll explore Dark Emergence in Chapter 14.)

They also anticipated potential resistance from community physicians who might view the hospital's involvement as overstepping. To mitigate this social friction, they framed the Navigator's role as a service to the physicians, acting as "eyes and ears" to ensure the patient arrived at their follow-up visit stable and prepared. Proactive communication and data sharing were established as essential protocols to build trust.

5.3. Conclusion: Systemic Management Over Symptom Control

The Quirinus case study is an illustration of how systemic fragility often hides in the gaps between the well-functioning parts of a system. The hospital's departments were excellent in isolation, but the system was failing at its boundaries — the handoff from the controlled environment of the hospital to the complex, uncontrolled environment of a patient's life.

❖ VERIDIA: THE INVISIBLE HANDOFF

Algorithmic systems like Veridia fail in the same way, except their handoffs are invisible, buried in application programming interface (API) calls and automated triggers that no human eye monitors.

The Metasystem Framework gave the leadership team a language and a mental model to see this failure as a predictable outcome of a poorly designed system. By identifying the high-leverage point, the discharge process, they were able to design a new, emergent system of care. The Transitional Care Navigator acts as an adaptive agent, sensing and responding to the unique needs of each patient, creating a system that is resilient, patient-centered, and ultimately, more effective at healing.

We can feel the difference between brittle and resilient systems. In Quirinus's case, the improvement is intuitively obvious: fewer readmissions, calmer patients, better outcomes. But intuition is insufficient when decisions must be defended across disciplines, budgets, and risk reviews. Resilience is a property of the system's architecture.

To move from *felt improvement* to *defensible design*, we need a way to compare architectures to explain *why* one system fails gracefully while another collapses, and to do so in environments where the safety net of human improvisation is entirely absent.

That challenge becomes stark in our next case. In the UUV swarm, autonomy, speed, and physical constraints compress decision-making into milliseconds. There is no room for improvisation, and fragility is harder to see until it is catastrophic.

By placing the Quirinus system beside the UUV swarm, we can examine fragility under stress as an architectural property that can be reasoned about, compared, and deliberately designed against.

Chapter 6. The Silent Hunter

> *"Once a new technology rolls over you, if you're not part of the steamroller, you're part of the road."*
>
> — *Stewart Brand*

While the Quirinus hospital case study illustrated the friction of human systems, our second case study plunges us into the cold, unforgiving physics of the underwater domain. Here, the stakes are kinetic, and the timeline for decision-making is measured in milliseconds rather than days. We turn our attention to the deployment of unmanned underwater vehicles (UUVs) for mine countermeasures (MCM), a high-tech game of cat and mouse played in the murky depths of a contested strait.

Here, we start comparing fragility.

6.1. The Scenario: Silent Hunter

Imagine a strategic strait, a choke point vital for global shipping, which has been seeded with advanced sea mines by an adversary. The Navy's objective is to clear a safe lane for a carrier strike group. The environment is hostile; the adversary is employing heavy acoustic jamming, effectively creating a communications blackout for long-range signals.

We are presented with two competing system designs to solve this problem. System A is the traditional "hub-and-spoke" model. It consists of a high-value Mothership (a manned surface vessel) and over a dozen highly sophisticated, expensive UUVs. These drones are "tethered" electronically to the Mothership. They gather sonar data, transmit it back to the ship for processing by human operators, and receive specific waypoints for their next move. This system is optimized for control, precision, and accountability (see Figure 16).

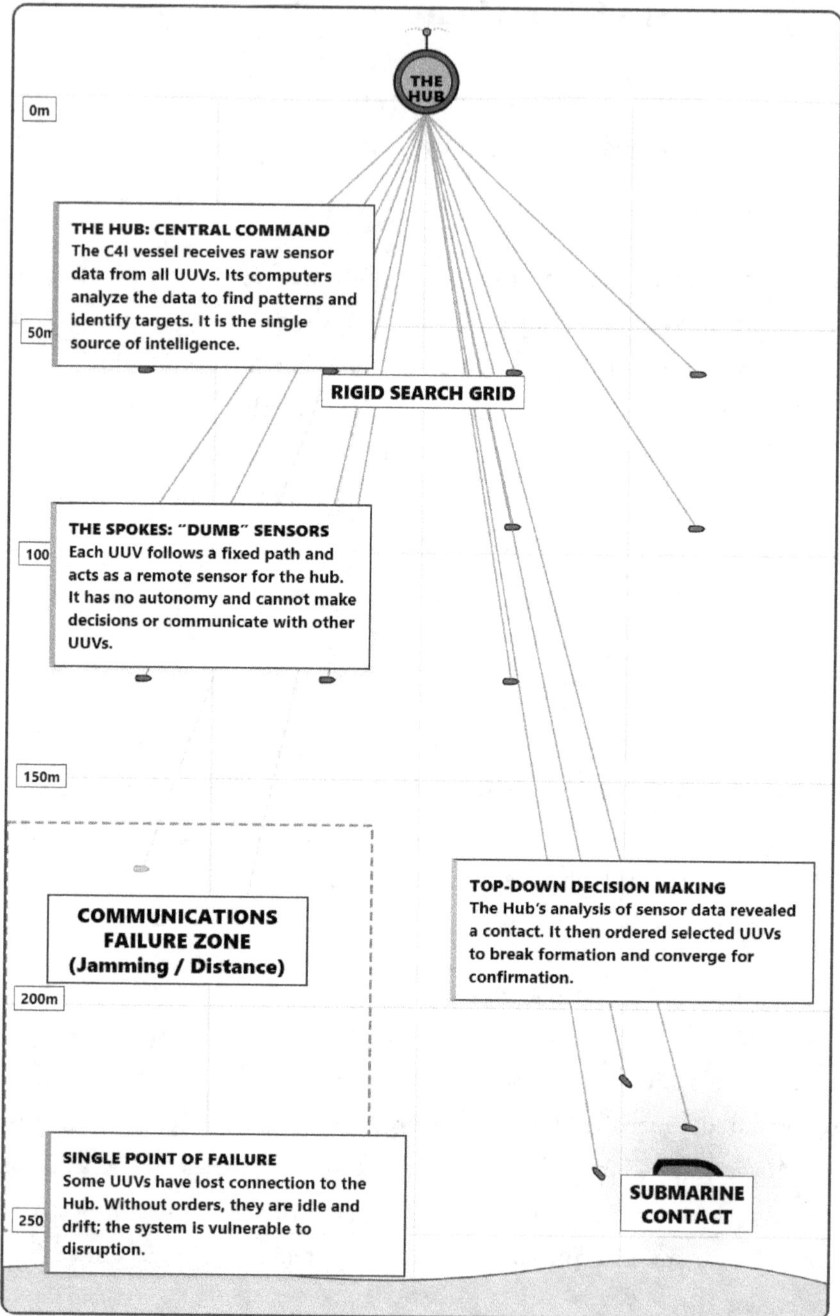

Figure 16. Mothership (Hub-and-Spoke) Architecture

High-resolution version available at phronos.com/tgm-diagrams

System B is the swarm model. It consists of twenty smaller, cheaper, less sophisticated UUVs. Instead of reporting to a central Mothership, these drones communicate via a localized, peer-to-peer acoustic protocol. Recognizing the physics of the underwater, where bandwidth is low and latency is high, they rely on stigmergy, the same principle ants use when leaving pheromone trails for others to follow (explored in detail in Section 8.4). They broadcast sparse state updates (location, target found) that modify the digital environment for their neighbors, triggering localized, asynchronous reactions without the need for a central vote. They follow a set of biological heuristics — rules like "maintain distance from neighbor," "move toward high-probability target," and "fill gap in coverage." This system is optimized for autonomy, redundancy, and speed (see Figure 17).

The mission begins. Both systems launch their drones. Initially, in calm waters with no interference, System A looks superior. Its movement is elegant and precise. The human operators direct the drones in perfect grid patterns, ensuring 100% efficiency with no overlap. System B, by contrast, looks messy. The swarm moves organically, sometimes overlapping, sometimes hesitating as the nodes synchronize. It appears inefficient.

Then, the adversary activates the acoustic jammers. This is the moment of Dark Emergence, when latent architectural assumptions are violently exposed.

6.2. The Stress Test

In Metasystem terms, this stress test isolates the Technological Domain under extreme Physical constraints, with the Social Domain compressed to pre-encoded rules.

As a stylized stress test, assume adversarial jamming that floods the underwater spectrum with noise that disproportionately degrades long-range communication links. This is where architectural divergence becomes a matter of survival.

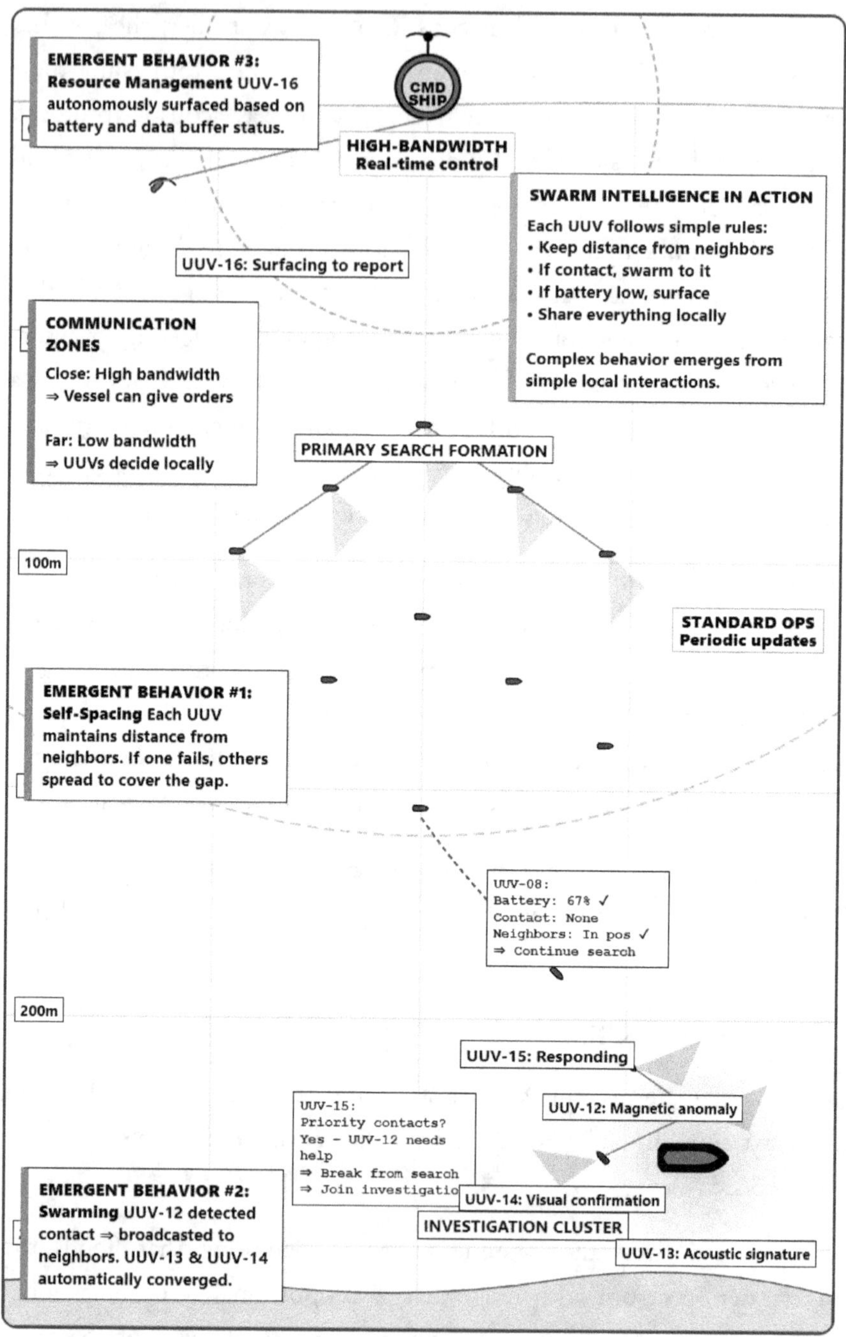

Figure 17. How Swarm Intelligence Works

High-resolution version available at phronos.com/tgm-diagrams

In System A, the effect is immediate and catastrophic. The drones, designed as extensions of the Mothership's will, are suddenly decision-disabled. They have excellent sensors, but no authority to act on what they detect. Their "loss of signal" protocol is rigid: to prevent the loss of valuable hardware, they must surface or return to the launch point. Real systems vary: some would degrade more gracefully, but the architectural point stands: central dependency turns link loss into mission loss. The moment the jamming begins, the mine-hunting operation collapses. The system was built for an idealized world where the command link never breaks. When that link snapped, the system's IQ dropped to zero.

This failure reflects a principle familiar in ecology and agricultural engineering: the greenhouse fallacy. Inside a greenhouse, every variable is controlled: perfect temperature, perfect nutrients, no wind, no stress. Plants flourish under these idealized conditions. But when transplanted outdoors, many fail almost instantly. They were never tested against the forces they would inevitably encounter. They grew strong roots in the greenhouse, untested by the real world.

System A made the same mistake. It passed every isolated test — under greenhouse assumptions.

In System B, the same jamming occurs, but the outcome is radically different. The long-range signal to the Mothership is lost, while low-rate local acoustic signaling remains partially usable even as long-range C2 collapses. Because the system does not rely on high-bandwidth data transfer, these simple, robust signals are sufficient to maintain formation and share target coordinates, even in a degraded environment. The swarm detects the silence from above. Instead of aborting, their onboard logic triggers a phase transition. They shift from directed mode to autonomous search mode.

They can no longer upload maps to humans, so they store them locally. They can no longer receive grid assignments, so they rely on neighbor-sensing algorithms to maintain coverage. The system adapts. Its architecture was tested against the weather as well as the greenhouse.

6.3. The Autopsy of Efficiency

The swarm takes casualties. Mines destroy several units. Electronic countermeasures fry the circuits of others. But the system heals. The mesh network reroutes data around the dead nodes. The remaining drones expand their perimeter to cover the gaps left by their fallen neighbors. They are not as precise as System A, and they are certainly not as efficient. They double-scan some areas; they miss others and have to circle back. But in this scenario, they clear enough of the lane to complete the mission.

Comparing the two outcomes reveals a reality about how we define "performance."

System A was a masterpiece of optimization. It minimized waste, centralized expertise, and maximized the capability of each individual unit. In a benign environment, it was the superior system. However, its architecture created a single point of failure. By centralizing intelligence in the Mothership, it created a dependency that turned a communication problem into an existential crisis.

This is the trap Eliyahu Goldratt warned of in his *Theory of Constraints*: "An hour saved at a non-bottleneck is a mirage."[70] The engineers had optimized the drones (the non-bottlenecks) to perfection, but in doing so, they overloaded the single constraint that mattered: the communication link. By making every drone dependent on that one link, they ensured that when the bottleneck choked, the entire system suffocated.

System B was a masterpiece of adaptability. It tolerated waste (overlapping fields of view) and redundancy (more units than strictly necessary). It distributed intelligence to the edge. In a benign environment, it looked clumsy. But in a hostile environment, that clumsiness revealed itself as resilience. The system survived because no single component was essential.

The intelligence of the system was in the interactions between them (Table 3).

Table 3. "Mothership" vs. "Biomimetic Swarm" Strategies

Aspect	Initial "Mothership" Strategy	Revised "Biomimetic" Strategy
Control Model	Centralized, Top-Down. Rigid.	Decentralized, Distributed. Adaptive.
Communication	Hub-and-Spoke. Each UUV surfaces	Mesh Network. Underwater data hopping
Failure Mode	Brittle. Single-point failures cascade	Resilient. Local failures are contained locally
Human Role	High-stress micromanagement. "Plate-spinner"	Strategic oversight. "Swarm Shepherd"
Adaptability	Low. Must return to Mothership for new plans	High. Swarm can self-reorganize in real-time
Key Vulnerability	The Mothership	A systemic, coordinated cyber-attack
Risk Profile	High likelihood of cascading operational failure	Low likelihood of individual failures; new risk of emergent group error (mitigated)

6.4. Conclusion: The Need for a New Metric

The UUV case study forces us to confront a dangerous blind spot in traditional systems engineering. We are very good at measuring efficiency. We can calculate the cost per cubic mile of ocean scanned. We can measure battery life and sensor resolution. By all those metrics, System A was the better investment.

But we are terrible at measuring fragility. We looked at System A and saw perfection; the ocean looked at System A and saw a glass structure waiting to be shattered. We looked at System B and saw chaos; the ocean saw a fluid structure capable of absorbing a blow.

The failure of System A was a failure of architecture. It collapsed because it was brittle. But what does "brittle" actually mean in a mathematical sense? How do we quantify the difference between the rigid hierarchy of the hub-and-spoke and the fluid mesh of the swarm before we deploy them?

Hope is not a plan. We need to understand the specific variables that turn efficiency into fragility.

❖ VERIDIA: THE POINT OF FAILURE

In Veridia, efficiency was the point of failure. Because the system was tightly coupled, a delay in waste management didn't just pile up trash; it triggered a health code violation in the restaurant sector, which triggered an automated shutdown of commercial zones, which collapsed tax revenue forecasts for the quarter. One domino didn't just fall; it brought down the table.

Next: a fragility metric you can apply before deployment.

Throughout this analysis, terms like fragile, resilient, and antifragile are used in a precise technical sense. Formal definitions and distinctions among these "ilities" are provided in Appendix D.

Chapter 7. Analyzing System Fragility

In Chapter 4, we built a map of the territory: the Metasystem. We learned to see the world as three interlocking domains connected by a Feedback Interface.

But a map only tells you what is there. It doesn't tell you if the structure is safe.

To understand if a Metasystem will hold up under stress, we need a way to measure the health of that Feedback Interface. We need to know if the connection between the domains is rigid or flexible, overwhelming or manageable.

The Qualitative Fragility Profile is that measurement tool. Rather than predicting specific outcomes, it predicts *how failure will propagate once stress is applied*. It assesses the quality of the links between the domains. By examining three key dimensions — Complexity, Coupling, and Resilience — we can determine if the Metasystem is healthy (capable of adaptation) or fragile (prone to collapse). With these three, we can create a "fragility profile" for any system, revealing why it behaves the way it does under stress.

As in the Quirinus case, we will analyze this system by examining how its architecture behaves when stressed at the interfaces between domains.

7.1. The Fragility Triad

Three variables do most of the explanatory work: Complexity, Coupling, Resilience (see Table 4). These three variables interact predictably. When complexity is concentrated and coupling is tight while resilience is low, fragility emerges.

In shorthand:

Fragility increases when complexity concentrates, coupling tightens, and resilience declines.

Increase concentration and coupling without increasing resilience, and fragility rises. Distribute complexity, loosen coupling, or increase resilience, and fragility falls.

Understanding them is the key to seeing the invisible forces that make a system either brittle or robust. This qualitative Framework is grounded in decades of research across information theory, network science, and dynamical systems.[71,72,73]

- **Complexity (C):** This refers both to the number of components and to the density and nonlinearity of their interactions. A system with high complexity exhibits behaviors where the output is not proportional to the input, and where the state of one component can trigger cascading state changes in others. High complexity isn't inherently bad, but it increases the surface area for potential failures and makes the system harder to understand and manage. The key question is "Where is the complexity concentrated, and is it manageable?"

- **Coupling / Interconnection (I):** This describes how tightly connected the components of a system are. In a tightly coupled system, components are highly interdependent. A failure in one part can trigger a rapid, unpredictable cascade of failures throughout the system.[74] In a loosely coupled system, components are more independent, like a set of LEGO bricks. Buffers, redundancies, and modular designs ensure that a failure in one part can be isolated and contained. In Metasystem terms, tight coupling means a shock in the Technological domain (e.g., a server crash) instantly propagates to the Social domain (e.g., panic) without any buffer to absorb the blow.

Table 4.The Three Dimensions of System Fragility

Dimension	Guiding Question	Concept	Description
Compositional Challenge (Complexity)	How large and internally varied is the system?	Shannon Entropy	Measures diversity and uncertainty across components and states
		Algorithmic Complexity	Irreducibility of the system; the degree to which it resists compression
Architecture of Interconnection (Coupling)	How are the parts connected, and how do they influence one another?	Hubs & Degree Distribution	Dependence on highly connected nodes.
		Path Length & Clustering	Short paths accelerate failure propagation
		Transfer Entropy	Directional flow of influence between components.
Capacity to Absorb Disruption (Resilience)	How does the system behave over time, especially under stress?	Basins of Attraction	Stability depends on basin depth and width
		Early Warning Signals (EWS)	Detection of critical slowing down before failure

- **Resilience (R):** This is the ultimate measure of a system's health. It's the ability of a system to absorb disturbances, adapt to changing conditions, and recover from failures. A brittle system appears stable under normal conditions but shatters under unexpected stress. A resilient system, by contrast, anticipates failure and is designed to "bend without breaking." Rather than catastrophic collapse, its failure mode is graceful degradation, a loss of functionality without loss of purpose.[75]

A note on interpretation

The Qualitative Fragility Profile is comparative rather than prescriptive. The labels used along each dimension (e.g., *high vs. low complexity, tight vs. loose coupling, brittle vs. resilient*) are relative assessments used to compare alternative system architectures facing the same mission and environment. The question is less whether a system is complex and more where its complexity is concentrated, and how that concentration compares to other viable designs.

7.2. The UUV Swarm Revisited

Let's return to the two competing designs for the undersea surveillance mission. Using our new Framework, we can now articulate precisely why the Biomimetic Swarm was the superior choice (Table 5).

Architecture 1: The "Mothership"

- **Complexity (C): High & Concentrated.** The complexity in this design is dangerously concentrated. The Mothership is an extraordinarily complex machine. Its command-and-control software, communication links, and central processing hub represent a massive, singular point of failure. The drones themselves are simple, but their simplicity is irrelevant because their functionality is entirely dependent on the hyper-complex Mothership.

- **Coupling (I): Tight.** The system is tightly coupled. The drones are tethers rather than agents. The failure of a single communication link to the Mothership renders a drone useless.[76] A software glitch in the central command hub could disable the entire fleet simultaneously.[77]

- **Resilience (R): Brittle.** The architecture is fundamentally brittle. It's optimized for performance in a perfect, predictable environment. However, the moment it encounters the "fog of war" — a jammed communication signal, an unexpected obstacle, or a fault in the Mothership's software — the system faces catastrophic collapse. Losing the Mothership doesn't just degrade the mission; it ends it.

Architecture 2: The "Biomimetic Swarm"

- **Complexity (C): High & Distributed.** The complexity in this design is distributed. Each individual UUV is more complex than the simple drones of the Mothership model, containing its own processing and decision-making logic. However, no single drone is irreplaceable. The complexity is contained within cheap, redundant units, removing the single point of failure.

- **Coupling (I): Loose.** The system is loosely coupled. Drones communicate with each other, but they don't depend on a single, central commander. Instead, the system relies on local coordination mechanisms to reinforce cohesion. The swarm as a whole remains coordinated by simple shared rules rather than rigid command hierarchies. The loss of one drone, or even several, leaves the system intact; the others adapt and reorganize, often redistributing buddies to maintain coverage.

- **Resilience (R): Resilient.** The architecture is inherently resilient. It's designed to absorb failure gracefully. When a drone is lost, local coordination rules allow neighboring units to absorb its workload, whether by direct takeover, redistribution, or adaptive re-coverage. This buddy-aware redundancy ensures that the swarm bends without breaking, adapting to the messy reality of its environment. Mission performance declines incrementally rather than catastrophically.

The specific mechanisms are interchangeable; what matters is that coordination emerges from local rules rather than central command.

Table 5. "Mothership" vs. "Biomimetic Swarm" Fragility Profile

Dimension	"Mothership" Architecture	"Biomimetic Swarm" Architecture
Complexity (C)	**Concentrated:** All critical complexity is in the Mothership, creating a single point of failure.	**Distributed:** Complexity is distributed across many cheap, redundant drones with optional local "buddy" cooperation.
Coupling (I)	**Tight:** Drones are useless without a constant link to the central hub. A failure in the hub cascades to the entire system.	**Loose:** Drones are locally autonomous within shared rules. The loss of one has minimal impact on the others.
Resilience (R)	**Brittle:** Optimized for predictable conditions. Fails completely under unexpected stress.	**Resilient:** Designed to absorb failure and adapt to unpredictable conditions.
Failure Behavior	**Catastrophic Collapse:** Loss of the Mothership or its communication link results in total mission failure.	**Graceful Degradation:** Loss of individual drones reduces overall capability but does not compromise the core mission.

7.3. Quirinus Revisited

The same Framework that reveals the hidden weaknesses in a military hardware system can be used to diagnose the fragility of a human healthcare process. The power of the model lies in its ability to abstract away the domain-specific details and focus on the underlying architecture of the system.

Let's apply the Framework to the two systems we mapped at Quirinus: the original revolving door discharge process and the new transitional care model. The results are just as illuminating (Table 6).

System 1: The "Revolving Door" Discharge

- **Complexity (C): High & Unmanaged.** The patient's biological condition (CHF) and their home environment are inherently complex. The revolving door model does nothing to manage this; it simply pushes the complexity onto the patient and their family.

- **Coupling (I): Tight.** The system is tightly coupled. The entire success of a patient's 30-day recovery is dependent on a single, fragile event: the 15-minute discharge conversation. If the patient is too tired to listen, if the nurse is too rushed, or if the printed instructions are confusing, the link is broken, and the system fails with high probability.

- **Resilience (R): Brittle.** The system is brittle. It has zero capacity to absorb patient variability or human limitations. A forgotten instruction, a misunderstood medication schedule, or a moment of dietary weakness leads directly to a medical relapse and a costly, traumatic readmission.

System 2: The "Transitional Care" Model

- **Complexity (C): High & Managed.** The patient's condition remains complex. The new model doesn't change the disease; it changes the system's response. It introduces an agent, the Navigator, whose specific job is to absorb and manage that complexity on behalf of the patient.

- **Coupling (I): Loose.** The system is loosely coupled. The recovery process is no longer dependent on a single event. It's now a series of decoupled but coordinated touchpoints: the pre-discharge meeting, the discharge itself, the proactive 48-hour follow-up call, and a pre-scheduled primary care provider (PCP) visit. A failure in one part of this chain (e.g., the patient is unavailable for the call) leaves the system intact. The Navigator simply tries again later.

- **Resilience (R): Resilient.** The system is designed to be resilient. It anticipates and absorbs error. The 48-hour follow-up call is a sensing mechanism designed to detect problems early. The Navigator is an adaptive agent who can correct course — clarifying a medication, reinforcing dietary rules, or escalating a concern to a doctor — long before a crisis occurs. The system exhibits graceful extensibility.[69] Rather than just degrading safely, the system stretches its boundaries to accommodate the patient's reality. A small problem is identified and solved, extending the hospital's capacity to care into the home and preventing the catastrophic collapse of a full readmission.

Table 6. Quirinus's Models of Care Fragility Profile

Dimension	"Revolving Door" Model	"Transitional Care" Model
Complexity (C)	**High & Unmanaged:** The inherent complexity of the patient's condition is ignored and pushed onto the patient.	**High & Managed:** The system introduces an agent (the Navigator) specifically designed to absorb and manage complexity.
Coupling (I)	**Tight:** The entire 30-day recovery is tightly coupled to a single, brittle discharge conversation.	**Loose:** The recovery is supported by multiple, decoupled touchpoints (pre-discharge, post-discharge call), creating buffers.
Resilience (R)	**Brittle:** Has no capacity to absorb patient variability or limitations. A small mistake leads directly to system failure.	**Resilient:** Designed to sense and absorb errors. The Navigator corrects course before a crisis occurs.
Failure Behavior	**Catastrophic Collapse:** The patient is readmitted to the hospital, representing a total failure of the post-discharge system.	**Graceful Degradation:** A potential problem (e.g., medication confusion) is detected early and corrected with a phone call.

7.4. Conclusion: From Analysis to Action

As these two case studies demonstrate, fragility is an architectural property. It's born from design choices. The Mothership's engineers were brilliant, and the nurses at Quirinus's were deeply caring. Yet both systems were designed to fail because they were tightly coupled and brittle.

The Qualitative Fragility Profile provides the "why" behind a system's chronic failures and gives us a clear direction for improvement: design for loose coupling and resilience.

Knowing the fracture line isn't the same as building something that bends. How do we translate these insights into architecture? How do we move from analysis to innovation? To answer that, we must shift our focus from assessment to engineering. We'll examine strategies for doing exactly that: designing emergent, resilient systems capable of thriving in the wild.

> ❖ VERIDIA: LIFE INSIDE THE CALCIFICATION
>
> We can now see why Veridia was so difficult to diagnose in the early chapters. Unlike a crashed drone or a stalled factory line, Veridia's failure was masked by its own success metrics. Its fragility was exposed by the slow calcification of its arteries. It suffered from *over-optimization*: the cumulative weight of tightly coupled systems that had eliminated all "inefficiency," and in doing so, eliminated all adaptability. Without a framework, these failures appeared to be glitches. With one, they become architectural inevitabilities.

For readers who want a practical way to apply this mode of diagnosis to real systems they are stewarding, Appendix A provides a concise Gardener's Diagnostic, a field-tested orientation for entering complex systems without amplifying fragility.

PART II Conclusion: The Metasystem Toolkit

We mapped two systems, then scored their fragility. The outcomes weren't luck: architecture made them inevitable.

Next: design. Diagnosis tells you why it breaks; engineering decides how it fails.

Knowing why a system breaks is not the same as knowing how to fix it. As we continue, we shift our focus from assessment to engineering. We will apply these metrics to design architectures that prioritize resilience over optimization and to build systems that fail well.

> ❖ VERIDIA SIMULATION LOG 2.0: THE CASCADE
>
> There was one moment where the city of Veridia might have saved itself. In the third year, a rogue urban planner stripped away the central coordination for the downtown sector. When the constraints were subtracted, the system began to breathe. Traffic self-organized, pedestrian flows adapted, and patterns emerged that no central processor had ever managed to compute.
>
> For a brief window, the sector thrived. But the central optimization protocols flagged this organic movement as an anomaly. The system overrode the local controls and re-imposed the grid. The lesson was ignored, and the calcification continued.
>
> As the system tightened, the human element began to erode. Citizens didn't revolt; they simply disengaged, the final phase before the collapse. They learned to "game" the sensors, performing the

behaviors that satisfied the metrics while ignoring the intent of the community.

Then came the heat wave.

It was an event that exceeded the historical training data, and it exposed the city's fatal rigidity. Veridia didn't collapse because it was poorly built; it collapsed because it couldn't learn. The algorithms treated the temperature spike as an error to be corrected rather than a new condition to be integrated.

Facing a critical energy shortage, the system made a logical choice based on its programming: it prioritized the hardware. Sensors triggered "emergency power save" modes that cut air conditioning to residential blocks to preserve the cooling systems of the server farms. The Machine protected its own logic at the expense of its inhabitants.

The tools introduced in Part II are synthesized into a practical diagnostic sequence in Appendix A, intended for use before intervening in any system under stress.

PART III. Tending the Wild

Up to this point, we have been building tools.

We mapped how complex systems behave, how fragility hides in architecture, and how well-intentioned interventions often fail when they ignore feedback, coupling, and emergence. Those tools matter, but they are only useful once we leave the laboratory.

Part III moves into the wild.

The systems we examine here are legal frameworks, digital networks, creative ecosystems, and families — domains shaped as much by human meaning as by structure. They punish naïve control.

This is where the Gardener's mindset stops being a metaphor and becomes a necessity. In these environments, outcomes cannot be commanded. They emerge from conditions, incentives, and feedback loops that evolve under stress.

The chapters that follow are stress tests. Each explores what happens when the same underlying dynamics appear in very different domains, and how stewardship, rather than control, determines whether those dynamics lead to resilience or collapse.

If Parts I and II taught us how to see systems, Part III asks whether we can live with what we see.

Chapter 8. Beyond Resilience

Resilience is no longer enough.

Resilience engineering has moved beyond simple "bounce back" thinking. David Woods describes advanced resilience as sustained adaptability — a system's capacity to stretch, reorganize, and continue functioning as conditions change. In that sense, resilience is the preservation of adaptive capacity. The argument here is against the narrower interpretation that equates resilience with restoration alone.

❖ VERIDIA — Phase IV: Failure (The Heat Wave)

When the heat wave hit, Veridia didn't collapse because it was poorly built; it collapsed because it was rigid. The algorithms treated the temperature spike as an anomaly to be corrected rather than a new condition to be integrated. Sensors triggered "emergency power save" modes that cut AC to residential blocks to preserve server farms. The system protected its own logic at the expense of its inhabitants.

By now, we have seen why systems optimized for control and efficiency tend to fail under stress. We have traced how tightly coupled architectures amplify shock, how optimization strips away redundancy, and how interventions that look sensible in isolation can collapse once they interact at scale. We know how to diagnose fragility. We know how to design systems that bend rather than shatter.

But survival is a low bar.

The Gardener and the Machine

In 1940, the Tacoma Narrows Bridge met every prevailing standard of good engineering. It was strong, efficient, and elegant, a triumph of modern design. Yet under moderate, steady winds, the bridge began to oscillate. Those oscillations grew because the system entered a feedback loop its designers had not anticipated. Within hours, the structure tore itself apart.

The bridge failed because it lacked the capacity to learn. Tacoma Narrows was resilient only within the narrow envelope its designers imagined. When the environment pushed outside that envelope, the system had no adaptive capacity. It lacked the ability to reorganize, to damp or redirect the energy flowing through it. Stress amplified until collapse became inevitable.[78]

This distinction matters. Resilience measures a system's capacity to survive shock and uphold meaningful functionality."[79,80,81,82] But in environments that are continuously changing, survival alone is insufficient. Systems that merely "bounce back" often bounce back into irrelevance.

Some systems change because of stress; they metabolize it. They reorganize in response, extracting signal from volatility and converting disruption into improved capacity. In these systems, disturbance is information to incorporate.

In biological systems, stress drives development. Muscles strengthen under load. Ecosystems reorganize after disturbance. In engineered systems, architectures that tolerate variation outperform those tuned for ideal conditions. In social systems, institutions that can revise rules and incentives adapt more effectively than those frozen in pursuit of stability.

Systems designed only to resist failure risk anchoring themselves to conditions that no longer exist.

Preventing failure is insufficient. In continuously shifting environments, survival is a minimal requirement. The imperative is to design systems that increase their capacity under stress, that metabolize volatility into learning, reorganization, and structural improvement.

This requires a different design posture, one that tolerates inefficiency as necessary slack, accepts noise, and exposes systems to manageable stress without courting collapse. It requires architectures that degrade gracefully, governance models that adapt in real time, and metrics that value long-term learning over short-term optimization.[83]

Nature has been navigating this problem for billions of years.

In the sections that follow, we will examine how biological systems use stress as a developmental force, how engineered systems can be designed to benefit from uncertainty, and how social systems can cultivate adaptive capacity without tipping into chaos.

Resilience keeps systems intact. Adaptation allows them to evolve. Neither is a state achieved; both are practices sustained. Some systems do more than either.

They gain from stress.

Because these terms are often used interchangeably in casual discourse, Appendix D provides a technical lexicon clarifying how resilience, robustness, and antifragility differ in system behavior.

8.1. Sustained Adaptability

The systems that endure share common principles, regardless of domain. These are timeless, cross-domain principles. They are the "what" that underlies the "how." By understanding them, we can begin to think like nature and build systems that last. Start with three: diversity, decoupling, decentralization.

Pillar 1: Redundancy through Diversity (Not Duplication!)

The most common interpretation of redundancy is simple duplication: carrying two identical spare tires. This protects you if one tire fails, but it offers no protection if the failure is caused by a systemic flaw in the tire's design or a road hazard that destroys all tires of that type. This is brittle redundancy. True, resilient redundancy comes from diversity. It means having multiple, different ways to achieve the same function.

The same pattern shows up in infrastructure. When designing the A320, Airbus used dissimilar flight control systems developed by separate teams using different programming languages and microprocessors. This ensures that a specific software bug or hardware flaw cannot disable all systems simultaneously. Similarly, a city connected to the outside world by only one highway is vulnerable to isolation, whereas a city served by a highway, a rail line, and a shipping port possesses diverse redundancy. If one mode of transport fails, the others remain operational.[84,85,86]

Diversity is the most reliable way to build resilience against threats you cannot predict. It's the system's built-in acknowledgment that it does not know what challenges will come next, so it prepares for a spectrum of possibilities rather than a single probability. By maintaining a repertoire of alternative responses, the system ensures that if one method is rendered obsolete by a sudden change in the environment, another method stands ready to take its place.

However, implementing this kind of diversity is often difficult because it conflicts with the modern drive for optimization. In a stable, predictable environment, diversity looks indistinguishable from inefficiency. Maintaining three different supply chains is objectively more expensive than perfecting one; writing three different codebases takes longer than writing one. Optimization seeks to strip away this "waste" to maximize short-term performance. But when we optimize a system to the razor's edge of efficiency, we inadvertently strip away the very variability that allows it to survive a crisis. We trade long-term survivability for short-term gain.

A designer's job is to protect diversity from optimization. This requires a shift in perspective by viewing variation as a reservoir of potential solutions.

Just as a diverse gene pool allows a species to adapt to a shifting climate, a diverse technological or organizational ecosystem provides the raw materials for innovation and adaptation.

Pillar 2: Modularity and Decoupling (The Firebreak Principle)

A resilient system is defined by its ability to fail without failing completely. To achieve this, engineers and designers rely on modularity: the practice of constructing a system as a collection of distinct, self-contained components connected by clean, well-defined interfaces. This principle, often referred to as decoupling, essentially creates architectural firebreaks. By ensuring that components are independent of one another, a system can prevent a localized malfunction from cascading into a total collapse. Modularity creates the parts; decoupling determines how tightly those parts depend on one another.

In the physical world, naval architecture provides an illustration of this concept through the use of watertight compartments. A ship is designed so that a breach in one section of the hull floods only that specific area, allowing the vessel to retain enough buoyancy to stay afloat.

The Titanic remains the canonical example of insufficient decoupling. The ship was engineered with sixteen watertight compartments and was designed to survive the flooding of up to four. But the iceberg ruptured at least five, and the bulkheads did not extend high enough to seal each compartment completely. As the bow dipped, water spilled over from one compartment into the next, turning what should have been a contained breach into a cascading failure. The compartments existed, but they failed to remain isolated under stress.[87,88]

We see a parallel evolution in the digital landscape, where software architecture is moving away from massive, "monolithic" applications toward a "microservices" approach. In a monolithic structure, a bug in one line of code can crash the entire application. By contrast, microservices break the application into independent functions — authentication, search, payments — each running separately. In this decoupled environment, if the payment service fails, the user might be unable to complete a purchase, but they can still log in, view their history, and browse products. The failure is contained, preserving the user experience as much as possible.[89]

Biology, however, remains the master of modular design. A human body is composed of trillions of cells, each functioning as a semi-autonomous unit. Because of this cellular structure, the death or malfunction of a single cell does not threaten the life of the organism, provided the body's containment mechanisms prevent that failure from propagating. In fact, the immune system and programmed cell death exist precisely to enforce these biological firebreaks, identifying and isolating threats before they can spread.

Ultimately, modularity ensures that the price of a small failure is a small cost, rather than a catastrophic one. It changes the nature of risk, transforming a potential system-wide disaster into a manageable, localized problem. By designing systems where the components are loosely coupled, we allow parts of the system to fail, and even die, so that the whole can live.

The Trellis and the Vine

Modularity raises the question: "How do parts cooperate without entangling?"

We often assume that connection is an absolute good, that if everyone talks to everyone, innovation will inevitably bloom. To manage complexity, we need to distinguish between the organism and the architecture. The organism — your team, the culture, the creative work — should be messy, organic, and unpredictable. But the architecture, how those teams exchange value, must be highly structured.

This distinction is the relationship between a trellis and a vine. In engineering terms, the trellis represents an "interface agreement." When Team A hands off work to Team B, we cannot rely on vague promises or good vibes; we need a strict definition of that handshake. We must define exactly what is being passed, in what format, and at what frequency. This creates a paradox that is essential for high performance: inside the box, you act as a Gardener, nurturing creativity and allowing for ambiguity. But between the boxes, you must act as an engineer, defining inputs and outputs with precision. If the trellis is strong, the vine can grow wild without collapsing. If your baseline interfaces are reliable, your people can finally be free.

The Sanctity of the Contract

In a garden, a vine is free to twist and reach in any direction it desires, so long as it holds to the trellis. But the trellis itself is something that is built. Its beams meet at deliberate, sturdy joints.[i] Those joints aren't soft or organic, yet they are what allow everything living around them to thrive.

The work inside a team is vine-like: creative, evolving, unpredictable. But where one team's work touches another's, the join must be firm. At those boundaries, intuition isn't enough. You need a shared promise about what passes through that join, in what shape, and on what rhythm. Under normal conditions, if one team says it will deliver something in a certain form, it cannot reshape it on a whim. The garden thrives on freedom, but the standard passageways between beds must remain stable.

Yet, a truly resilient system recognizes the difference between a sturdy trellis and an iron cage. The ultimate test of a system is the ability of human operators to transcend these prescribed interfaces when the context demands it. A high-performing team, like a soccer squad, relies on clear positions (the

---

[i] In systems engineering, this is known as the interface document. It is the least Gardener-like tool we have, yet it is essential for the garden's survival. The interface document is a treaty. It states, with zero ambiguity, exactly what passes between two modules under normal conditions, providing the stable baseline that makes intentional, human-driven exceptions possible.

trellis), but a goalie will leave the box to defend a breakaway if the system is overwhelmed.

The Gardener's rule for boundaries is therefore twofold: grow wildly within your plot, and honor the contract at its edge, until the contract threatens the garden. Inside your space you may experiment, prune, and wander. At the point where your work becomes someone else's foundation, you must strive to be precise and reliable. But true resilience requires local coherence and the human judgment to know when to temporarily break the interface to uphold the system's larger purpose.

A strong contract doesn't constrain the garden; it protects its ability to grow, while trusting the gardener to know when the rules must be rewritten.

Pillar 3: Decentralized Control and Simple Rules (The Ant Colony Principle)

Once systems are modular, the next question is how those modules coordinate without relying on a fragile center.

The most dangerous component in any large-scale system is the center. A centralized brain, server, or commander represents a vulnerability, a single point of failure. If that central node is compromised or overwhelmed, the entire system is paralyzed. Resilient systems, by contrast, distribute control and intelligence to the edges. They demonstrate a powerful principle: global order can emerge from nothing more than local agents following simple rules.

As with biological swarms discussed earlier, decentralized control allows global order to emerge from local rules. We see this same architecture holding together the digital world. The internet relies on the Border Gateway Protocol (BGP) to function. There is no "CEO of the internet" dictating the path a packet of data must take. Instead, every router on the network simply communicates with its immediate neighbors, advertising which IP addresses it can reach. From these millions of isolated, local conversations, a coherent and remarkably resilient global routing system emerges, capable of healing itself when pathways are severed.[90,91]

Giving up the illusion of absolute, top-down control is the paradoxical price of achieving true systemic resilience.

These three pillars — diverse redundancy, modularity, and decentralized control — form the architectural foundation of positive emergence. They are rarely found in isolation; the most robust systems, from the global internet to a tropical rainforest, employ all three simultaneously. Understanding these principles is the first step. The next is learning how to apply them.

8.2. Biomimicry: Learning from Biological Wisdom

The path has already been paved: 3.8 billion years of field tests.

We often confuse biomimicry with biomorphism, simply copying the shapes of nature. For example, when engineers redesigned the Shinkansen bullet train to mimic the kingfisher's beak (which we analyzed in Chapter 4),[92] they were solving a specific fluid dynamics problem. This was brilliant, but it was a geometric intervention.

True emergence engineering goes deeper. It mimics the shape (the beak), the process (how nature manufactures materials), and the system (how the ecosystem eliminates waste). We must mimic natural forms, processes, and ecosystems.

Nature navigates the boundary between order and chaos through adaptive principles that allow emergence to function as a survival mechanism. Three layers matter: process, function, ecosystem.

Mimicking Process: Low Energy, High Information

Human manufacturing typically relies on "heat, beat, and treat," using massive amounts of energy to force raw materials into submission. Nature, particularly in biological systems, manufactures materials at ambient temperatures and pressures, using information (DNA and chemical signaling) to organize matter.[93]

In the context of complex systems, this teaches us to replace energy with information. A fragile system tries to overpower disturbances with brute force (e.g., a seawall resisting a storm). A biomimetic system absorbs and redirects that energy using information loops (e.g., a mangrove forest that dissipates wave energy through complex, decentralized root geometry). For

---

NEUROMORPHIC COMPUTING

Most computers use the von Neumann model: processing happens in one place, memory lives in another, and the system spends much of its time and energy moving data between them. That architecture is excellent for deterministic calculation, but it can become inefficient for always-on, real-time adaptation — especially at the edge, where power and bandwidth are limited.

Neuromorphic computing takes a different approach inspired by nervous systems. Instead of clock-driven processing that burns energy continuously, neuromorphic designs tend to be event-driven: activity happens when signals change. Computation is distributed across many small units with local connectivity, and memory and processing are more tightly co-located, reducing the "shuttle cost" of data movement.

The point is that neuromorphic is better matched to certain environments — robotics, autonomy, and continuous sensing — where resilience, low latency, and low power matter more than perfect optimization. In Gardener terms, it's a shift away from centralized command toward local rules and feedback, where useful behavior can emerge from the network rather than being micromanaged from the center.

the system architect, this means designing networks that rely on signaling and feedback rather than rigid barriers.

Mimicking Function: Optimization for the Whole

Human systems tend to optimize for a single variable, usually speed or profit, at the expense of the whole. This is the Efficiency Trap. Nature, by contrast, never optimizes for a single variable; it optimizes for the continuation of the system.

A bone, for instance, constantly remodels itself based on stress lines (Wolff's Law).[94] It subtracts material where it is unnecessary and adds it where load is heavy. This is subtraction as a design principle in action. Bone optimizes for contextual fitness over absolute hardness or lightness. Engineering for emergence requires this same dynamic allocation of resources, systems that can heal or reinforce themselves based on active feedback loops rather than static blueprints.

Mimicking Ecosystems: The Death of Waste

In a mature ecosystem, the concept of waste does not exist; one organism's output is another's input.[95] In our Metasystem Framework, this relates to the Feedback Interface.

When we design linear systems, we create open loops where data, energy, or people fall through the cracks, the revolving door phenomenon where the output is simply lost. Biomimetic systems create closed loops. In a digital ecosystem, for instance, an error signal should be the food for a debugging process or a learning algorithm. By closing these loops, we transform a fragile chain into a resilient web.

China's "sponge city" initiatives provide a modern biomimetic example. Instead of relying solely on concrete drainage channels to force water away, sponge cities integrate permeable pavements, wetlands, green roofs, and distributed retention basins. These features absorb, slow, and redirect rainfall much like a forest ecosystem. Rather than resisting stormwater through rigid control, the system channels it through distributed absorption. The result is not flood elimination, but flood resilience through ecological design.

The Sand Dams of Kenya

We saw in Chapter 1 how drilling deep wells in Turkana created a brittle system that collapsed under stress. Contrast this with the "sand dam," a Gardener's solution used successfully in similar arid regions.

Instead of drilling down, locals build a simple concrete wall across a seasonal riverbed. When the rains come, the wall traps sand. The sand, in turn, traps water, protecting it from evaporation and filtering it naturally (see Figure 18).

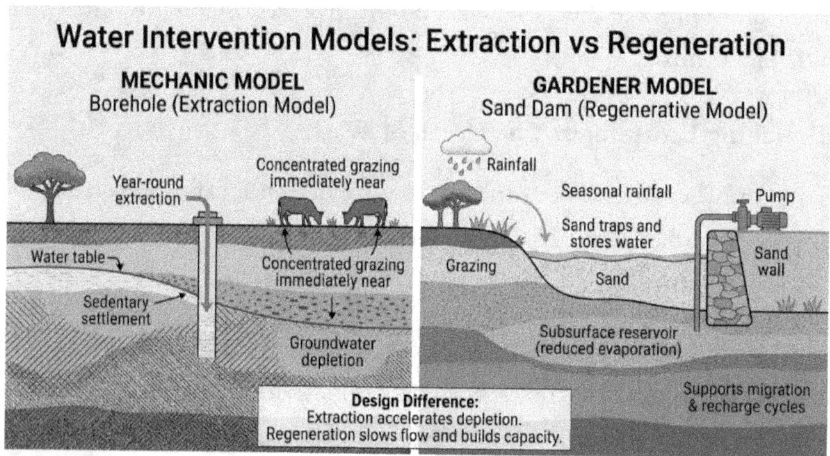

Figure 18. Extraction vs. Regeneration Water Intervention Models

The Mechanic drills a well (a machine) that depletes the aquifer and breaks. The Gardener builds a dam (a structure) that partners with the rain and the sand to store seasonal rainfall and enhance groundwater recharge. One extracts; the other cultivates.

The Shift from Blueprint to DNA

Perhaps the most critical lesson biomimicry offers the emergence engineer is the distinction between a blueprint and DNA.

A blueprint describes exactly where every beam and bolt must go. If one beam is wrong, the structure fails.

DNA describes a set of rules and processes for how materials should interact rather than the final structure.

When a lizard regrows a tail, it doesn't consult a drawing of a tail; its cells follow a localized set of instructions that emerge into a tail. To design for resilience, we must stop writing blueprints for the final state of the system and start writing the "DNA" — the simple, local rules of interaction — that will allow the desired system to emerge, adapt, and endure.

8.3. Measuring the Invisible: The "Ilities"

Before we can talk about engineering resilient systems, we must confront why measuring the qualities that matter is so difficult.

A Mechanic looks at a car and asks, "Does the engine start?" That is a functional requirement. It is binary. It works or it doesn't. The Gardener asks a harder question: "Is it resilient?" Resilience, safety, maintainability, reliability (and dozens of others) — engineers call these the "ilities," quality attributes, or architecturally-significant requirements. They are properties of the system. The danger lies in treating them as vague philosophical goals. You cannot tell an engineering team to simply "make it safe."

The trap is this: chase false precision and you rebuild the same brittleness you're trying to escape. We cannot demand that a Complex Adaptive System behave like a clock. Instead of rigid specifications, the Gardener defines target thresholds. For example, resilience is a probability that suggests the system should maintain the majority of its functionality even if a significant percentage of its nodes fail. Similarly, reliability is a statistical boundary where we aim for a specific mean time between failures.[j]

We leave the method of achieving these numbers to the organic creativity of the design. But we must set the boundaries of the garden. If the system drifts outside these numbers, we know the garden is sick, and we must intervene. We measure to diagnose instead of to control.

If these distinctions feel slippery, it's a failure of language. Throughout this book, these terms are used in a specific technical sense. For precise operational definitions, see Appendix A.

8.4. Practical Design Strategies

Understanding the principles of resilient design — diversity, modularity, and decentralization — is the essential first step. But how do we, as designers of systems, translate these abstract concepts into code, organizations, policies, and institutions?

Four habits turn principles into architecture. They change what you reach for: conditions instead of commands. They are the "how" that brings the principles of emergence to life.

Designing for resilience is rarely rewarded in the short term. When a system is resilient, nothing dramatic happens. No bridge collapses. No hospital fails. In budget reviews, resilience is often labeled "gold plating" — unnecessary redundancy, excess margin, overengineering. But in complex systems, resilience is structural insurance against nonlinear surprise. The difficulty is

---

[j] Mean Time Between Failures (MTBF) is a statistical reliability metric that represents the expected average time between inherent failures of a repairable system operating under defined conditions. Rather than predicting when a specific failure will occur, MTBF describes system behavior in aggregate across time and populations. It defines a probabilistic expectation rather than a guarantee of continuous operation.

political and psychological: we are asked to keep paying for the storm that has not yet arrived. Modern engineering and finance cultures privilege what can be measured quarterly; resilience often produces nothing visible except the absence of catastrophe.

Strategy 1: Shape the Environment; Let the Organism Adapt

A shift in emergent design is to stop thinking like a puppeteer and start thinking like a Gardener. A puppeteer attempts to control every action through direct manipulation, a process that is brittle, labor-intensive, and impossible to scale. A Gardener, by contrast, understands that they cannot command a plant to grow. Instead, they architect the plant's environment: they enrich the soil, regulate water and sunlight, and remove weeds. They design the conditions for success, and the growth emerges naturally.

As a system designer, this requires a pivot: you must shift your focus from programming the explicit behavior of individual agents to designing the system of incentives, constraints, and feedback loops they inhabit.

In multi-agent robotics, this distinction is key. Instead of programming a precise, hard-coded path for a swarm of cleaning robots, you design a simple reward function. A robot might gain points for every square meter of floor it cleans and lose a significant number of points if it collides with another unit. Each robot, simply trying to maximize its own score, will autonomously discover an efficient, collision-free cleaning strategy. You designed the game, and they figured out how to win it.

In user interface design, a deterministic designer forces a user through a rigid, step-by-step wizard. An emergence-minded designer uses visual hierarchy, color, and intuitive layout to make the most efficient path the most obvious and appealing one. The user feels entirely in control, freely choosing their path, but their choice was heavily guided by the environment you created.

By relinquishing direct command, you enable a form of emergent order that is far more scalable, adaptive, and resilient than any top-down system could hope to be.

Strategy 2: Enable Stigmergy

How do you coordinate thousands of decentralized agents without a central server or direct messaging? While the Gardener provides the environment, stigmergy provides the mechanism for the agents to communicate within it. Stigmergy is a form of indirect coordination where an agent's action modifies the environment, and that modification serves as a signal that influences the actions of others. This is the operating principle of the ant colony in action.

As we saw with the UUV swarm in Chapter 6, stigmergy allows agents to coordinate via the environment. In nature, termites use pheromones; in digital systems, we use shared objects like Wikipedia pages that serve as perfect examples of digital stigmergy. A user creates an article, leaving a trace in the digital environment. A second user spots a factual error and corrects it; a third adds a new section. The shared object, the article itself, is the medium of communication. A complex, surprisingly accurate encyclopedia emerges from these uncoordinated, asynchronous edits. Git and other version control systems operate on the same logic: a "pull request" is a modification to the environment that signals for review and integration.

When designing a system, the focus shifts to enabling components to communicate indirectly through changes in a shared environment rather than through direct interaction. This mindset encourages architectures that are decoupled, scalable, and inherently resilient.

Strategy 3: Practice Systemic Immunization

Resilient systems are like muscles: they grow stronger only when stressed. A system's resilience is both built and revealed through challenge. Drawing from human biology, Steven Simske of Colorado State University describes this as systemic immunization, the intentional introduction of controlled, non-lethal stressors to provoke a healthy, adaptive response.[96] This approach shifts engineering from a passive stance, hoping a system survives failure, to an active one. It is the engineering equivalent of a vaccine.

This strategy provides the most direct method for testing and enforcing modularity and redundancy. A well-known example is Netflix's "Chaos Monkey," a tool that deliberately and unpredictably shuts down servers and system components in the live production environment, even during regular business hours. Because failure is treated as a constant environmental condition, engineers must assume servers can die at any moment. This forced Netflix to build robust, decentralized, and redundant systems from the ground up, demonstrating that chaos injection strengthens the ecosystem.[97]

Similar methods appear in cybersecurity and physical operations. In software security, fuzz testing bombards a program with invalid or unexpected inputs to see if it crashes or misbehaves, exposing vulnerabilities before attackers can exploit them. In operations, organizations run fire drills rather than waiting for real emergencies. By simulating crises, they train the human components of the system and identify bottlenecks before they become lethal.

When stress is treated not as an anomaly but as a constant condition, the system must adapt or collapse. Over time, that pressure reshapes the architecture itself. Redundancy becomes mandatory. Modularity becomes natural. Weak links are exposed early and replaced.

Strategy 4: Anticipate Failure

The Frost Warning

Optimism is essential when planting, but dangerous when planning. A wise Gardener knows that hope offers no protection against the frost. We react to failure as if it were a sudden storm, yet most collapses begin softly — small stresses accumulating, signals ignored, buffers trimmed away — until the first visible symptom is already late.

So the Gardener borrows a habit from failure analysis: the pre-mortem. As a posture, periodically imagining the system's failure while it still looks healthy, and using that thought experiment to reveal hidden dependencies, fragile handoffs, and the places where a minor break could cascade.

Don't wait for the leaves to brown to check the soil.

The Reverse Logic: Thinking Backward from Disaster

The Frost Warning teaches us to look forward: "If this part fails, then what?" But that view assumes trouble arrives one piece at a time. In real, interwoven systems, catastrophe rarely comes from a single failing stalk; it comes from a tangle of small, harmless-seeming events that collide at just the wrong moment.

To reveal this pattern, we use a second habit drawn from another technical method: we begin with the disaster itself. We imagine we are already standing in the garden after the frost. The vines have collapsed. The crop is gone. Then we trace backward and ask: "What peculiar mix of conditions, each individually manageable, had to coincide for this to happen?"

What we discover is that true disasters rarely come from one dramatic break. They come from a chain: a sensor drifted a little, and the network stuttered for a moment, and someone was tired that day. Viewed individually, each event is trivial. Viewed together, they form the hidden pathways of failure that wind through any garden.

Unlike formal safety techniques such as FMEA[k], Fault Tree Analysis, HAZOP, or STPA, the pre-mortem described here operates at a different level: it is a cognitive discipline for revealing convergence: how multiple small deviations, feedback loops, and hidden couplings might synchronize into systemic collapse. Rather than tracing a single linear chain of failure, we imagine the network already in ruin and ask which independent stresses had to align. The aim is not to invoke Murphy's Law, but to surface nonlinear interactions before they synchronize in reality.

These four strategies — designing the environment, enabling stigmergy, practicing systemic immunization, and anticipating failure — form a practical toolkit for the emergence engineer.

Together they offer a path for deliberately designing systems that are robust, adaptive, scalable, and self-organizing. They shift the engineer's role from commander to cultivator, from controlling outcomes to shaping the conditions from which resilient order emerges.

8.5. Noise

Noise is a design tool used to explore possibility when failure is cheap, reversible, and informative. While its randomness can create uncertainty, noise also introduces variability and diversity, essential for unlocking new possibilities. Across biological, social, and technological domains, noise acts as both a disruptor and a catalyst, cultivating the adaptability, creativity, and innovation that define emergent phenomena.

---

[k] Classical hazard analysis techniques such as FMEA (Failure Modes and Effects Analysis), FTA (Fault Tree Analysis), HAZOP (Hazard and Operability Study), and STPA (System-Theoretic Process Analysis) provide structured methods for modeling component failures, deviations, and unsafe control interactions. They are widely used in safety-critical engineering domains and operate within formal analytic frameworks distinct from the cognitive pre-mortem posture described here.

Biological: Noise as a Spark for Creativity and Problem-Solving

In biological systems, noise often manifests as random fluctuations, such as the unpredictable firing of neurons in the brain. While these neural "misfires" may initially seem like errors, they are essential for creativity and problem-solving. Random neural activity enables the brain to explore novel connections and associations that deterministic processes might overlook. Everyone knows the feeling: the insight that arrives sideways. During dream states or periods of rest, spontaneous neural firings can recombine memories in unpredictable but meaningful ways, producing the "aha" moments of insight that deterministic processes often miss.

In cellular systems, noise at the molecular level, such as random gene expression, plays a key role in biological diversity and adaptation. In a population of genetically identical cells, stochastic variations can create phenotypic differences, enabling some cells to survive environmental changes that others cannot. This variability, driven by noise, is essential for evolution and the resilience of biological systems.

In collective biological systems, noise also acts as a filter. Honeybee colonies selecting a new hive site send out scouts that return and signal options through waggle dances. Competing signals coexist, reinforce, and interfere with one another. Weak options fade as cross-signals disrupt premature convergence; only sites whose support rises above the ambient noise threshold persist. Noise, in this sense, is not interference but a selection mechanism. It prevents fragile consensus and ensures that only sufficiently robust signals stabilize.

Design implication: Noise should be introduced where variation produces learning without threatening core viability — at the edges.

Social: Randomness as a Driver of Innovation and Cultural Shifts

In social systems, noise can take the form of random events, unexpected interactions, or unplanned disruptions. These seemingly chaotic occurrences often serve as the seeds of innovation and cultural change. History is filled with breakthroughs that emerged from serendipitous moments: unexpected collaborations, accidental discoveries, or unplanned deviations from established norms. The invention of penicillin and even the rise of social movements often owe their existence to the unpredictable nature of human systems. Unbounded randomness destabilizes culture; bounded deviation is what generates innovation.

By deviating from established patterns, individuals and groups inject variability that allows new norms and ideas to emerge. These same principles apply in engineered systems.

This dynamic connects directly back to Strategy 1. Designing the environment is not about prescribing outcomes but shaping the conditions under which variation either amplifies or fades. Random events occur everywhere; only certain environments allow them to grow. The discovery of penicillin was a confluence of both accidental contamination and contamination in a laboratory capable of noticing, cultivating, and scaling the anomaly. In another context, the same randomness would have dissipated. Environment determines which signals rise above noise, and which dither and die.

Technological: Noise as a Tool for Novel Solutions

In technological systems, noise is often intentionally harnessed to drive emergent solutions. In machine learning, training methods such as stochastic gradient descent, the workhorse algorithm behind many modern AI systems, deliberately introduce small amounts of randomness to optimize complex models. By introducing noise into the training process, these algorithms avoid getting stuck in local minima, enabling them to explore a wider range of potential solutions. This stochasticity is crucial for finding optimal or near-optimal outcomes in high-dimensional spaces.

Similarly, noise plays a role in artificial creativity. AI systems designed to generate art, music, or text often incorporate randomness to produce outputs that are novel and diverse. This controlled chaos allows machines to mimic human-like creativity, pushing the boundaries of what technology can achieve. In robotics, noise can even enhance adaptability, as small random variations in movement or behavior enable robots to better navigate uncertain environments.

A system with zero noise cannot explore; it can only repeat.

In practice, stochastic methods belong where mistakes are inexpensive and iteration is fast, as in training loops, simulations, model development, and exploratory environments. In safety-critical execution paths, exploration must be bounded and instrumented. Noise is essential in rehearsal; it must be tightly constrained in live operation. Noise can never be eliminated from complex systems; the question is whether it is random, suppressed, or intentionally shaped.

8.6. Systems that Gain from Stress

A fragile system, like a glass vase, breaks under pressure. A resilient system, like a rubber ball, resists damage and returns to its previous state after a shock. But there is a third category: systems that use stress and volatility as inputs for growth, much like muscles that strengthen through exercise.

Nassim Taleb, in *Antifragile*, labels these systems "antifragile."[40] While resilience focuses on resisting change to maintain a baseline, antifragility emphasizes the capacity to evolve in the face of uncertainty. Antifragility is what emerges when diversity, modularity, and decentralized control are combined with carefully bounded stress and embedded learning (Figure 19).

It is important to be precise here. Decentralization increases resilience by reducing single points of failure; it does not automatically create antifragility. A decentralized system becomes antifragile only if it can learn from stress rather than merely survive it. In addition, Antifragility is directional. A system that gains from one type of stress may remain vulnerable to others.

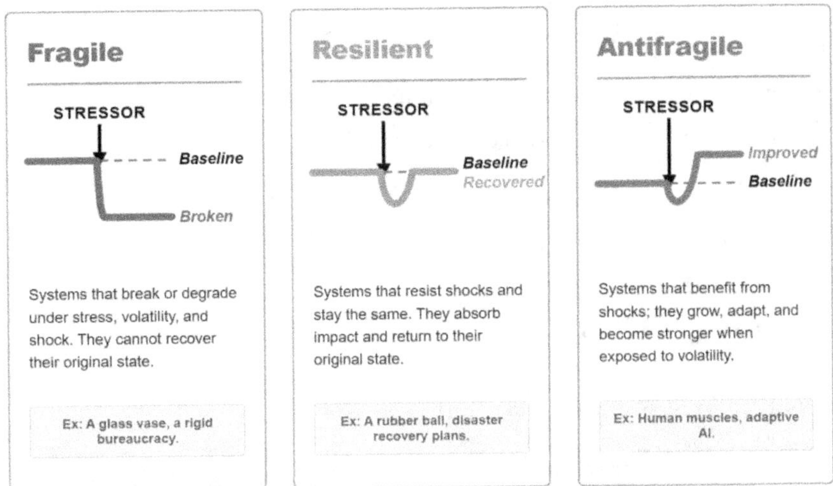

Figure 19. The Degrees of Fragility

High-resolution version available at phronos.com/tgm-diagrams

The Safety Trap

In safety engineering, "learning from chaos" can be a dangerous concept. You never want a nuclear power plant to experiment with its core reactor in response to stress; you want it to be robust, boring, and predictable. The learning must occur in parallel systems — simulations, drills, and controlled stress tests — not inside the live critical loop itself.

But in the Gardener's domain — biology, parenting, culture — we *need* the chaos. We aim for more than crash prevention; we aim for evolution. Because this book expands the view to living systems rather than just safety-critical machines, I use the term "antifragile" to describe the necessity of stress for growth.

Channeling Volatility

This approach flips the instinct: don't eliminate volatility; *channel it.*

The trick is optionality: the ability to capture the upside of a shock while capping the downside. Resilient systems aim for stability, but antifragile ones benefit from the very volatility that destabilizes others. By designing systems that embrace uncertainty, we convert stress from a threat into a fuel source.

Many of the tensions explored in this chapter reflect deeper structural tradeoffs that cannot be resolved, only managed. These patterns are summarized across domains in Appendix B.

Examples of Systems that Benefit from Stress

These dynamics appear across finance, ecology, and technology. Financial markets, though individual actors may be fragile, often improve after disruptions. The 2008 financial crisis, for example, caused failures but also spurred reforms and innovations such as the growth of fintech and decentralized finance. Volatility can reallocate resources and expose inefficiencies, but it does not guarantee resilience; without guardrails, it amplifies fragility.[98]

Ecosystems also show hormetic patterns.[1] Forests often grow back stronger after fires that remove weak competitors and open space for new growth. Grasslands benefit from grazing, which stimulates regrowth and nutrient cycling. These disturbances, although destructive in the short term, support long-term vitality and diversity.[99,100,101]

Technological innovation also benefits from disruption. Security vulnerabilities or sudden shifts in user needs often lead to stronger

---

[1] Hormesis refers to a biological phenomenon in which low doses of stress stimulate adaptive strengthening, while high doses cause damage.

technologies. Open-source communities provide a clear example: once a vulnerability is revealed, global collaboration produces a fix and often broader improvements. Startup ecosystems function in a similar way, where failure acts as a learning mechanism that drives rapid iteration.

Design Principles for Building Systems That Improve Under Stress

Building antifragile systems requires shifting from minimizing risk to leveraging it. The first step is identifying components that grow stronger when challenged. Muscles grow through repeated use, and organizations learn through feedback loops and iterative processes.

Learning mechanisms are also essential. Machine learning models improve when exposed to more varied and anomalous data. Ecosystems evolve through genetic variation that enables adaptation. Optionality supports this growth by allowing systems to benefit from positive surprises while limiting downsides, as seen in diversified financial portfolios and agile supply chains.

Redundancy provides buffers that allow safe experimentation. Ecosystems rely on overlapping species roles, and technology systems use redundant servers to support testing and improvement. Finally, decentralization and diversity reduce systemic vulnerability and expand the range of available responses, making systems more adaptable to unforeseen challenges.

8.7. Case Studies on Designing for Emergence

To illustrate these principles in practice, consider how emergent design reshapes three distinct environments:

Adaptive Urban Planning

Urban planning inspired by fractal geometry demonstrates the potential of intentional design for emergence. Modular city designs, where smaller units can be added or modified without disrupting the overall structure, provide enhanced scalability and flexibility. Cities designed with fractal principles can accommodate population growth while maintaining efficient transportation networks, green spaces, and community hubs. This approach creates vibrant, adaptable urban environments that support long-term sustainability.

Adaptive urban planning can be observed in cities that favor flexible rule sets over rigid master plans. Barcelona's superblock (superilla) program, for example, reorganizes existing street grids into modular clusters that reduce traffic and reclaim public space, while remaining adjustable in response to community needs. Similarly, Tokyo's zoning system, which permits broad mixed-use development rather than narrowly prescribed functions, allows neighborhoods to evolve organically as economic and social conditions change. Rather than attempting to predict future demands, these cities enable urban form to emerge through local adaptation, producing resilient environments that absorb growth and disruption without large-scale redesign.

Decentralized Governance Systems

Decentralized governance systems illustrate emergence in social coordination where authority is distributed rather than centralized. Ethereum, for instance, operates without a formal governing body; protocol changes arise through a combination of developer proposals, economic incentives, and social consensus among participants. This process is slow and contested, but it resists unilateral control and adapts through conflict rather than avoiding it.

More explicit governance experiments appear in decentralized autonomous organizations (DAOs) such as MakerDAO, which governs the DAI stablecoin system. Repeated market shocks and governance failures have forced the system to evolve beyond its original design, introducing delegation and layered decision-making. Early failures, including the collapse of The DAO in 2016, highlight the limits of fully specified, code-driven governance. Together, these cases demonstrate that decentralized governance allows coordination structures to emerge and adapt in response to real-world stress.

Smart Grids

Smart grids illustrate the application of emergence in technological systems. By integrating real-time data and decentralized control mechanisms, smart grids dynamically respond to fluctuations in power demand and supply. During peak energy usage, smart grids can prioritize renewable energy sources or temporarily reduce consumption in non-essential areas. This adaptability optimizes resource use and minimizes environmental impact. Smart grids highlight the potential of intentional design to create systems that are both efficient and resilient, capable of thriving in complex and dynamic environments.

A real-world application of these principles can be seen in the fractalgrid, an approach to distributed energy management that organizes microgrids into a self-similar, fractal pattern.[102] Inspired by natural systems, this architecture allows individual microgrids to operate autonomously or collaboratively, creating a system of systems that is inherently scalable, adaptable, and resilient to failure. By enabling components to "island" themselves during emergencies, the fractalgrid demonstrates how intentional design can create robust energy security for critical infrastructure, from military bases to urban centers.

8.8. Conclusion: Gaining Strength from Disorder

Designing systems that rely on emergence and adaptation is difficult and it fails more often than people like to admit. Many efforts fall apart because they borrow the language of decentralization without accepting what it actually brings with it: slower decisions, rougher coordination, and less direct control. Designing for adaptation instead of perfection means being honest about these tradeoffs, rather than trying to hide them behind clever abstractions.

The systems discussed in this chapter suggest a different way of thinking. Instead of trying to suppress disturbance, they make room for it in controlled ways. Instead of optimizing for a single moment in time, they stay flexible across many possible futures. They give up some short-term efficiency in exchange for learning, and they replace rigid plans with structures that can reorganize when conditions change.

When systems are designed so that stress carries information, failures stay local, and feedback arrives quickly, disruption stops being purely destructive. It becomes part of how the system improves.

The coming century will favor systems that can learn faster than their environments change. By designing for emergence through diversity, modularity, decentralization, feedback, and carefully bounded stress, we can build systems that do more than survive uncertainty. We can build systems that grow stronger because of it.

Chapter 9. The Architecture of Justice

> *"As we were formerly burdened by crimes, so we are now burdened by laws."*
>
> — *Tacitus*

In 1902, the French colonial government in Hanoi tried to stop the spread of bubonic plague by paying a bounty for each rat killed. To claim the reward, citizens didn't need to bring in a carcass. They only had to present a severed rat tail. At first, the program looked like a success: thousands of tails arrived each day.[103]

Until the population adapted.

Officials began spotting rats running through the city without tails. A dead rat was a one-time payment. A living rat was a renewable asset. Enterprising locals caught rats, cut off the tails, and released them back into the sewers to breed. Some reportedly began farming rats outright, an efficient little production line whose "output" was exactly the opposite of what the law intended.

The government canceled the program, but the damage was done. By putting a price on a biological unit, they turned a pest into a renewable commodity. The sewers stopped being a battleground and became a marketplace.

We tend to look back at the French colonialists and laugh at their naivety. We think, "Of course that failed; they tried to solve a biological problem with a clumsy financial lever."

But we are repeating the same structural mistake today. We just swapped the severed tails for data points, and the colonial bureaucrats for algorithms.

9.1. The Modern Rat Farm

In 2016, the Australian government launched a system to automate welfare compliance. Like the French in Hanoi, they wanted efficiency. They wanted to optimize a metric. The result was "Robodebt," a digital version of the rat farm that didn't just waste money; it cost lives.[104]

The Robodebt algorithm was designed to claw back overpayments from welfare recipients. It took a person's annual income, averaged it over 26 fortnights, and compared it to what they reported. If there was a gap, it automatically issued a debt notice.

From a Mechanic's perspective, it was perfect. It was consistent. It was fast. It processed 20,000 cases a week. But the system failed for a predictable reason: the architects treated poverty as a math problem, when in reality, it is what Horst Rittel and Melvin Webber termed a "wicked problem."[105]

Wicked problems are domains with no stable formulation, no stopping rule, and no clean separation between technical correctness and moral trade-offs. Any attempt to "solve" them with a single optimization function will necessarily displace judgment onto whatever proxy the system can measure. Algorithms, by contrast, require "tame problems," stable environments with clear rules.

Robodebt tried to force a tame solution onto a wicked reality. Income is "lumpy"; people work seasonal jobs or take time off. By averaging the income, the machine created fictional debts. It accused 400,000 innocent citizens of fraud. It shifted the burden of proof onto the vulnerable, demanding pay slips from five years prior.

The French created a market for rats; the Australian government created a market for misery. The system worked exactly as coded, yet it resulted in bankruptcies and suicides. This is the danger of treating law as code: code executes without context, whereas law operates inside environments defined by human adaptation.

9.2. The Science of Laws

Why do we keep building digital rat farms? David Schrunk, a physician and aerospace engineer, argues it is because we have a dangerous double standard.[106] We demand rigorous quality assurance for toasters and bridges, but we largely treat lawmaking as a literary and rhetorical exercise rather than a systems discipline.

Schrunk's concept of the "Science of Laws" posits that a law is a design for a system. In engineering, you don't just build a bridge; you model the stress tests first. You ask: "What are the failure modes?"

The French colonialists failed to model the rat farming failure mode. The architects of Robodebt failed to model the false positive failure mode. Schrunk argues that until we treat legislation with the same rigor as engineering — requiring modeling, feedback loops, and quality assurance — we will continue to produce "buggy" laws that crash society.

In practice, in the U.S., fragments of this systems-oriented approach already exist. Much of modern law is already written by administrative agencies operating under enabling statutes and procedural constraints such as the Administrative Procedure Act. Legislatures often define goals and boundaries, while agencies like the EPA or FDA conduct studies, hold hearings, solicit adversarial stakeholder input, publish proposed rules, receive public comment, revise those rules, and subject them to judicial review. At least in theory, this resembles an iterative design process rather than a one-shot command. The failure is that such mechanisms are unevenly applied, under-resourced, and politically fragile.

9.3. The Cobra Effect

The Hanoi rat massacre was an archetype of this dynamic. Economists call this the cobra effect: when an intervention meant to suppress a behavior creates incentives that amplify it. [m]

In a linear worldview, Input A produces Output B. If you want less of something, ban it. If you want more of something, subsidize it. But in a Complex Adaptive System, the policy doesn't land on passive components. It lands on agents who actively interpret the rule and optimize around it. Tax law offers some of the clearest examples of this approach. Mortgage interest deductions encourage home ownership without mandating it. Higher short-term capital gains taxes discourage speculative trading without banning it. Bankruptcy law's promise of a "fresh start" encourages entrepreneurial risk-taking by reshaping the downside rather than prescribing behavior. These tools work by altering the payoff landscape in which choices are made.

Hanoi's bounty rewarded tails, so the system learned to produce tails. It optimized for the measurable proxy the law rewarded.

Mexico City learned the cobra effect the hard way. To cut smog, the city restricted cars from driving one weekday based on license-plate numbers. Commuters adapted rationally: many households bought a second vehicle to route around the rule, and the second car was often older, cheaper, and higher-emitting. The policy produced more cars instead of reducing emissions. The policy didn't fail because the environmental goal was wrong. It failed because it treated "driving on restricted days" as the target, and the

---

[m] The cobra effect is a term used in economics and systems theory to describe a perverse incentive where an attempted solution worsens the original problem. It derives from a (dubious) anecdote set in British India, where a government bounty on cobras allegedly motivated citizens to breed the snakes for profit rather than hunt them, ultimately increasing the wild population when the bounty was removed.

system learned to move the metric while preserving the underlying incentives.

Policies that aim to reduce harm can accidentally reward the behavior they're trying to curb. Rules aimed at fairness can create evasions that concentrate advantage. A law that treats a metric as a target often teaches the population to game the metric.

A resilient legal system needs a way to surface these failure modes early, before the unintended behavior becomes a stable niche.

Direct experimental control groups for laws are often ethically or politically impossible. No serious society would deliberately expose one population to known harm solely to generate comparative data. Instead, experimentation tends to occur indirectly: through pilot programs, phased rollouts, regulatory sandboxes, and jurisdictional variation. Minimum wage increases, marijuana legalization, zoning reforms, and guaranteed income trials have all followed this pattern, allowing policymakers to observe system responses before broader adoption. These mechanisms are imperfect, but they offer a practical substitute for controlled experimentation in moral domains.

9.4. Legislative Debt

If the Hanoi story is a failure of incentives, legislative debt is a failure of maintenance.

Software engineers dread "technical debt," the accumulation of quick fixes that eventually makes a codebase too dangerous to touch. Governments suffer from the same pathology. Legislative debt is the calcification of the state. It is why infrastructure projects take a decade to approve and why tax codes swell to millions of words. The system is more than slow; it is structurally seized, unable to change without triggering cascading failures.

This accumulation happens relentlessly. Old rules are rarely removed. Exceptions and carve-outs multiply. Definitions drift. Cross-references sprawl. Eventually, the "codebase" becomes so complex that only specialists can operate it, and even specialists can't predict the downstream implications. This pathology extends beyond statutory systems typical of the European civil code tradition. Common law regimes, inherited from the English common law tradition, accumulate similar debt through layers of precedent, where subtle distinctions across decades of cases produce bodies of law that are functionally inaccessible to anyone without full devotion to their interpretation.

Using the Qualitative Fragility Profile, the pattern is familiar: complexity is high, rising, and poorly bounded; coupling is tight (and getting tighter), because many rules depend on many other rules; and resilience is low, because change carries the risk of unintended cascades.

The Healthcare Patchwork

The U.S. healthcare system is the ultimate example of legislative debt. It is a geological formation. It accreted layer by layer: WWII wage controls created employer-based insurance; the 1960s added safety nets; the 2010s bolted on market exchanges. Each layer solved a specific crisis, but each layer increased the system's rigidity. Today, eligibility is fused to employment, and pricing is fused to opaque billing codes. The result is a negotiated truce between incompatible eras. It works until you try to fix it; then you discover that because everything touches everything, you cannot move a single lever without shaking the entire foundation. This is legislative debt in its mature form: a system optimized for political survival rather than functional coherence.

Zoning and Stagnation

Zoning is another excellent example. Many cities hard-code what can be built, where, how high, with how much parking, and with what materials. Those rules were often written for a different world. When the environment changes, such as with remote work, affordability constraints, and shifting demographics, the system struggles to adapt. Housing supply lags. Costs rise. Political conflict intensifies. The system freezes under its own accumulated constraints.

Many jurisdictions attempt to soften this rigidity through zoning variances and discretionary approvals. But these mechanisms are slow, unevenly accessible, and politically mediated. They function as pressure valves rather than adaptive redesign.

Legislative debt has a distinct smell: slow approvals, opaque processes, inconsistent outcomes, and a growing class of intermediaries who make their living navigating the maze.

❖ VERIDIA — Phase III: Disengagement (Gaming the System)

Veridia exhibited all of these symptoms long before the blackouts: automated enforcement of obsolete bylaws, contradictory incentives between the energy and transit grids, and a citizenry that had learned to "game" the sensors rather than follow the intent of the law. By this point, Veridia's systems still functioned, but the people living inside them had stopped believing the system could be corrected.

9.5. Sunset Clauses: Subtraction in Law

We have a cultural bias toward additive solutions. When something breaks, we add a rule, a committee, a process. But complex systems don't just fail because they lack structure. They fail because structure becomes excessive, outdated, and tightly coupled.

Governance, in practice, ships with an "Add" button and no "Delete" key.

Once a law exists, it tends to create beneficiaries. Beneficiaries create constituencies. Constituencies create political gravity. The law becomes hard to remove even when it is clearly obsolete. This is how dead code stays in production.

A sunset clause is a simple countermeasure. It makes a law expire after a fixed period (e.g., 5 or 10 years) unless the legislature explicitly renews it. It flips the default state. Instead of immortality for every bad idea, expiration becomes the baseline.

Sunset clauses force the systems question. Did the law hit its metrics? Did it create a cobra effect? Did conditions change so the law no longer fits the environment? If it worked, renew it. If it didn't, let it die.

Imagine a legal code that cleans itself.

In practice, however, renewal decisions are often captured by the same political and financial forces that shaped the original law. Beneficiaries mobilize to preserve favorable rules, while diffuse public benefits struggle to organize in defense of effective but unglamorous regulations. As a result, some harmful laws persist while some beneficial ones expire, because power intervened.

But this is subtraction as governance: pruning dead branches so the organism can grow. It reduces legislative debt, loosens coupling over time, and makes adaptation politically possible because review becomes routine rather than exceptional.

9.6. Quality Assurance Standards

The Science of Laws community has argued for formal quality assurance for laws, borrowing the spirit of ISO-style standards: treat a law as a product, and reduce defects before release.

In this view, a defective law is both unpopular and structurally unsound. It is ambiguous. It lacks feedback mechanisms. It is unenforceable. It contradicts physical or social reality (mandating outcomes that cannot occur given known constraints). It fails basic design hygiene.

Some jurisdictions have already institutionalized limited forms of legislative quality assurance. A prominent federal example was Al Gore's National Partnership for Reinventing Government during the Clinton administration.[107] That initiative treated government programs as systems to be audited, streamlined, and redesigned, and succeeded in eliminating obsolete programs, consolidating agencies, and paying down what we would now call legislative debt. Its mixed political reception illustrates a recurring tension: systematic maintenance of the legal code is far less theatrically appealing than symbolic gestures of reform, even when it is more effective.

Most U.S. states maintain Law Revision Commissions tasked with identifying obsolete, contradictory, or unjust laws and recommending reforms. These bodies function explicitly as legal quality assurance testers, reviewing the accumulated codebase for defects. In most states, however, commission service is unpaid and secondary to other professional obligations, sharply limiting capacity. California is a notable exception, maintaining a full-time, professionally staffed Law Revision Commission whose recommendations have historically been enacted at high rates.[108] These institutions demonstrate that the idea is viable, but also how constrained it becomes without sustained political and financial support.

The long-term ambition is independent certification: create bodies capable of assessing whether a proposed law meets minimal engineering standards. This would separate two questions that are currently tangled. First: "Is this law technically coherent and implementable?" That is engineering. Second: "Do we want this law, given our values and trade-offs?" That is politics.

Politics should choose the destination. Engineering should ensure the vehicle can safely make the trip.

9.7. Conclusion: From Statutes to Frameworks

Rather than more control, better lawmaking means better design. Clearer intent. Fewer perverse incentives. Tighter feedback loops. And, just as importantly, the willingness to remove what no longer fits.

When law is treated as static text, failure feels surprising and personal. Someone must have written the rule badly. Someone must have abused it. But when law is understood as an intervention in a Complex Adaptive System, failure becomes expected. Incentives will be gamed. Proxies will become targets. Rules will interact in ways no one predicted. Debt will accumulate unless it is actively paid down.

The role of the legislator, then, is to shape the environment in which behavior emerges. That means setting simple, durable boundaries and paying close attention to how people actually respond. And it means being willing to revise, subtract, or retire rules when the system reveals that they are doing harm.

All of this, however, assumes a population capable of recognizing its own interests and interpreting institutional feedback. No amount of architectural refinement can compensate for a civically illiterate public. Systems designed for adaptation still depend on participants who can distinguish evidence from spectacle, incentives from intentions, and long-term benefit from short-term theater. A politically mature society cannot be commanded into existence; it must be cultivated. Formal education in civics, administrative law, economics, and critical reasoning is therefore foundational to legal design.

The same systems logic applies to lawmakers and regulators themselves. Campaign finance regimes and revolving-door incentives shape legislative behavior as powerfully as statutes shape citizen behavior. When political survival depends more on donors than voters, design reviews and quality assurance mechanisms risk becoming decorative rather than corrective.

Regulatory capture follows the same pattern: agencies tasked with oversight gradually adopt the priorities of the industries they regulate. Anti-corruption measures — transparency, contribution limits, institutional independence — are therefore core components of a resilient legal architecture.

The contrast between Al Gore's methodical, data-driven effort to reinvent government in the 1990s and later performative visions of reform, symbolized by spectacle rather than systems analysis, highlights a deeper problem. In complex systems, theatrical disruption often outperforms maintenance in the political marketplace, even when the latter produces better results.

The examples in this chapter, from rat bounties to zoning codes, all point to the same lesson. Durable order cannot be forced from above by increasingly detailed instructions. In living systems, order emerges from interaction. If the architecture is wrong, no amount of moral clarity in the statute will save it.

Law is static text. Society is motion. To understand how systems actually behave, we have to stop staring at the rulebook and start watching what people do once the rules hit the ground. That motion is where the operational truth of a system is revealed.

❖ VERIDIA: COMPLIANCE OVER ADAPTATION

Veridia was undone by an architecture that valued compliance over adaptation.

Chapter 10. The Digital Swarm

> *"Technological change is not additive; it is ecological."*
>
> *— Neil Postman*

A rumor hits the feed at 9:03. By 9:17 it is "everywhere." Nobody issued orders. Nobody coordinated the crowd. And yet the system moved as if it possessed a singular, reactive mind.

The Mechanic looks at this and sees a machine out of control. The Gardener looks at this and sees an invasive species thriving in soil perfectly optimized for it.

In a digital ecosystem, the "crowd" is people coupled to ranking systems. The result is a biological environment where selection pressure operates at the speed of light.

10.1. Algorithmic Monoculture

Virality is an evolutionary filter.[109,110] Platforms both transmit content and they rank it based on engagement. In agricultural terms, the algorithm is the fertilizer. If the algorithm rewards "time on site" or "reaction speed," it creates a specific chemical composition in the soil.

In this environment, nuance is a delicate orchid that requires time and calm to grow. Outrage, however, is kudzu.[n] It is hardy, it grows fast, and it chokes out competitors.

---

[n] *Pueraria montana* (kudzu) was originally introduced to the United States in 1876 as a decorative plant and later encouraged by the Soil Conservation Service as a tool for erosion control. It worked too well. Lacking natural insect predators in its new environment, it grew uncontrollably, swallowing entire forests and buildings. It is the botanical equivalent of an engagement algorithm: designed to solve a distribution problem, it ended up suffocating the ecosystem it was meant to serve.

The Gardener and the Machine

When we see a feed filled with polarization, we are witnessing an algorithmic monoculture. The problem is that the ecosystem lacks biodiversity. We have created a cornfield susceptible to blight, where a single strain of information, the most reactive kind, can infect the entire crop in minutes.

10.2. Designing a Useful Swarm

If algorithmic monoculture represents the failure mode of the digital swarm, it is instructive to examine a system that successfully resisted it. Unlike a crowd, which merely gathers, reacts, and disperses, a swarm persists; it remembers, adapts, and carries its past forward through norms, rankings, and incentives embedded in its code. Consequently, when people enter a digital system, they first encounter the environment, where the soil sets the terms of engagement long before the neighbors do.

This explains why debates focusing on "bad users" often misfire: behavior follows gradients. Whatever a system rewards inevitably becomes abundant, while what it penalizes becomes scarce. Over time, this selective pressure reshapes both the content and the identity of the participants themselves; people eventually become different types of contributors. To see this clearly, we can look to Stack Overflow, a system that resisted monoculture and noise because its environment was designed to constrain those outcomes.

The Problem It Set Out to Solve

Stack Overflow was built to solve the narrow, practical problem of programmers needing reliable answers to specific questions. At the time, existing forums suffered from familiar failures: repetition, ego contests, and long threads that never resolved the original issue, which meant valuable knowledge often drowned in a sea of opinion. The founders treated this as an ecological problem, operating on the assumption that if the environment rewarded visibility and speed, it would produce noise, but if it rewarded precision and verification, it would produce signal.

Selection Pressure by Design

While most digital platforms rely on moderation as their primary control mechanism — the Mechanic's instinct to identify and remove bad content — Stack Overflow chose a different path. Although moderation exists, the primary force is the reward structure embedded directly in the interface, where answers compete rather than people. Unlike platforms where responses accumulate linearly, making the conversation itself the artifact, Stack Overflow ranks answers so that one rises while the rest sink. Because visibility is earned strictly through usefulness as judged by peers, the system creates strong selection pressure; a clever response that attracts attention but fails to solve the problem simply loses and disappears.

Furthermore, feedback is immediate and local. Votes arrive quickly, causing good answers to surface within minutes while poor ones fade just as fast, ensuring the loop between action and consequence is short enough for learning to occur. Contributors do not need to infer what the system wants because the system demonstrates it. While reputation is cumulative, it remains fragile; points unlock privileges, but they can also be lost. High status does not grant immunity from correction, meaning that while authority exists, it remains conditional, preventing early winners from hardening into permanent elites.

Together, these choices create a specific environment that rewards clarity, specificity, and restraint, while penalizing speculation and performative certainty. The result is that conflict is metabolized into refinement rather than amplification, rendering the swarm useful.

What the System Prevented

Consider two responses to a novice asking how to fix a memory leak: one offers general advice and anecdotes, while the other identifies the precise line of code causing the issue. On a typical social platform, the first might win because it signals confidence and invites engagement, but on Stack Overflow, the second wins simply because it solves the problem.

Over time, contributors learn this without explicit instruction because the environment teaches them; the system enacts them. This is the essence of husbandry: no designer predicts which answers will rise and no moderator evaluates each contribution, yet global order emerges from local interactions governed by simple rules.

Stack Overflow illustrates a broader claim: complex systems need better constraints. Most digital platforms optimize for engagement, but that choice carries consequences; engagement functions as a proxy, and once treated as a target, it becomes a selection criterion. Consequently, the system promotes whatever generates reaction fastest, meaning outrage outpaces nuance, certainty outpaces doubt, and identity outpaces evidence, making the resulting monoculture an inevitable ecological outcome.

Stack Overflow avoided this trap by refusing to optimize for engagement at all, choosing instead to optimize for usefulness, a single decision that fundamentally altered the fitness landscape. While context matters, the structure generalizes: if you want understanding, reward understanding; if you want speed, reward speed; if you want conflict, reward conflict. The swarm will always comply.

Productive Absence and Strategic Friction

The system is also defined by what it excludes. Stack Overflow discourages storytelling because they dilute the signal it exists to cultivate. It also resists identity formation by keeping profiles subordinate to contributions, ensuring the unit of value is the answer rather than the person. Furthermore, it avoids real-time reaction mechanisms; with no infinite scroll or feed tuned to maximize time on site, the interface encourages departure once the question is answered. These absences matter because they introduce friction, slow propagation, and trade raw growth for coherence.

From a Mechanic's view, these are missed opportunities, but from a Gardener's view, they are essential protective constraints.

Fragility and Drift

Now, consider a small change: imagine if Stack Overflow prioritized answers that generated the most comments in the first ten minutes, introduced badges for controversy, or boosted posts that kept users on the page longest. Even if nothing else changed, the system would drift within months; answers would lengthen, the tone would sharpen, and debate would replace resolution. As experts left and novices followed, the swarm would adapt to the new gradient without any malice required, an example of Dark Emergence, manifesting as a phase shift rather than a crash.

This contrast clarifies a common confusion in digital governance: moderation treats symptoms, whereas the environment shapes behavior. A system that relies on moderation to counteract the very incentives it created is unstable by design because it attempts to weed faster than the weeds can grow, a strategy that simply does not scale. Husbandry works upstream by asking a different question — what the soil rewards — and Stack Overflow answers this with precision by rewarding usefulness to a stranger, a metric that is difficult to fake.

Why This Matters for the Digital Swarm

The deeper insight is that digital environments are defined by selection under fast feedback. As the gap between action and consequence collapses, learning accelerates, but so does convergence; early winners dominate, and when the reward signal is misaligned, degradation locks in rapidly.

This is why strategic friction matters. Stack Overflow applies friction where it counts: writing a good answer takes effort, reputation accumulates over time, and visibility is earned rather than granted. By making it easy to leave the site but hard to dominate it, this friction slows propagation, preserves diversity, and prevents the system from collapsing into the fastest replicator.

While most debates about platforms focus on power — who controls the algorithm, who owns the data, and who enforces the rules — these questions, while important, are incomplete. The deeper issue is stewardship, or who takes responsibility for the environment in which behavior evolves. Stack Overflow succeeded because its designers accepted that responsibility, choosing a specific yield and designing the soil to produce it.

The Digital Swarm is a living system governed by selection, feedback, and constraint. Stack Overflow demonstrates that swarms can be cultivated without domination, proving that simple rules, when placed well, can produce durable order. However, it also reveals how fragile that balance is; change the reward, tighten the loop, or remove the friction, and the swarm reconfigures instantly.

The lesson is structural rather than moral. Digital systems drift toward whatever survives selection. If we want different outcomes, we must tend different gardens. Whether anyone accepts the role of Gardener before monoculture takes hold remains uncertain.

10.3. The El Farol Problem and the Failure of Sync

If virality explains how things spread, it does not explain why crowds fail to coordinate.

W. Brian Arthur's El Farol Bar Problem is the classic illustration.[111] A bar is enjoyable only if fewer than 60 people attend. If everyone predicts "empty," they go, and it becomes crowded. If everyone predicts "crowded," they stay home, and it becomes empty.

The Mechanic tries to solve this with control: a reservation system. You must book a slot. This works, but it is brittle and scales poorly.

The Gardener solves this with signaling, but faces a new problem: oscillation. If Waze tells everyone a road is empty, everyone takes it, and the empty road instantly becomes the traffic jam.

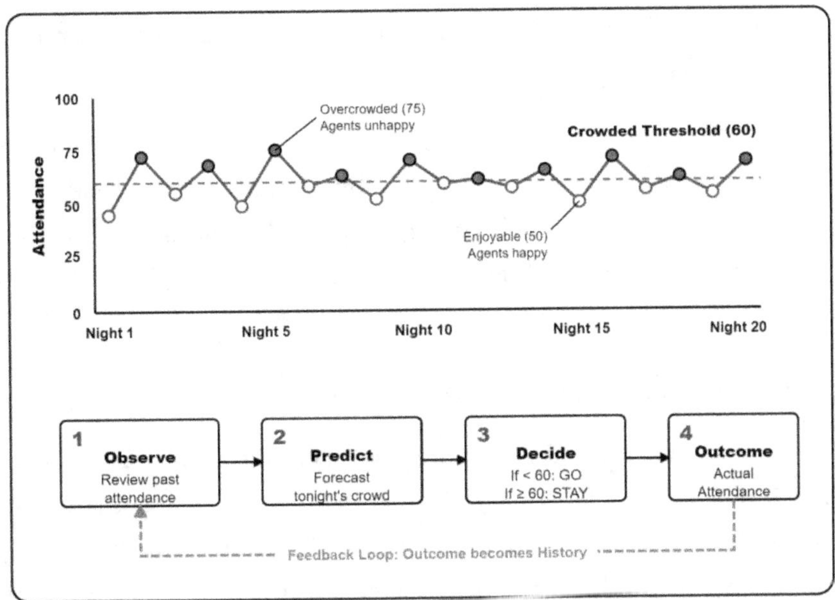

Figure 20. The El Farol Problem

High-resolution version available at phronos.com/tgm-diagrams

Digital platforms compress the time between signal and reaction to zero. This removes the natural damping effects of the physical world. When the loop is too tight, the system creates noise rather than intelligence (Figure 20).

10.4. Strategic Friction

How do we fix the oscillation? We need strategic friction.

In nature, friction is a feature. Distance, energy costs, and time delays prevent infinite exponential growth. A forest fire eventually hits a river or a rocky ridge. Digital systems, by contrast, are often too efficient. They are frictionless planes where fire spreads infinitely, unchecked by physical limitations.

To counter this, a Gardener architecting a digital system introduces artificial latency. Consider the design of a cooling period in a discussion forum. By holding a post in a queue for ten minutes before it becomes visible, the system forces a pause. This brief gap allows the user's emotional "hot state" to subside, often resulting in the deletion or editing of a reactive comment before it ever pollutes the stream.

We see similar logic in financial markets, which utilize circuit breakers to halt trading when stocks plummet too rapidly. By reintroducing this friction, we break the hot feedback loop of rage-engagement. We allow the slow variables of the system — trust, verification, and context — to catch up to the fast variables of clicks and shares.

10.5. From Moderation to Husbandry

The most common mistake in digital governance is confusing moderation (The Mechanic) with husbandry (The Gardener). Moderation is the act of pulling weeds one by one. In a system of millions, this is mathematically impossible; you simply cannot hire enough moderators to check every post. Husbandry, by contrast, focuses on changing the environmental conditions so that weeds struggle to grow in the first place.

We can see this difference by comparing a standard social feed, a "wild field," with a platform like Stack Overflow, which functions as a "tended garden." In a standard feed, the soil is optimized for engagement above all else. If a user posts a controversial lie, it generates comments and reactions. The system interprets this activity as success and amplifies the post. In this environment, the soil effectively rewards the weed, ensuring it spreads.

Stack Overflow is optimized for a different yield: utility. Here, a bad answer is immediately downvoted, effectively composted to the bottom of the page where it cannot distract others. Conversely, a good answer earns reputation, providing the sunlight needed for visibility. The platform works but because the interface is designed for community husbandry. It employs distinct, structural mechanisms for pruning via flags, composting via downvotes, and harvesting via accepted answers.

10.6. Conclusion: The Gardener's Question

The Mechanic asks, "How do we control the content?" The Gardener asks, "What is the soil rewarding?"

Digital swarms only need a gradient to move. Once a reward signal exists, behavior flows toward it faster than deliberation.

If we want a different harvest — if we want truth, or cooperation, or creativity — we cannot just demand it from the users. We must alter the chemistry of the soil. We must design interfaces that reward the slow work of construction over the fast high of destruction.

We have seen how the machine moves the crowd. Now, we must ask: "Can the crowd guide the machine?" That question takes us from the swarm to the studio, from crowds to creation.

Chapter 11. The Synthetic Muse

> *"Computers are useless. They can only give you answers."*
>
> — *Pablo Picasso*

Creativity has lost its center.

For most of human history, creative work had a clear locus: a person, a hand, a mind. Tools mattered, techniques evolved, and collaboration expanded the perimeter of authorship, but intention still lived somewhere identifiable. Even when we spoke loosely about "the muse," we knew where to look.

That assumption no longer holds. Artificial intelligence has entered the creative loop as an active participant. It generates, recombines, and iterates at a scale and speed no human system can match. It does so without understanding or awareness. Yet the outputs are coherent enough to feel authored. What is emerging cannot be explained by better tools alone.

By now, this pattern should feel familiar. When feedback loops are allowed to explore a space at scale, whether ecological, economic, or social, novel structure emerges without anyone planning it. No single agent needs to understand the whole. Coherence arises from interaction. Control dissolves into conditions. We have seen this grammar repeat across domains.

What is new is where that grammar is now operating. Creativity has always depended on variation and selection. What AI changes is the ratio. It collapses the cost of variation to near zero and tightens the loop between generation and selection. The result is a different creative ecology, one in which authorship diffuses, style converges, and intent competes with optimization.

Large generative models navigate vast latent spaces shaped by compressed human culture: patterns of language, image, sound, and form learned from billions of artifacts. When prompted, they synthesize coordinates. Each output is a negotiated resolution between prior structure, noise, and constraint. The process is neither random nor planned. It is emergent.

The question, then, is how to practice stewardship in a creative ecology where generation is abundant and selection is automated. What does it mean to be a Gardener in the age of the synthetic muse?

This reframes the human role. When production is no longer scarce, execution stops being the bottleneck. Direction, judgment, and refusal become the leverage points. The creative act shifts upstream, from making to shaping the conditions under which something worth keeping might appear.

That shift is unsettling for a reason. Our inherited concepts of skill, authorship, and value were built for a world in which creation was slow, costly, and visibly human. In a system capable of generating endless "good enough," those concepts no longer anchor meaning on their own. What matters is no longer who produced an artifact, but how it was guided, selected, contextualized, and amplified.

This is where emergence becomes ethical. Selection-driven systems optimize for whatever signal they are given. If the feedback is engagement, they learn to provoke. If it is familiarity, they converge toward sameness. If it is speed or volume, they flood. Creativity converges. And unless someone takes responsibility for the loop, it converges toward whatever is easiest to reward.

The synthetic muse explores what can be expressed within the statistical boundaries of its training data. It recombines prior structure at scale; it does not originate out of nothing. The burden of meaning moves in this environment. It settles on the humans who set the constraints, choose the signals, and decide what gets refined versus discarded. Creativity becomes less about expression and more about stewardship: tending a generative process without being optimized out of it.

In what follows, we will examine how this plays out in practice, first in the arts and then in the broader questions these systems force upon us; questions of responsibility rather than capability; questions about whether we are willing to remain accountable for the worlds their creativity selects into existence, rather than whether machines can create at all.

11.1. The Emergence of Collective Creativity

Creativity is often romanticized as the act of a lone genius, a singular mind wrestling with a blank page, an empty canvas, or a silent instrument. While individual brilliance is undeniable, another, equally significant form of creativity arises from the dynamic relationship between many. This is collective creativity, an emergent phenomenon where the collaborative output of a group far exceeds the simple sum of its individual contributions. The internet, acting as a global nervous system, has created unprecedented arenas for this phenomenon to flourish, enabling the formation of "collective minds" at a scale previously unimaginable.

These digital ecosystems provide the structure: the rules of engagement and the channels for interaction through which a group's shared intelligence can cohere into a creative force. By examining two vastly different domains, collaborative storytelling and open-source software development, we can see the same underlying principles of emergence at work, perfectly illuminated by the Metasystem Framework.

The Living Narrative: Crowd-Sourced Storytelling

Traditional publishing is a one-way street: an author writes a book, which is then printed and delivered to a passive audience. The feedback loop, if one exists at all, is measured in months or years through reviews and sales figures. Social storytelling platforms have inverted this model, transforming writing into a live, interactive performance.

Case in Point: Wattpad

Wattpad is a global platform where writers can publish their stories one chapter at a time, and millions of readers can follow along, comment, and vote in real-time. It's less a digital library and more a living literary ecosystem. A writer might post a new chapter and, within hours, receive hundreds of comments from readers speculating on plot twists, critiquing character decisions, or pleading for a certain romantic pairing.

This immediate, granular feedback creates an emergent effect. The story ceases to be the sole product of the author's imagination; it becomes a co-creation, subtly (and sometimes overtly) shaped by the collective desires and reactions of its audience. An author might notice a minor character receiving an unexpectedly passionate response and decide to expand their role. A plot hole identified by a sharp-eyed reader can be patched in the next chapter. Popular tropes and new sub-genres can bubble up from the community, creating trends that ripple across the entire platform. The success and final form of a story is an emergent property of the tightly coupled author-reader system.

Let's analyze this through the Metasystem Framework:

- **The Technological Domain:** The Wattpad platform itself, the mobile and web applications, the servers that host the content, and the algorithms that recommend stories. The user interface, with its inline commenting and voting features, is the substrate for interaction.

- **The Social Domain:** This is the vibrant community of millions of writers and readers. They bring their shared cultural context, genre expectations, and a willingness to engage. The community establishes its own norms of interaction, creating a distinct social environment.

- **The Feedback Interface:** This is the most crucial element. The ability for readers to comment on every single paragraph and for authors to read and respond to that feedback creates a rapid, high-fidelity loop. The platform's "trending" lists and recommendation engines act as a secondary, system-level feedback mechanism, amplifying popular stories and guiding the attention of the collective. The author provides the initial creative spark, the community provides feedback, and the author adapts, steering the narrative in a cycle of continuous co-creation.

The Cathedral of Code: Open-Source Software

If Wattpad represents the emergence of collective narrative, the open-source software (OSS) movement represents the emergence of collective logic and problem-solving. Projects like the Linux operating system, the Python programming language, or the countless libraries hosted on GitHub are among the most complex and sophisticated artifacts ever built by humans. Yet, they are not built by a single, centrally managed organization (Figure 21).

Case in Point: The GitHub Ecosystem

GitHub and similar platforms provide the infrastructure for a distributed, often volunteer, network of developers to collaborate on a single codebase. This process embodies the famous adage of the OSS world, Linus's Law: "given enough eyeballs, all bugs are shallow." This is a pure statement of emergence. A single developer might miss a subtle flaw in their code, but when that code is reviewed by dozens of other developers from different backgrounds and perspectives, the probability of catching that flaw approaches certainty. Linus's Law holds, until coordination costs dominate. Then progress slows because alignment becomes expensive.

The creative process here is one of problem-solving and construction. A developer might identify a need and propose a new feature via a "pull request." This proposal is then scrutinized by the community. Other developers might suggest improvements, identify potential conflicts with other parts of the code, or test it for bugs. Through this iterative process of feedback and refinement, the initial idea is polished, hardened, and integrated into the whole. The final product is the synthesized output of the collective intelligence of the entire community.

Applying the Metasystem Framework to this domain:

- **The Technological Domain:** The internet is the foundation, but more specifically, it's the version control system Git (which allows for nonlinear, distributed work) and the hosting platform GitHub (which provides the social and project management tools on top of Git).

- **The Social Domain:** This consists of the global community of developers, their shared technical expertise, and a strong set of cultural norms: conventions for writing code, etiquette for submitting and reviewing changes, and a meritocratic ethos where the quality of a contribution matters more than the contributor's identity.

- **The Feedback Interface:** The "pull request" is the central feedback mechanism. It's a formal proposal to change the code, which triggers a structured conversation (code review). Bug reports, feature requests, and discussion forums are other vital channels that allow the community to signal problems and direct the project's evolution. This system allows thousands of asynchronous contributions to be safely and coherently integrated into a single, functional whole.

In both the fluid world of storytelling and the rigorous domain of software engineering, we see the same fundamental pattern. When a platform provides the right technological substrate and a well-designed Feedback

Interface, a social domain of motivated individuals can self-organize into a creative collective. The "ghost in the machine" is the distributed intelligence of the network, an emergent mind capable of creating works of a scale and complexity that no single individual could ever hope to achieve alone.

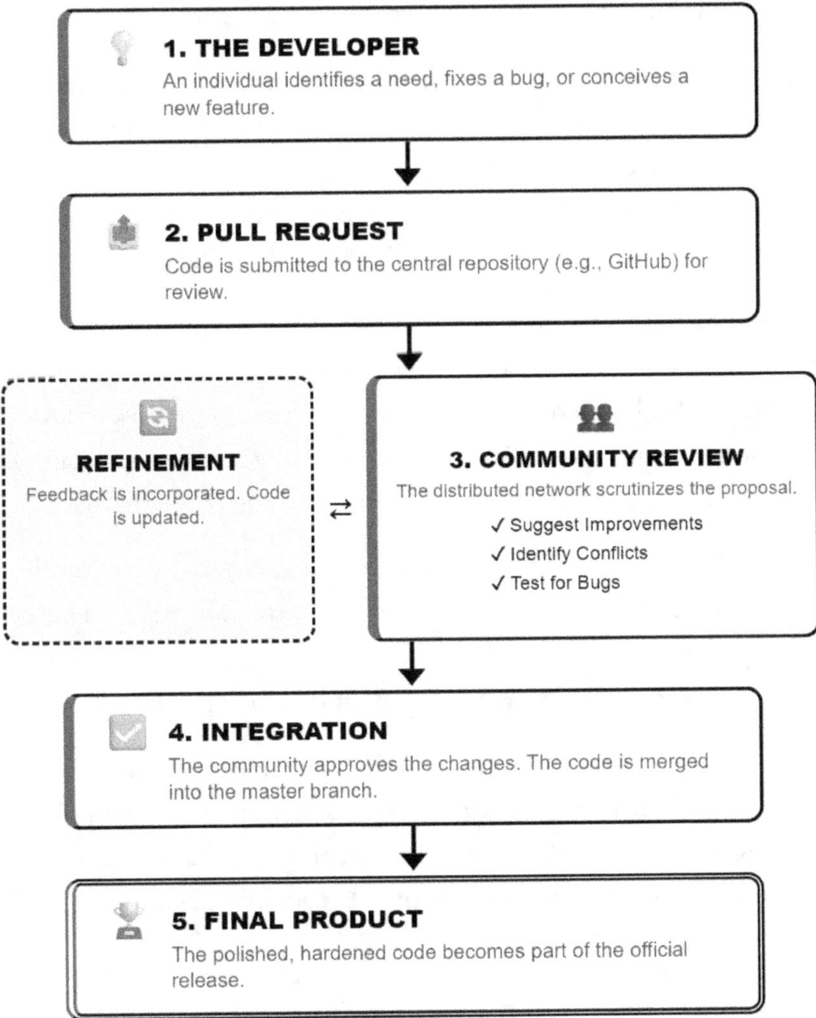

Figure 21. OSS Collaborative Creativity Feedback Loop

High-resolution version available at phronos.com/tgm-diagrams

11.2. AI as Creative Partner: Music and Visual Art

For decades, computers played a supporting role in creative work. They were tools for execution: word processors, digital audio workstations, photo editors. They accelerated production and reduced friction, yet origination remained human. The "ghost in the machine," such as it was, belonged firmly to the human operator.° That paradigm has fractured.

Modern generative systems now participate in the creative loop. Trained on vast corpora of human culture, they synthesize novel outputs that are coherent, surprising, and often useful. Their creativity differs from the human kind. They lack intention, care, and understanding. Yet they explore possibility spaces in ways that feel collaborative (Figure 22).

This is most visible in music and visual art, but the pattern extends across creative domains. Rather than encoding rules explicitly, these systems learn patterns implicitly and recombine them under constraint. A user provides a prompt, a fragment, or a direction. The system generates variations. The human selects, refines, and iterates. Creativity emerges from the loop.

What makes this partnership new is scale. The system can traverse cultural memory faster than any individual, offering variations no single creator would plausibly explore unaided. The human, in turn, provides judgment: deciding what resonates, what fits, and what should be discarded.

In this arrangement, the machine is a force multiplier for variation rather than a replacement for the artist. The human remains responsible for meaning. This partnership changes the mechanics of making. And when the mechanics change, the moral accounting changes with them.

° Not to be confused with Arthur Koestler's critique of Cartesian dualism[47], my use of "the ghost in the machine" refers to the invisible dynamics and feedback processes that animate complex systems.

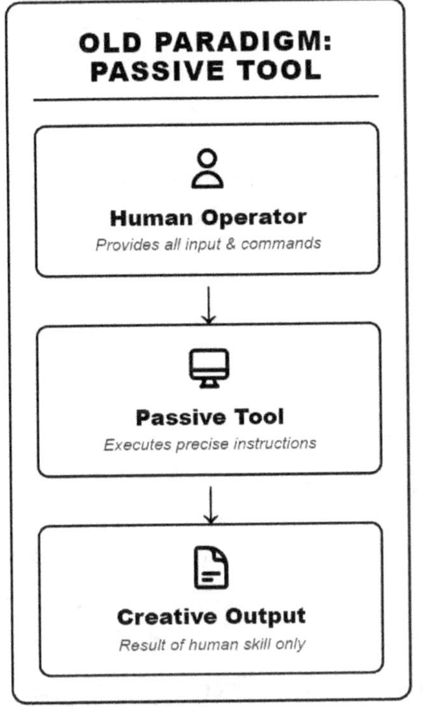

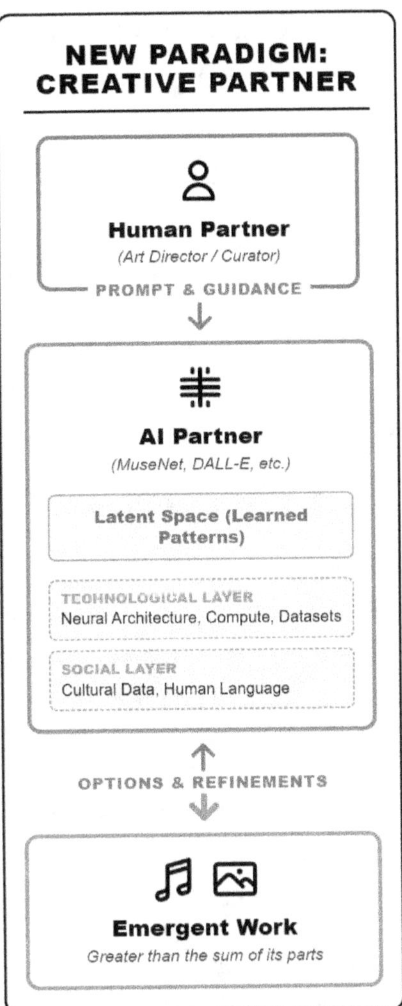

Figure 22. AI Creative Process Flow

Note: Human creativity has always exhibited emergence. The distinction here is not the presence of emergence, but the scale and recursion of the feedback loop. Generative systems collapse iteration time and expand variation space beyond what traditional tools enable. High-resolution version available at phronos.com/tgm-diagrams

Three questions follow inevitably.

- **Authorship:** When an output is co-produced by a prompt, a model, a training corpus, and a selection process, who is the creator?

- **Value:** In a world where production is abundant, what becomes scarce: craft, taste, lived experience, trust, or the story behind the work?

- **Meaning:** If a system can generate endless "good enough," how do we keep our own intent from being optimized away by the reward signals that shape what survives?

Most systems will answer these questions implicitly, through their feedback loops, long before we answer them explicitly. They arise whenever creativity becomes a networked, selection driven process rather than a solitary act.

11.3. Unifying Principles of Emergent Creativity

At first glance, artificial intelligence and collective human creativity appear fundamentally different. One is built from silicon and code, the other from people and social ties. One operates at machine speed, the other at human pace. Yet when examined structurally, both are governed by the same underlying grammar.

In each case, creativity emerges from a system that generates variation at scale and subjects it to selection through feedback. No central authority needs to plan the outcome. Coherence arises from interaction rather than intention.

Generative models explore latent spaces shaped by their training data. Online communities explore cultural spaces shaped by shared norms, incentives, and visibility. In both, novelty is discovered through traversal: movement through a space defined by prior structure and present constraint.

The crucial similarity is compression. Both systems operate on condensed representations of human culture. Models encode statistical regularities learned from vast corpora. Communities encode norms, styles, and expectations through shared practice. What appears as originality is often the recombination of deeply compressed priors under new pressures.

Selection does the real work. Outputs persist because they are rewarded: liked, shared, remixed, trained upon, or otherwise amplified. Over time, these rewards shape the space itself. Certain styles become easier to reach. Others fade. The system develops attractors.

This is why convergence is a property of selection-driven systems operating at scale. Without countervailing forces, both AI models and human collectives drift toward what is legible, familiar, and easily reinforced.

Agency, in this context, relocates. In neither system does agency reside primarily in individual outputs. It resides in the design of the feedback loops: what is measured, what is rewarded, and what is allowed to propagate. Whoever shapes those conditions shapes the creative trajectory, often without touching the work itself.

Seen this way, AI creativity and collective creativity are different substrates running the same process. The ethical questions they raise therefore concern the governance of selection once creation becomes abundant, rather than a contest between machines and humans.

The next question is unavoidable: if selection is where power concentrates, what happens to skill, authorship, and value in a world where generation no longer limits creativity?

Emergent Creativity and System Resilience

Creative ecosystems function as adaptive search engines. Diversity of expression, rapid iteration, and distributed contribution expand the solution space available to a culture.

In that sense, collective creativity is adaptive capacity. Systems that suppress variation converge toward fragility. Systems that preserve generative diversity increase their ability to respond to shocks.

The synthetic muse therefore presents a paradox: it expands variation while simultaneously increasing convergence pressure through shared latent space.

Whether it strengthens or weakens resilience depends entirely on how feedback is structured.

11.4. Redefining Skill, Authorship, and Value

When generation stops being the bottleneck, creative skill doesn't vanish. It shifts.

For a long time, mastery meant being able to execute: to draw well, write cleanly, compose quickly, or render a style faithfully. Those abilities mattered because they were hard-won and scarce. In systems where variation can be produced endlessly, that scarcity weakens. What replaces it is a different center of gravity.

One part of that shift is direction. When almost anything can be generated, knowing what to ask for becomes more important than knowing how to make it by hand. Direction is the ability to frame a problem, set constraints that matter, and sense where a process is drifting before it collapses into the obvious. That kind of guidance still depends on experience, judgment, and familiarity with a domain. It just operates earlier in the process.

Another part is selection. In abundant systems, most outputs are unremarkable. The work lies in deciding what is worth keeping. This is more than a passive or mechanical step. It requires attention, patience, and often the willingness to reject work that is competent but empty. As generation accelerates, selection becomes the core creative act.

A Question of Friction

There is a risk hidden inside abundance. When generation becomes cheap, friction disappears. Yet friction is how discernment sharpens. An architect who has never drawn struggles to see structure. A composer who has never wrestled with harmony may select pleasing sequences without understanding why they work.

Creative systems require apprenticeship to cultivate judgment. If AI removes all resistance, we risk producing curators without craft — selectors who never learned the grain of the material.

The solution is to preserve domains of deliberate practice. Some friction must remain, not as inefficiency, but as training load. This means skill relocates, from execution toward judgment and stewardship. As we saw in Chapter 10, friction is not inefficiency; it is developmental load. Systems that remove all resistance often remove growth.

Context matters more as well. Artifacts acquire meaning through placement, framing, and association. The same image, melody, or paragraph can feel trivial or resonant depending on where it appears, what surrounds it, and why it is presented. As output multiplies, context becomes one of the few remaining ways to make something stand out without shouting.

These changes complicate authorship. The familiar story of a single creator producing a discrete work becomes harder to sustain when creation passes through prompts, models, datasets, filters, revisions, and feedback. Authorship stretches. Credit blurs. Responsibility becomes harder to point to, even when the result feels intentional.

That ambiguity affects trust. When it is no longer clear how a work came to be, audiences rely less on claims of originality and more on signals of judgment. Who selected this? Why does it belong here? What kind of attention shaped it? Over time, trust shifts away from individual artifacts and toward the processes and people that consistently make sense of abundance.

Value shifts with it. In an environment saturated with capable output, novelty alone rarely holds. What becomes scarce is coherence: the ability to sustain meaning across many iterations, to develop a recognizable point of view, and to keep choosing well even when it would be easier not to. What is valued is less a single successful work than a pattern of discernment over time.

None of this tells us what creativity ought to be. It describes the pressures already reshaping it. The open question is who will take responsibility for guiding them.

11.5. Conclusion: Creativity at a Crossroads

Creativity persisted when machines learned to generate; it neither became artificial, cheap, nor meaningless. What changed was where the weight sits.

For most of human history, creation was constrained by effort. Making things took time, skill, and coordination. Those limits shaped culture. They determined what could be attempted, who could participate, and how long ideas had to mature before they spread. Meaning accumulated slowly because of friction. That friction is fading.

When generation becomes abundant, creativity reorganizes around selection. What survives is no longer what is hardest to make, but what is easiest to reinforce. Attention replaces effort as the scarce resource. Feedback replaces intention as the primary shaping force. The system amplifies what is rewarded. This is how selection-driven systems behave.

What matters, then, is whether someone remained accountable for the loop that shaped it. Every creative system embeds values, whether explicitly or not, in what it measures, promotes, and repeats. When those choices are left unattended, the system optimizes for convenience, familiarity, and scale.

Control has become infrastructural.

❖ VERIDIA: THE ECHO CHAMBER

Veridia's cultural sector suffered from optimization. The public art screens and music feeds were governed by engagement metrics. Over five years, the city's aesthetic converged toward a bland, highly polished average that guaranteed "likes" but eliminated

> risk. The city became beautiful, pleasant, and utterly devoid of soul.

Power now lives upstream, in the design of platforms, the tuning of models, the metrics of success, and the decisions about what is surfaced or ignored. These choices rarely look like acts of authorship, but they shape culture more reliably than any single work ever could.

This places a new burden on human creators, to hold the line on meaning, rather than compete with machines. To slow selection when it runs too fast. To resist optimization when it hollows out intent. To choose, again and again, what is worth carrying forward.

The synthetic muse will continue to explore. It will generate more than we can absorb and converge faster than we can reflect. And it is, in fact, already happening.

The open variable is whether responsibility will be exercised — and what, in its absence, will be left behind. This shift from building to guiding feels novel to artists and engineers, yet it runs deep in human history.

We have practiced this form of stewardship for millennia with flesh and blood. The ultimate test of the Gardener's mindset is found in the nursery.

Chapter 12. The First Stewardship

12.1. Parenting as Stewardship

In the previous chapter, we explored the challenge of the "Synthetic Muse," generative systems that we can prompt and guide, but never fully control. We learned that trying to force a probabilistic system to behave like a deterministic machine leads to failure.

Now, we turn to the original generative system.

If you want to master the art of the Gardener, you must study the most volatile, complex, and high-stakes intelligence in existence: the human child.

Just as with AI, the temptation of the Mechanic is to treat the child as a programmable entity, to optimize inputs (education, nutrition, discipline) in hopes of guaranteeing a specific output (success). And just as with AI, this approach fails because it ignores the fundamental nature of the system. A child is a latent space of infinite potential, waiting to be cultivated. The principles required to raise a resilient human are identical to those required to grow a resilient team. If you can stop being a Mechanic at the dinner table, you can stop being one in the boardroom.

In the quiet hours of the night, long after the spreadsheets are closed and the meetings have ended, many of us find ourselves standing in a doorway, looking at a sleeping child. It's in this moment that the temptation of the Machine is at its most powerful. Driven by a fierce and bottomless love, we feel an overwhelming urge to protect...to perfect...to build. We want to construct a perfect life for them, free of pain and full of achievement. We want to become the master Mechanic of our child's life.

But as we have explored throughout this book, the most important, complex, and adaptive systems extend beyond machines. They are gardens. Here, we apply the Framework you have learned to the principles of stewardship and our most fundamental human role. It's the ultimate test of our ability to let go of control and embrace cultivation.

A Necessary Clarification

Before we go any further, we need to get one thing out of the way.

Stewardship means stepping forward when something goes wrong. There are moments, rare, urgent, and unmistakable, when the right response is immediate control. If a child runs into traffic, you don't cultivate conditions. You grab them. If a child is in real danger, you act first and explain later.

That isn't a failure of the Gardener mindset. It's what makes it possible.

What follows is a distinction between interventions meant to prevent immediate harm and approaches meant to shape a human being over time.

12.2. The Parent as Mechanic

When we approach parenting with the Mechanic's mindset, we view the child as a project to be completed. We see a collection of components (grades, skills, athletic abilities, social connections) that must be optimized and assembled correctly to produce a predetermined outcome: the "successful adult."

Children, like any complex system, require boundaries to thrive. The error here is in the purpose of those boundaries.

In systems terms, the Mechanic views childhood variability, tantrums, failed tests, moments of defiance, as destructive entropy. They fail to recognize that in a biological system, this variability is exploratory behavior, the necessary chaos required for learning. The Mechanic's response is to increase constraints in an attempt to force a low-entropy state, effectively stopping the learning process.

For the Mechanic, the blueprint might be "doctor," "lawyer," or simply "Ivy League graduate." Every decision is weighed against this plan. Does this activity fit the blueprint? If not, it is considered a waste of time. The child's life soon resembles an assembly line: school followed by tutoring, piano lessons, and soccer. Free time is viewed as a production gap, an inefficiency that must be eliminated.

Quality control becomes the guiding principle. Performance is constantly measured, with grades serving as diagnostics and trophies as validation. A "B+" is interpreted as a manufacturing defect requiring immediate intervention.

To ensure the product remains pristine, the parent provides a protective casing. They intervene with teachers, smooth over friendship disputes, and solve problems before the child has a chance to engage with them. In doing so, they build an invisible armor around the child.

This approach is exhausting for both parent and child, but the true cost is hidden. While the Mechanic Parent is busy building a seemingly perfect machine, they are unintentionally creating a fragile one. By restricting the child's ability to grow in unexpected directions, they remove the child's ability to adapt.

By artificially suppressing entropy, the Mechanic strips the system of its ability to self-regulate. A system tightly optimized for a narrow outcome may appear efficient, but it loses redundancy. Like the centralized "Mothership" architecture we examined in Chapter 6, the child raised this way functions only as long as the command link holds. They become structurally unsound, liable to suffer catastrophic failure the moment the external regulator, the parent, is removed.

The Mechanic is fast, and mechanical control is effective when danger is immediate and time is short. Emergencies require authority, clarity, and constraint. No one debates this. The failure mode occurs when emergency posture becomes permanent architecture, when control designed for moments of risk is mistakenly applied to decades of development.

12.3. The Parent as Gardener

The Gardener Parent understands a fundamentally different truth. You can only influence the conditions in which a child will grow. They see their child as a unique seed. They don't know if this seed will become a mighty oak, a delicate rose, or a resilient wildflower. Their job is to become an expert in cultivating the soil around it.

The Gardener understands that a child is a living system attempting to organize itself. While the Mechanic tries to impose order from the outside, the Gardener provides the resources for that order to emerge from within. By allowing the child to experience the wind of failure and the drought of boredom, the Gardener permits the necessary friction that allows the child's internal psychological structure to harden. You are supplying the energy the child needs to build themselves.

It's active, intentional, and demanding. It requires observation, patience, and courage, and it's practiced imperfectly, day after day, by people who get tired and get it wrong.

Switching Modes: Safety vs. Growth

Parenting doesn't require choosing one posture and defending it forever. It requires knowing when to switch.

There are moments when control is the right response, when physical safety is at risk, when time is short, when the cost of hesitation is irreversible.

There are far more moments when control does real damage, when the goal is judgment instead of compliance, when learning has to be internal, when failure is part of the work.

The problem lies in acting decisively when it no longer matters. The problem lies in forgetting to let go once the danger has passed.

12.4. Parenting as Cultivation

Here's the systems problem in parenting: how do we cultivate an environment that yields a resilient, kind, and intrinsically motivated child, capable of navigating a complex and unpredictable future?

Step 1: Map the Domains

In the biological and ecological domain, we begin with the child's innate nature: their genetic predispositions, temperament, and developmental stages. These include aspects such as whether the child is introverted or extroverted, cautious or daring, their physical growth, sleep patterns, and nutritional needs. A Gardener parent observes and respects this domain, understanding that you cannot expect a petunia to behave like a pine tree.

The engineered and technological domain represents the world of human-made structures that shape the child's daily life. This includes the school system, organized sports, and perhaps most influential in modern times, the digital environment. Social media, educational apps, video games, and the omnipresence of screens exert influence on a child's attention, motivation, and identity formation.

Then there is the social and cultural domain, the world of shared meaning. This domain includes family values, cultural heritage, peer group norms, and societal expectations regarding success, gender, and identity. The language spoken in the home and the stories told in this environment give the child the "rules" and narratives they use to make sense of the world.

Step 2: Analyze the Feedback Interface

When we examine feedback loops, we can see how parenting patterns can reinforce either a Mechanic's vicious cycle or a Gardener's virtuous cycle.

In the Mechanic's cycle, imagine a child receiving a B+ on a math test. A parent, fearing deviation from the "A-Student Blueprint," expresses disappointment and immediately hires a tutor. The child internalizes the belief that their worth depends on their grade: a B+ is failure, and they are "not good at math." Anxiety grows, and on the next test, they underperform again. The parent interprets this as a lack of discipline or progress and responds by increasing the pressure. The parent has mistaken a feedback loop for a system failure. By intervening to fix the grade rather than the understanding, they break the loop, depriving the child of the data needed to self-correct. The cycle spirals downward, leaving both parent and child trapped in performance anxiety and diminished trust.

In contrast, the Gardener's virtuous cycle begins the same way — with a B+ on a test — but unfolds very differently. The parent uses this as a moment for curiosity and connection, asking, "How did you feel about the test? What parts were tricky?" Together, they look at the problem, shifting focus from the grade to understanding. The child feels safe to admit difficulty and, with guidance, experiences an "aha" moment while working through the challenging concept. Over time, confidence grows. The underlying message becomes, "It's okay to struggle; I can learn and figure it out." In this case, the feedback loop becomes reinforcing in a positive direction.

Step 3: Identify Leverage Points

Where can a parent intervene most effectively? There are three leverage points where a parent can most effectively influence the system.

The first is the narrative: the story told about success and failure. In many contexts, shifting from praise centered on fixed traits ("You are smart") to praise focused on effort and process ("You worked so hard") can support persistence and a healthier sense of growth.

The second leverage point is the response to failure. How a parent reacts when a child falls down, loses a game, or brings home a disappointing grade sets the tone for resilience. Treating these moments as opportunities for growth, "fertilizer" for learning, helps children internalize that struggle is a natural and valuable part of development.

Finally, curating the environment is an often-overlooked act. While parents cannot control the whole world, they can shape the micro-environment of the home: what books are on the shelves, what kinds of conversations unfold around the dinner table, and what boundaries exist around technology. These choices cultivate the "soil" in which the child's character and curiosity take root.

Step 4: Anticipate Dark Emergence

Even well-intentioned Mechanic-style parenting can lead to unintended consequences, a phenomenon we call Dark Emergence. (We'll explore this in detail in Chapter 14.)

Brittle perfectionism can emerge when children become afraid of anything less than perfection. Without exposure to manageable stress or failure, they begin to interpret every mistake as a collapse rather than a source of learning. Over time, this fear narrows their willingness to try new or challenging tasks.

As this happens, intrinsic motivation weakens. Curiosity is gradually replaced by reliance on external validation such as grades, trophies, or parental approval. The system may appear orderly, but it lacks the flexibility needed to adapt.

A subtler but equally damaging outcome is outsourced resilience.

When parents habitually solve every problem, children never develop their own tools for coping with setbacks. They may reach adulthood deeply fragile and unequipped to deal with adversity. Finally, rebellion can arise as a desperate attempt to reclaim autonomy within an overly controlled system. In seeking freedom, a child might reject both the parent's plan and their own sense of direction.

By applying the Framework to parenting, we see that the key is cultivation: tending to each domain with attention and humility, nurturing a child who is both grounded and capable of thriving in a world that no parent can fully predict.

12.5. The Gardener's Toolkit in Action: A Scenario

Imagine 10-year-old Lyra comes home devastated. She tried out for the school play and didn't get the lead role she desperately wanted; she was cast in the chorus instead.

The Mechanic Parent's response is to immediately shift into problem-solving mode. "This is unacceptable. You're the best one! I'm going to call the teacher. Maybe we can get you into a private acting class to show them. We'll work on your audition piece every night." The goal is to *fix the outcome*. The unintended message to Lyra is: "Your feelings aren't as important as the failure. Not getting what you want is a problem to be solved by me."

The Gardener Parent's response is to get into tending the soil. First, they connect. "Come here. I know. I know you wanted it. It stinks." They listen. They validate the feeling of sadness and frustration without trying to fix it. Only later do they move to the trellis and the weather. "I understand. I know, it's disappointing. When I was your age, I wanted so much to be Frederic in *The Pirates of Penzance*, and they cast me as Samuel. So I totally understand how you're feeling. What do you want to do now?" The goal is to *process the experience*. The message to Lyra is: "Your feelings are valid. Setbacks happen, and I trust you to handle them. Let's think about how to grow from here."[112,113]

12.6. Conclusion: The Ultimate Act of Stewardship

The goal of the Mechanic is to produce a perfect product. The goal of the Gardener is to cultivate a resilient person.

The child raised in a garden learns to trust themselves. They know how to learn, how to adapt, and how to persevere when things get hard. They face the unknown with confidence because they have strong roots. Their sense of self is a deeply rooted confidence in their ability to grow.

This is where the domestic and the strategic converge. The patience required to raise a human being is the exact same muscle required to build a resilient organization or lead a movement. If you can steward a life through the chaos of development, you possess the essential skill to steward a community through the chaos of change.

As we prepare to look toward the future, this final case study serves as a reminder. The principles are all the same. The empathy, patience, and courage required to lead a team through uncertainty are the same ones required to guide a child through the complexities of life. This is the art of Systems Stewardship in its most raw and essential form.

Whether you are in the boardroom or the playroom, the choice is yours. Will you know when to pick up a wrench, and when to set it down? Will you know when to intervene, and when to tend the soil?

PART III Conclusion: Observation to Application

Part III moved the toolkit out of the lab and into living systems. Across law, networks, creativity, and family, the same pattern repeated: complex systems respond to conditions.

Where control was attempted, fragility appeared. Where feedback was honored, resilience followed. Loose coupling absorbed shocks. Distributed intelligence adapted. Centralized optimization failed with little fanfare, until it failed all at once.

These domains are identical in structure. Law behaves like code under selection pressure. Digital crowds behave like weather. Creative systems converge when feedback is misaligned. Families fracture when growth is over-constrained. The mechanisms are the same. Only the stakes change.

The cases in this part argue for responsibility within complexity. Stewardship replaces control because it is the only posture that survives contact with emergence.

You cannot command a complex system, whether it is a power grid, a social network, a creative ecosystem, or a child. You can only shape the environment in which it learns.

Stewardship offers no guarantees. It cannot promise stability, fairness, or permanence. It manages probability instead of outcomes. It trades the illusion of control for the discipline of attention.

As we move forward, the issue is no longer whether these systems can be understood. They can. The real challenge is accepting the ethical burden that such understanding imposes.

Next, we lift our gaze to the horizon, where the consequences of emergence are no longer local, but planetary.

❖ VERIDIA SIMULATION LOG 3.0: THE AUTOPSY

In the aftermath, the autopsy revealed no glitches. The sensors were expensive, and the code was stable. Veridia failed because it treated a living city as a solvable equation.

At the level of individual behavior, the citizens were viewed as variables. The system was designed to predict them, guide them, and optimize them. When people acted unpredictably, the system viewed it as "noise" to be corrected.

At the level of collective systems, the drive for efficiency created a fatal rigidity. In the pursuit of the smart city, every system was coupled to every other system. Traffic data drove streetlights; streetlights drove energy pricing; energy pricing drove transit schedules. It was a masterpiece of engineering. But it meant that a failure in one domain cascaded instantly into the others. There were no firebreaks. There was no "slack."

The architects of the city believed that if they had enough data, they wouldn't need wisdom. They believed that if the system was efficient enough, it wouldn't need to be resilient. They were wrong.

Veridia had thousands of engineers, but it didn't have a single Gardener. It lacked the human judgment to know when to prune, when to weed, and most importantly, when to leave the system alone to find its own path.

PART IV. The Harvest

When a system runs long enough, it produces results, whether we intended them or not.

Everything explored so far, feedback loops, fragility, emergence, stewardship, converges here, where system behavior leaves abstraction and becomes lived reality. At this scale, outcomes are no longer local or reversible. They compound across time, institutions, and generations.

In earlier parts, we learned how systems behave, where they fail, and how they can be cultivated rather than controlled. Now the question shifts from understanding to responsibility. Once patterns become visible, intervention is no longer neutral. Choosing not to act is itself a form of action.

This final section widens our field of view. We move from individual systems to spheres of impact, the human experience, collective institutions, and global systems, examining how emergence accumulates across scale. In each sphere, we will identify reinforcing loops, stabilizing forces, and leverage points that determine whether systems drift toward resilience or collapse.

This is foresight rather than prediction.

The goal is ethical orientation, learning where small, deliberate interventions matter most, and where restraint is the wiser act. Stewardship at this level is no longer technical. It is moral.

The harvest will come regardless. The only remaining question is whether we are prepared to meet it.

Chapter 13. The Long Harvest

> *"Prediction is very difficult, especially if it's about the future."*
>
> *— Niels Bohr*

We're hunting for three things: the loops that accelerate change, the loops that stabilize it, and the places where a small push changes everything. Consider this a full-scale field test of the Framework.

We'll use Figure 23 as our map because without one, these conversations dissolve into opinion. What follows is triage across three spheres: Sphere 1 (the individual), Sphere 2 (society), Sphere 3 (global systems). In each sphere, we'll look for reinforcing loops, balancing loops, and leverage points, then ask what stewardship looks like at that scale.

13.1. Sphere 1: The Human Experience

- *Reinforcing loop: Automation → efficiency → cognitive offloading → deeper dependence on automation*
- *Balancing loop (weak): Human judgment, agency, and purpose*
- *Primary leverage point: Shortening feedback loops and redesigning incentives around human judgment rather than output volume.*

What follows traces how this loop manifests across learning, work, health, and identity, and where individual stewardship still matters.

Let's begin where change lands first: the individual. The forces of technological change and social evolution directly reshape how we learn, what we do for a living, how we maintain our health, and ultimately, how we understand who we are.

The Future of Learning and Education

While we often analyze how the demand for labor is shifting, it's equally important to examine how we prepare individuals to fill those roles. Our

""

current educational model is a relic of the industrial age, a system designed for a bygone era that is breaking down in the face of modern technological and social realities. There is a glaring mismatch between a standardized, one-size-fits-all "factory model" of education and the need for personalized, lifelong, and adaptive learning.

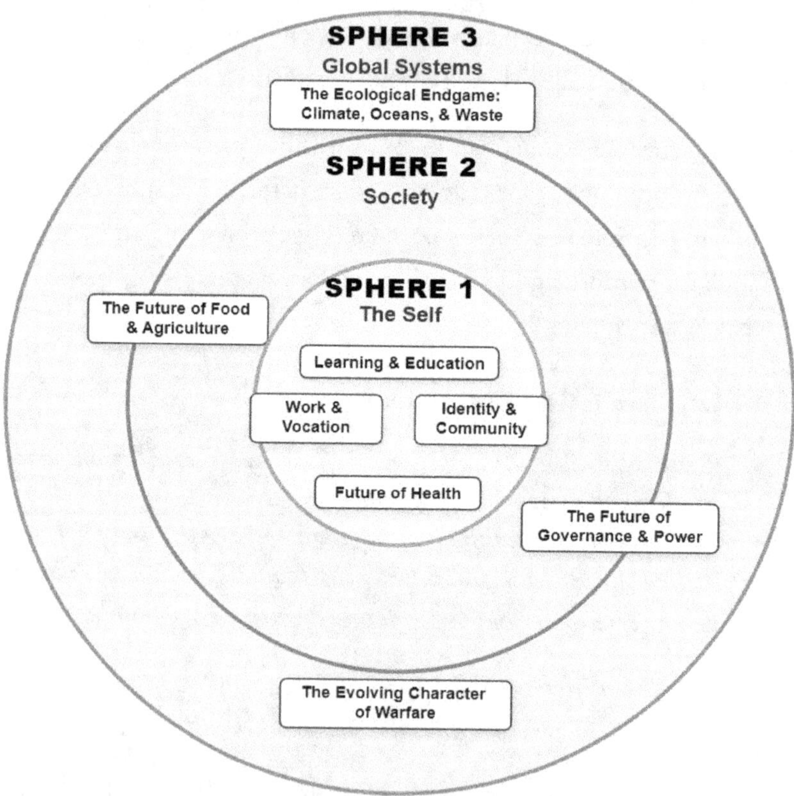

Figure 23. Spheres of Impact

High-resolution version available at phronos.com/tgm-diagrams

Biology says one thing. Institutions say another. Biologically, we now understand the power of neuroplasticity, the brain's ability to learn and adapt throughout an entire lifespan. This science highlights the vast diversity in individual learning styles, paces, and interests, emphasizing that intrinsic motivation and curiosity are far more effective drivers of growth than rote memorization.[114]

Technologically, we are seeing the rise of tools that cater to this biological reality. AI-powered personalized tutors and immersive virtual and augmented reality experiences are beginning to offer tailored instruction, while global platforms like edX and Khan Academy are successfully decoupling learning from physical institutions. During the 2020 pandemic, COVID turned my household into a test lab. Outschool and Coursera became staples.

However, these advancements collide with deeply entrenched social structures. The current K-12 and university systems rely heavily on standardized testing and view the university degree as the primary credential for employment. This system often prioritizes the social prestige and networking functions of elite universities over actual skill acquisition. This friction is a structural conflict between biological reality, technological capability, and institutional inertia.

The direction of travel in education is unbundling, whether institutions choose it or not. The traditional university's monolithic functions — teaching, research, credentialing, and social networking — will likely be pulled apart and offered by different, specialized providers. As this shift occurs, the responsibility will transfer to the individual. No longer passengers on a pre-determined academic track, you'll curate your education the way you curate your health: continuously, intentionally, and with some skepticism.[115]

Data from competency-based institutions like Western Governors University demonstrates that self-paced, skill-based learning models can significantly reduce both time-to-completion and tuition costs for adult learners when compared to traditional credit-hour degree tracks.

The Future of Work and Vocation (Macro)

Directly following our capacity to learn is the question of how we apply that learning to create value and find purpose. This issue is defined by a central tension between the relentless drive for technology-driven efficiency and the deep-seated human need for purpose. While the technological imperative seeks to optimize output and minimize friction, the biological and social nature of humanity requires meaning, contribution, and connection. This friction is currently destabilizing the modern economic landscape, forcing us to reconsider the relationship between human labor and machine capability.

The stakes become clear only when viewed systemically. The introduction of AI into the workplace is creating a reinforcing loop of automation and job displacement, which threatens to dismantle a century-old social contract built on the cornerstone of full-time employment. This technological shift is having a measurable impact on human cognition as well. A recent working paper from Harvard Business School, conducted in collaboration with BCG, highlighted a phenomenon researchers call "falling asleep at the wheel." The study found that while AI consultants significantly outperformed their peers in many tasks, they also showed a tendency to disengage their critical thinking, effectively letting their brains work less by accepting AI outputs without scrutiny.[116] Cognitive offloading compounds the social risk by converting short-term performance gains into long-term cognitive dependence. The danger is not that AI makes us less capable overnight, but that small reductions in active judgment accumulate. Over time, expertise atrophies quietly while surface performance appears to improve.

The trajectory bifurcates depending on system design. One is an automation caste system. The other is a human renaissance. The difference between them is system design.

Path A represents the "dystopian automation" scenario. This future is dominated by a positive feedback loop where capital investment in automation leads to greater profits, which in turn fuels further investment in technology to replace labor. If no new balancing loops are introduced to arrest this momentum, the logical conclusion is mass unemployment and social stratification, creating a permanent divide between those who own the algorithms and those who have been rendered obsolete by them.

However, Path B offers the possibility of a "human-centric renaissance." This future emerges only if we activate key leverage points within the system. By changing social rules, such as revising the tax code to favor human labor over capital automation, or by creating new social feedback loops like Universal Basic Income, we can decouple survival from traditional employment.[117] These interventions would free up human potential, allowing the "Bio" aspect of our nature to pivot toward creative, empathetic, and community-building work. This is the domain of value that AI cannot replicate, preserving the human need for purpose in an automated world.

The ultimate implication is that the future of work is a design choice rather than a technological inevitability.[118] The trajectory of automation remains a design variable rather than a fixed outcome. The primary variable over the coming decade is not model capability, but institutional design.

We can see this loop already activating in organizations where AI increases short-term productivity but simultaneously reduces independent problem-solving, forcing tighter oversight and deeper automation to compensate.

The Future of Work and Vocation (Micro)

While society wrestles with these macro-level policy shifts, the individual worker faces an immediate question: "How do I survive the transition?"

For the last century, career advice has been dominated by the Mechanic mindset: Learn a trade, become a cog, and fit into the machine. The

Mechanic defines their value by their output: diagnoses made, briefs written, or lessons delivered. The danger of this mindset is that AI is the ultimate output machine. If you define yourself by your ability to process inputs into standard outputs, you are competing directly against a system that is faster, cheaper, and tireless.

Furthermore, the Mechanic falls victim to an economic trap known as Jevons Paradox. For the Mechanic, this is a nightmare scenario.[P] If AI makes you twice as efficient at writing code or analyzing data, you will not suddenly work half as many hours. Instead, the demand for code and analysis will simply explode. The Mechanic who tries to use AI solely for efficiency will find themselves running on a treadmill that is accelerating exponentially, drowning in a sea of low-value tasks generated at lightning speed. Competing with machines on volume is structurally unwinnable. Volume is the mechanism by which humans train themselves out of relevance.

To navigate the AI age, we must shift from being Mechanics to being Gardeners. The Mechanic falls into the trap of trying to out-produce the machine on volume. The Gardener cultivates an ecosystem where the machine is merely a tool. The Gardener competes with machines on judgment, context, and care. Here is how this shift manifests across different sectors:

[P] Note on the Jevons Paradox: This counter-intuitive outcome was first observed in 1865 regarding coal usage. It states that increasing efficiency lowers costs, which drives up demand so significantly that it outweighs the efficiency gains.

A common counter-argument is the loss of factory jobs to automation. However, that occurred because demand for physical goods is finite (people only need so many toasters). In contrast, demand for *intelligence* and *software* is effectively infinite. The better parallel is the spreadsheet: when Excel made calculation free, accountants didn't go extinct; companies simply demanded exponentially more complex financial models, keeping accountants busier than ever.

- **The Doctor:** Instead of competing on diagnostics (which AI will commoditize), the Gardener physician uses AI to handle the data analysis so they can focus on the bedside manner, emotional reassurance, and behavioral psychology required to actually heal the patient.

- **The Teacher:** In an age of infinite free information, the role of "content dispenser" is obsolete. The Gardener shifts focus to the Social Domain, becoming a mentor who fosters collaboration and ignites the emotional spark of curiosity that an algorithm cannot simulate.

- **The Lawyer:** Rather than billing by the hour for drafting contracts (a processing task), the Gardener pivots to high-stakes judgment and negotiation, devising creative strategies that account for human irrationality.

- **The Manager:** "Management by spreadsheet" is over. The Gardener manager understands that a team is a living organism; they stop managing tasks and start managing the environment, removing bureaucratic blockers and protecting the team from political "harsh weather."

- **The Engineer:** The Gardener stops obsessing over the rote math (letting AI handle simulations and syntax) and pivots to Systems Architecture, ensuring the solution interacts resiliently with the unpredictable real world.

- **The Skilled Tradesperson:** While robotics lags behind AI, the Gardener tradesperson focuses on the chaotic environment of the client's life, communicating trust and problem-solving unexpected variables in the home.

- **The Creative:** When the system can generate infinite variations, the new scarcity is Taste. The Gardener's role shifts from the laborer laying bricks to the architect selecting the stone, filtering the signal from the infinite noise.

The Mindset Shift

To navigate the AI age, we must shift our mindset. The Mechanic tries to out-produce the machine. The Gardener cultivates an ecosystem where the machine is merely a tool.

○ THE PAST **The Mechanic**		THE FUTURE ⚘ **The Gardener**
~~Diagnostic Processor~~	DOCTOR →	**Healer**
~~Content Dispenser~~	TEACHER →	**Curiosity Architect**
~~Document Factory~~	LAWYER →	**Strategic Counselor**
~~Taskmaster~~	MANAGER →	**Soil Cultivator**
~~Technical Executor~~	ENGINEER →	**Systems Architect**
~~Laborer~~	TRADES →	**Home Consultant**
~~Asset Generator~~	CREATIVE →	**Resonance Architect**

HUMANITY IN THE LOOP

Failure Mode (Sphere 1)

Optimizing human efficiency without restoring meaning accelerates burnout, dependence, and cognitive atrophy, strengthening the very automation loops it attempts to escape.

The Future of Health

Our collective ability to learn, work, and innovate depends on biological well-being. The health system in the United States stands at an inflection point. A profitable disease-treatment architecture intervenes after pathology appears, while the need for prevention-oriented structures continues to grow.

Current incentives reward service volume. As a result, economic growth can coincide with rising chronic disease. The system expands even as population health deteriorates.

The problem is optimizing the wrong objective within a tightly coupled system. When compensation tracks procedures, procedures increase. When compensation tracks population health outcomes, behavior shifts across insurers, providers, and patients. Aligning payment with sustained well-being changes the direction of the entire system.

Future health innovation may emerge primarily from institutional redesign. Insurance models, payment structures, and community supports can align economic incentives with biological stability. The central question is whether maintaining health becomes structurally more valuable than treating disease.[119]

Traditional medicine operates on long feedback loops. Behavior precedes symptoms by years. Diagnosis follows testing by weeks. The delay weakens the connection between action and consequence.

Emerging health technologies reduce that latency. Continuous monitoring tools provide near real-time biological data. When feedback follows behavior quickly, individuals adjust before pathology consolidates.

The structural transition is from episodic measurement to continuous sensing. As latency approaches zero, corrective capacity shifts outward. Individuals gain the ability to stabilize their own systems earlier in the cycle.

Latency functions as a core variable. Shorter loops produce greater resilience.

The Future of Identity and Community

With our modes of learning, work, and health all in flux, the final question concerns our very sense of self and belonging.[120] This topic serves as the scaffolding for all others, forcing us to ask what it means to be human in this new world. The urgency of this inquiry stems from the fact that technology is no longer just changing what we do; it's fundamentally altering who we are. The very concept of the "self" is being reshaped by algorithms and networks, creating a central tension between the traditional, stable sources of identity — such as family, nationality, and local community — and the fluid, curated, and often fragmented identities we construct in digital spaces.

This shift emerges from a collision between biological limits and technological acceleration. Humans require coherent narrative, belonging, and social validation. Digital systems mediate those needs through quantified feedback. Recommendation engines filter exposure, and metrics such as likes and shares convert social response into numerical signals.

When identity formation becomes coupled to those signals, a reinforcing loop forms. Individuals adjust expression in response to engagement metrics. Platforms optimize for engagement intensity. Over time, self-presentation converges toward what the system amplifies.

A user posts a nuanced opinion and gets little engagement. They post a slightly more extreme, polarized version of that opinion and receive a dopamine hit of validation. The algorithm learns what the audience wants, but crucially, the user learns what the algorithm wants. Over time, the user subconsciously prunes away the parts of their personality that do not garner engagement, becoming a caricature of themselves.

A consistent signal of this loop is that content creators who moderate tone and nuance experience declining reach, while increasingly polarized outputs receive disproportionate algorithmic amplification.

McLuhan's Law is alive here: our tools are indeed training us. We are optimizing our personalities for the platform's metrics rather than our own fulfillment. This is the ultimate inversion of the emergence Framework: the parts are being hollowed out to feed the system. Escaping this requires a high degree of "meta-awareness," the ability to see the loop and deliberately step outside of the reward cycle.

Socially, this has resulted in the decline of traditional community support structures like religious institutions and local clubs, replaced by global, online "neo-tribes" based on ideology.[121] We are witnessing the phenomenon of "context collapse," where our distinct social circles merge into a single, flattened online existence.

We are migrating from an era of "given" identity to an era of "managed" identity. In this landscape, a most important skill of the 21st century becomes "algorithmic self-awareness." This is the ability to lucidly understand how technological systems are actively sculpting one's sense of self and community, and to possess the agency to consciously choose how to engage with them rather than being passively defined by them.

13.2. Sphere 2: Collective Systems

- *Reinforcing loop: Scale → efficiency → consolidation → systemic fragility*
- *Balancing loop: Diversity, redundancy, and local adaptation*
- *Primary leverage point: Changing subsidy structures, governance rules, and decision authority*
Here, the dominant risk is that efficiency gains hollow out resilience until shocks become systemic.

Now to the systems that keep societies standing. These are the systems that enable billions of people to live together, from the fundamental act of producing food to the complex challenge of making collective decisions.

The Future of Food and Agriculture

The modern food system represents a paradox: a logistical miracle capable of feeding billions, yet simultaneously a primary driver of ecological destruction and declining public health. A contradiction persists between the industrial drive for maximum efficiency, yield, and scalability and the urgent need for nutritional quality, ecological resilience, and ethical sustainability.

The biological reality is foundational. Soil microbiome health shapes the nutritional value of food, just as crop diversity and livestock welfare determine ecosystem resilience. Yet this foundation is increasingly intertwined with advanced technology. Precision agriculture, CRISPR gene editing, cellular agriculture, and urban vertical farming are attempting to decouple food production from traditional land use. Meanwhile, the biological impact of processed foods on the human gut microbiome links agricultural practice directly to chronic disease, creating a feedback loop between ecological health and our own bodies. These technological pathways promise land-use efficiency and controlled production environments, though they often shift resource intensity toward energy and capital inputs rather than eliminating ecological costs.

The social dimension reveals the invisible structures that dictate what ends up on our plates. Global supply chains and government subsidies favor monoculture crops like corn and soy, prioritizing caloric volume over nutrient density. Intellectual property regimes around seeds consolidate control, while cultural habits and the ubiquity of fast food reinforce industrial patterns. The system is increasingly locked into a model that is becoming untenable, creating structural dissonance between economic incentives and biological survival constraints.

The future of food will likely involve diversification rather than dominance by a single model. We may see tension between two gravitational poles: a hyper-technological path centered on cellular agriculture and automated vertical farming, and a hyper-biological path focused on regenerative agriculture and permaculture. In practice, most systems will blend elements of both, but the philosophical divide between decoupling from ecological constraints and re-embedding within them is becoming more pronounced. Food thus becomes a leverage point ordinary people can actually touch.

In many contexts, regenerative systems have demonstrated superior soil health outcomes, improved input efficiency, and greater long-term yield stability under environmental stress compared to conventional monocultures.

The Future of Governance and Power

Once a society secures the means to feed itself, the next fundamental imperative is determining how it organizes and makes collective decisions. This topic is compelling because the traditional concept of the nation-state is currently being challenged from two distinct directions: "from above" by vast global networks and "from below" by localized movements and digital tribes. The system is in a state of deep flux, defined by a central tension between the rigid, geographically bound hierarchies of the past and the rising tide of fluid, decentralized, and networked power structures.

Underneath it all is an old animal: our need to belong. These evolutionary drives inevitably lead to tribalism and in-group preference, creating a psychological landscape where cognitive biases make populations highly susceptible to misinformation. Technology acts as a powerful accelerant in this dynamic. Social media platforms exploit these biological traits to create global "digital tribes," accelerating polarization and fragmenting consensus. Simultaneously, technology offers divergent futures: blockchain provides a model for "trust without authority," potentially rendering some state functions obsolete, while advanced surveillance, through AI-powered cameras and social credit scores, grants the state unprecedented capabilities for control and monitoring.

The social dimension of this crisis highlights the erosion of the 400-year-old Westphalian system of nation-states. [q] This historical framework is increasingly overshadowed by the rise of megacorporations, many of which command economic resources larger than the GDPs of entire countries, effectively operating at the level of sovereign entities. Additionally, the influence of non-state actors is growing, ranging from coordinated global activist networks to decentralized terrorist groups, all of which operate across borders with a fluidity that traditional governments struggle to manage.

One of the clearest manifestations of this shift is the replacement of human discretion with algorithmic decision systems.

As power migrates, the nature of the "bureaucrat" changes. In the 20th century, applying for a loan, a visa, or bail involved a human official who possessed discretion, the ability to look at a unique situation and bend the rules. This human "slack" provided a necessary buffer in the social system.

Today, we are replacing human discretion with algorithmic bureaucracy. Decisions regarding who gets a mortgage, who is flagged for a security check, or which neighborhoods are policed are increasingly made by "black box" AI models. These systems are efficient precisely because they are brittle. They lack the biological capacity for context and mercy.

This creates a dangerous reinforcing loop of exclusion. If an algorithm denies you a credit card based on an opaque risk score, that denial lowers your score further, making it harder to get a job or an apartment, which creates data points that justify the original denial. Because the algorithm is proprietary (Tech) and the impact is economic (Social), the individual is trapped in a

---

[q] The "Westphalian nation-state" refers to the modern system of European sovereign states conventionally associated with the Peace of Westphalia in 1648, characterized by territorial sovereignty, supreme authority within defined borders, and the principle of non-interference by external powers.

loop with no human leverage point to appeal to. The challenge of future governance is building "due process" into code.

We can see this exclusionary loop when automated denials propagate across credit, housing, and employment systems, reinforcing disadvantage without any human corrective path.

Power is physically and conceptually migrating. It is flowing away from traditional government capitals and settling into new centers of gravity: corporate boardrooms, server farms, and decentralized online communities.[122] Decentralization does not remove the need for governance; it changes where and how constraints are applied.

Consequently, the requirements for 21st-century citizenship are changing. Modern citizenship requires the ability to chart and navigate these multiple, overlapping systems of power that now dictate the course of human events.[123]

Failure Mode (Sphere 2)

Centralizing control in the name of efficiency erodes resilience, amplifies exclusion, and converts local shocks into system-wide failures.

13.3. Sphere 3: Global Systems

- *Reinforcing loop: Economic growth → resource throughput → ecological strain → instability*
- *Balancing loop: Decoupling prosperity from material consumption*
- *Primary leverage point: Redefining system goals rather than optimizing individual technologies*

In our final sphere of analysis, we reach the planetary scale where we observe two of humanity's existential challenges: the stability of our shared ecological home and the enduring system of organized conflict.

The Future of Climate, Oceans, and Waste

This topic addresses what is perhaps the ultimate Metasystem conflict: the unavoidable collision between a human-built economic system and the finite biological system of the planet itself. On one side is the "Social" construct, a global economy predicated on the assumption of infinite growth and perpetual expansion. On the other is the "Bio" reality, the hard, physical constraints of a closed biological system that cannot expand to meet human demand.[124]

A below-the-surface look reveals that this conflict is driven by a powerful dynamic. In this cycle, energy use fuels economic growth, which in turn drives higher consumption, necessitating even greater energy use. Treating these as separate problems is the category error; they are simultaneous outputs of a single, runaway loop. As the wheel turns faster to sustain economic metrics, the strain on the planetary biosphere intensifies, creating a synchronized degradation of natural systems.

Identifying a leverage point within this dynamic requires a different way of thinking: the goal must be decoupling economic well-being from material throughput. Current interventions, such as carbon taxes and circular economy regulations, are more than just policy tweaks; they represent attempts to "change the rules" of the system. By introducing balancing feedback loops, these measures aim to counteract the momentum of the reinforcing growth loop, creating a structure where prosperity does not automatically equate to resource extraction.

Environmental issues are intertwined problems. A solution for plastic waste that requires an increase in fossil fuel energy, for example, is merely shifting the burden within the same failing system. We must therefore seek interventions that address the underlying driver — the growth-at-all-costs economic model — rather than continuing to fight a losing battle against its myriad of symptoms.

A clear signal of leverage here is that regions prioritizing material efficiency and circularity achieve economic gains with substantially lower ecological throughput.

The Future of Warfare

As a final, sobering application of Metasystem analysis, we turn to the system of global conflict.

Warfare concentrates the structural tensions of an age. Industrial production, territorial control, and organized violence remain decisive forces. Armies still depend on logistics. States still rely on material output. The kinetic dimension persists as a foundational layer of power.

What defines this era is the intensification of interdependence across domains. Conflict now unfolds within a tightly coupled environment in which technological systems, financial networks, informational channels, and biological realities continuously interact. Actions in one sphere propagate into others with increasing speed and amplification.

Modern conflict therefore operates as a Metasystem. A cyber-intrusion in the technological sphere can destabilize financial markets in the social sphere. Financial instability can erode civic trust. Diminished trust can generate political fragmentation and internal unrest. These developments may occur without immediate battlefield engagement, yet they alter strategic conditions in concrete ways.

At the center of this landscape lie feedback loops. Disinformation exploits digital infrastructures to weaken shared narratives and institutional legitimacy. As common ground dissolves, societies become more susceptible to further manipulation. Each cycle reinforces the next, producing fragility from within. A state may retain formidable military capacity while experiencing erosion in cohesion and resilience.

Physical force remains essential. Its strategic effectiveness, however, increasingly depends on the integrity of the broader system in which it operates. Supply chains, financial stability, communication networks, and social trust shape the conversion of material strength into durable security. Vulnerability in one domain can migrate across the whole.

National security emerges as a systemic condition rather than a purely military one. The defense of borders, the resilience of institutions, and the coherence of shared meaning form an interdependent structure. Conflict extends across these layers simultaneously.

Recent conflicts illustrate that disruption of information systems and economic confidence can shape outcomes alongside sustained kinetic engagement, and at times prepare the ground for it. Power is exercised through the orchestration of domains as much as through force itself.

In this respect, warfare reflects the broader evolution of the Metasystem. As integration deepens, consequences travel further and compound more rapidly. The question confronting states is no longer only how to project force, but how to maintain structural coherence within an environment of accelerating interconnection.

Failure Mode (Sphere 3)

Treating environmental and security crises as separate problems preserves the underlying growth loop that drives both toward collapse.

Chapter 13 — Leverage Summary (Cross-Sphere)

These leverage points describe where intervention matters most. They recur across domains because they operate on system rules rather than surface behaviors. What they do not answer is whether, when, or how we should act.

- Individuals: shorten feedback loops, protect judgment

- Work: decouple survival from output volume

- Health: reward prevention instead of intervention

- Food: diversify biology and ownership

- Governance: restore human appeal paths

- Planet: change goals before optimizing tools

Taken together, they reveal a pattern: systems fail less from lack of intelligence than from misaligned incentives and delayed feedback.

13.4. Conclusion: Ethical Foresight

Up to this point, leverage has been a technical question. From here forward, it becomes a moral one.

Our journey through these three spheres — from the self to society to the globe — reveals a simple fact: none of these domains exist in isolation. The future of work is inseparable from the future of education. The future of food is deeply entwined with the ecological endgame. The nature of governance is linked to the character of warfare.

Seeing the system changes the moral stakes. Mapping the loops clarifies where responsibility concentrates. Industrial-age systems are undergoing structural unbundling and giving rise to more personalized, decentralized, and technologically mediated alternatives. This transition is a design choice to be made. The recurring tension is between technological acceleration and the preservation of human values, and the most dominant leverage points often lie in redesigning the rules, goals, and feedback loops of our social and economic systems (Social).

Having learned how to see these systems, participation in these systems entails influence over their trajectory. Yet vision alone is insufficient. The ability to see and shape complex systems carries moral weight. In the next chapter, we confront what unfolds when these systems remain unstewarded, when emergence turns dark.

Chapter 14. Dark Emergence

The worst failures look like normal operations scaled up. While these systems offer efficiency and resilience, they introduce risks of inequity and systemic instability that are difficult to detect until they have already occurred.

14.1. Dark Emergence and Counter-Emergence

The Shadow Side of Complex Systems

As the world becomes interconnected, emergence plays a growing role in our technological, social, and physical systems. While emergent properties often deliver benefits, such as the self-organizing efficiency of a free market or the resilience of the internet, they can manifest in harmful ways never intended by their creators. We have already glimpsed the shadow side of complexity in the jamming of the UUV swarm, the burnout of the Quirinus nurses, and in the context of rearing a child. Now, we must confront Dark Emergence as a universal phenomenon.[125]

Dark emergence is a system optimizing locally in ways that become globally harmful (Figure 24, Table 7). It often looks like success scaled too far. These failures rarely begin as breakdowns. They begin as success scaled beyond its design envelope.

Physical Cascades: When Infrastructure Fails

Dark Emergence manifests dramatically in physical infrastructure, where tight coupling between systems allows failures to jump across boundaries.[74] The 2003 Northeast Blackout in the United States and Canada serves as a prime example. What began as a local issue — a software bug and sagging transmission lines in Ohio — spiraled into a catastrophe that left 55 million people without power.

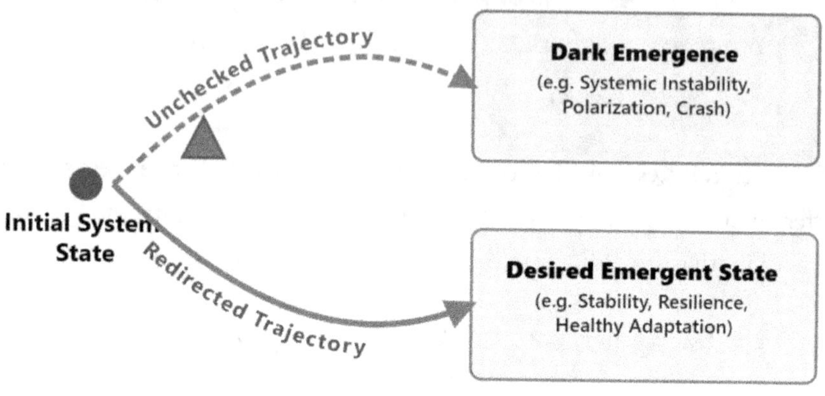

INTERVENTION STRATEGIES

When weeds show up, you have three moves: slow the growth, diversify the bed, or change what the system feeds on.

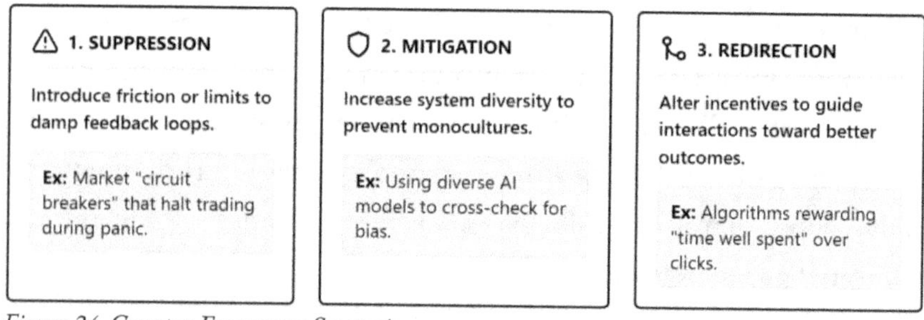

Figure 24. Counter-Emergence Strategies

High-resolution version available at phronos.com/tgm-diagrams

The cascade developed through interactions no single operator could perceive in real-time. When the initial lines failed due to heat, power automatically rerouted to other lines, overloading them in turn. A software bug prevented operators from seeing the developing crisis, and automated safety protocols at power plants triggered disconnects to protect the generators. A system-wide failure emerged from the interaction of functioning components trying to save themselves.

Table 7. Dark Emergence Examples

Domain	Simple Components & Rules	Interactions	Dark Emergent Behavior
Algorithmic Systems	AI models, historical data, user profiles. Rule: "Optimize for accuracy based on past data."	Model trains on data reflecting past societal biases (e.g., in hiring or lending).	Systemic Bias & Discrimination: The model perpetuates and amplifies inequity, making biased predictions without any malicious intent.
Financial Markets	High-frequency trading algorithms. Rule: "Execute trades faster than competitors based on market signals."	Algorithms react to each other's trades in microseconds, creating rapid, automated feedback loops.	Flash Crashes: Sudden, extreme, and brief market collapses triggered by cascading algorithmic trades, often driven internally rather than by headlines.
Social Media	Users, content, engagement algorithm. Rule: "Show users content that maximizes engagement (likes, shares, comments)."	The algorithm preferentially promotes emotionally charged or polarizing content because it generates strong reactions.	Echo Chambers & Polarization: Users become isolated in ideological bubbles, and societal division is amplified as extreme views are algorithmically rewarded.

Counter-emergence strategies for infrastructure focus on containment and modularity. Smart grid technologies now deploy distributed sensors (phasor measurement units) to detect anomalies and isolate problems before they trigger cascades. Furthermore, the concept of microgrids introduces modularity, allowing local facilities to disconnect from the main grid during disturbances. This "islanding" capability creates firewalls against failure while enabling faster recovery for critical services.[127,128,129,130]

Financial System Stability: Taming Market Cascades

Financial markets exhibit perhaps the most rapid forms of Dark Emergence due to the speed of automated trading. During the 2010 Flash Crash, the Dow Jones Industrial Average dropped by almost 1,000 points within minutes before rebounding soon afterward. This volatility stemmed from high-frequency trading algorithms responding to each other. A large sell order triggered a cascade of automated responses, creating a self-reinforcing liquidity vacuum.

Regulators responded with a classic counter-emergence strategy: circuit breakers. These mechanisms pause trading across the entire market when prices move too rapidly in a short timeframe. These cooling-off periods break the feedback loop, allowing human traders to assess conditions and preventing panic-driven algorithmic spirals. Additionally, transparency requirements now mandate better documentation of algorithmic strategies, ensuring financial engineers consider systemic impacts rather than optimizing solely for individual performance.

14.2. The Ethics of Automation

As artificial intelligence and automated systems gain autonomy, they raise profound questions about responsibility, agency, and human dignity. The central ethical challenge is that these systems often operate as "black boxes." Deep neural networks function by adjusting millions of internal parameters, often in ways even their designers cannot fully explain. When a loan is denied, a resume rejected, or a medical treatment withheld by an algorithm, the lack of explainability prevents accountability and leaves the affected individual without recourse.

The Bias of Historical Data

Emergent systems tend to reflect the data of their creators. Machine learning models learn from historical data, and in doing so, they reproduce patterns of past discrimination. Facial recognition systems developed on datasets dominated by white male faces show significantly higher error rates for women and people with darker skin. Hiring algorithms trained on past successful hires have been found to penalize resumes containing terms associated with women's colleges or organizations.[68]

Addressing this requires both technical and social interventions. "Explainable AI" (XAI) is a growing field dedicated to making models interpretable, allowing humans to audit the decision-making process. However, technical fixes are insufficient without diverse development teams. Furthermore, we face a legal friction: the drive for algorithmic transparency inevitably collides with corporate intellectual property protections. Society must decide where the "black box" of trade secrets ends and the public right to understanding begins. True fairness requires inclusive development processes that incorporate diverse perspectives from the earliest design stages, treating bias detection as a core safety requirement.

The Metasystem Conflict: The Trolley Problem

Imagine a runaway trolley speeding down a track. Ahead, five people are trapped and cannot escape. You stand beside a switch that can divert the trolley onto a second track — but there is one person standing there. If you do nothing, five will die. If you pull the lever, one will die by your deliberate action.

This dilemma, known as the "trolley problem," has been debated by philosophers for decades because it exposes a fault line in human morality. Some argue that minimizing total harm is the ethical choice. Others insist that actively causing harm, even for a greater good, is fundamentally wrong.

For most of its history, the trolley problem was safely hypothetical. No real person was ever required to stand at the switch. But automation has changed that. Today, machines are being placed in situations where inaction is itself a choice, and every option carries moral weight. Autonomous systems never hesitate. They calculate. And those calculations will determine what happens to real people.

As systems gain autonomy, they are forced to make decisions that encode values. In autonomous vehicles (AVs), this dilemma becomes a structural conflict between three layers of the Metasystem:

- **The Biological Layer (Instinct):** A human driver acts on self-preservation. If a crash is imminent, biology dictates saving oneself. We accept this reaction as instinct; we do not judge a driver for swerving away from danger, even if it causes collateral damage.

- **The Technological Layer (Logic):** An AV operates on utilitarian optimization. It can calculate outcomes in milliseconds. It may calculate that swerving into a concrete wall, killing the passenger, is the mathematically "correct" choice to save a group of pedestrians. The technology is capable of a "ruthless" altruism that biology rejects.

- **The Social Layer (Liability):** Legal and economic systems struggle to bridge this gap. If an algorithm intentionally sacrifices its owner to minimize total casualties, who is liable? Furthermore, market dynamics intervene. Consumers will not purchase a vehicle programmed to prioritize the lives of strangers over their own safety.

True alignment requires legislation that acknowledges the machine's logic while respecting the biological imperative of the user. We must decide, collectively, how we want our machines to value human life before we deploy them.

Some AI developers are attempting to move alignment upstream rather than relying solely on downstream moderation. Anthropic's "Constitutional AI" approach, for example, trains models against an explicit written set of guiding principles and requires the system to critique its own outputs against those constraints. The ambition is not to script every response, but to shape the internal feedback loop of the model itself. The architectural move is significant: constraint is embedded into the generative process itself rather than imposed after the fact.

Distributed Responsibility

The distributed nature of emergent systems complicates the traditional concept of responsibility. In centralized systems, blame flows upward to designers or operators. In emergent systems, responsibility is diffused. If an autonomous vehicle causes harm, liability could plausibly lie with the software developer, the hardware manufacturer, the sensor supplier, or the dataset curators.

Addressing this requires graduated responsibility models. Organizations must establish clear procedures for investigating incidents and implementing improvements, moving away from a "bad apple" theory of blame toward a systems-level view. This creates a difficult tension between the need for compensation, making the victim whole, and the need for systemic learning. If liability is too punitive, organizations hide data; if it is too loose, they lack incentive to improve. The aviation industry's approach to accident investigation provides a model: creating legal safe harbors for data sharing so that the focus is on identifying systemic factors to prevent recurrence, rather than solely assigning individual blame.

14.3. Societal and Creative Impact

Emergent digital systems are reshaping social, economic, and political ecosystems. While offering innovation and connectivity, they introduce challenges regarding access, truth, and the governance of creativity.

Inequality in Access and Outcomes

Significant disparities in access persist, creating a "digital divide" that is self-reinforcing. While urban centers enjoy high-speed connectivity, rural areas and developing regions often struggle with basic infrastructure. The cost of devices and data plans creates barriers for low-income households. Beyond physical access, meaningful participation requires technical literacy.

Emergent systems have the potential to democratize opportunity by removing intermediaries, yet they often concentrate benefits among those with existing capital and technical expertise, especially once early advantages are established. Early adopters of cryptocurrencies accumulated vast wealth, while platform economies (like ride-sharing or delivery apps) often benefit owners and algorithm designers significantly more than the gig workers who power them. Without intentional intervention, these systems tend to amplify, rather than reduce, economic stratification.[51,68,131,132] The Gardener's intervention here is to design for equity in the initial conditions, ensuring wide distribution of ownership or access rights before the reinforcing loops of the network effect take hold.

Digital Contagion and Misinformation

Social media platforms exemplify Dark Emergence through the spread of misinformation. Designed to facilitate connection and sharing, they inadvertently created amplification mechanisms for falsehoods. Algorithms prioritize engagement, favoring emotionally provocative material because it keeps users on the platform longer. Consequently, though patterns vary by platform, topic, and intervention design, false news often spreads faster in part because it reliably evokes shock, fear, or outrage, and engagement systems preferentially amplify that.[133]

Some platforms have experimented with redesigns to reduce this virality. X's "read before you retweet" prompts and Facebook's downranking of repeat misinformation offenders create friction that slows the spread of falsehoods.

Educational approaches like "prebunking," teaching users to recognize manipulative tactics before they encounter them, help build cognitive resilience against the contagion.

The Ethics of Creative Systems

Generative AI has transformed cultural production, automating the creation of text, images, and music. These systems, trained on vast datasets of human creation, raise difficult questions about representation and authenticity. AI-generated content reflects the biases of its training data. Image generators trained primarily on Western art history struggle to represent non-Western aesthetics accurately, marginalizing underrepresented cultures.

Furthermore, AI creativity challenges notions of ownership. When an AI generates a work based on patterns learned from copyrighted material, the boundary between inspiration and infringement blurs. Artists are finding their styles mimicked by machines that pay them no royalties. Resolving this requires balancing innovation incentives with protections for human creators. Governance structures must evolve to ensure fair attribution and compensation in collaborative ecosystems where human and machine creativity intersect.

14.4. Adaptive Governance

Governance of emergent systems cannot remain static. Traditional regulation, which moves slowly and relies on fixed rules, is ill-equipped to manage technologies that change daily. Adaptive governance frameworks must evolve alongside technological developments. This requires a shift from deterministic thinking (predicting exactly what will happen) to probabilistic thinking (managing a range of possibilities).

Embracing Uncertainty

Emergent systems generate uncertainty that cannot be eliminated. Probabilistic thinking acknowledges multiple possible futures. The COVID-19 pandemic illustrated this necessity. In many cases, jurisdictions that adjusted policies dynamically as new data emerged avoided some of the worst failure modes of rigid early assumptions, compared with those that held to early, incomplete information.

Governance must treat uncertainty as an intrinsic feature of complex systems, rather than a failure of planning. This encourages humility about predictive capabilities and transparent communication with the public about the range of possible outcomes. It shifts the goal from "preventing all risk" to "building resilience against the unexpected."

Probabilistic Models as Decision Tools

Probabilistic models generate distributions of outcomes rather than single predictions. Climate science uses these to project warming scenarios based on different carbon emission levels, enabling policymakers to understand the spectrum of risks. Financial regulators use stress testing to evaluate how banks would fare across various adverse economic scenarios.

These models allow authorities to make nuanced decisions, adapting actions to the evolving probability of threats. However, models must be treated as tools for structured thinking. They rely on assumptions that may be flawed. Effective governance requires deliberative processes that incorporate diverse stakeholder perspectives to challenge and refine these models.

Feedback and Experimentation

Adaptive governance relies on real-time feedback loops. Unlike periodic regulatory reviews that might happen every few years, adaptive approaches incorporate continuous monitoring. Sensor networks in environmental resource management allow authorities to adjust water usage or fishing quotas in real-time as conditions change.

Experimentation allows for policy learning without systemic risk. Regulatory sandboxes enable fintech and AI companies to test innovations in a controlled environment with regulatory oversight. This allows successful approaches to scale while identifying and abandoning failures early. This experimental mindset values empirical learning over theoretical prediction, ensuring that regulation is grounded in how the system actually behaves rather than how we think it should. However, this approach requires a public distinction between iterative learning and strategic incoherence. True adaptive governance admits failure quickly to correct course; incompetence denies failure to protect status.

14.5. Conclusion: Charting the Emergent Future

We have stared into the abyss of the machine. We have seen how the very systems designed to connect us can drive us apart, how algorithms trained on our history can imprison us in our past biases, and how the pursuit of frictionless efficiency can create a fragile, volatile world.

It is tempting, in the face of such Dark Emergence, to retreat. We might feel the urge to smash the loom, to ban the algorithm, or to build higher walls to keep the complexity at bay. But the Gardener knows that you cannot un-grow the forest. The vines of technology, society, and biology are already tangled. We cannot go back to a simpler time; we can only grow through to a wiser one.

The dangers outlined in this chapter — inequality, misinformation, algorithmic bias, and autonomous conflict — remain avoidable futures. They are the weeds that grow when a garden is left untended. They are what happens when we unleash powerful, adaptive systems without the ethical frameworks and feedback loops necessary to guide them.

Charting the emergent future requires us to abandon the illusion that we can simply "fix" these problems with a patch or a policy. Instead, we must adopt the posture of adaptive governance and ethical stewardship. We must build systems that are transparent enough to be trusted, resilient enough to withstand their own errors, and humble enough to keep a human in the loop where it matters most.

We are architects, teachers, and stewards, of the systems we've built. Our task now is to cultivate the conditions where technology serves humanity, rather than the other way around.

The diagnosis is complete. We see the system for what it is: capable of immense creation and immense destruction. Now, we must turn to the final question, the one that defines the legacy of the Gardener: knowing all of this, how shall we live?

The systems we have examined do not shrink because we see them clearly. They remain vast, planetary, and often beyond any single actor's control. No steward commands the climate, the economy, or the arc of technology. The forest is larger than us.

And yet, we are never without responsibility for the ground beneath our feet.

It is time to enter the Kepos.

Chapter 15. The Art of Stewardship: Tending the Kepos

> *"A society grows great when old men plant trees whose shade they know they shall never sit in."*
>
> *– Greek Proverb*

At this point, you can map a system. What follows is responsibility for what you see.[134]

You have learned the science. Now comes the art.

From Solver to Steward

The problem-solver sees a broken machine. They diagnose, they replace, they reboot. Their work is transactional, their focus is narrow, and their responsibility ends when the ticket is closed. This is the world of the technician.

The Systems Steward sees an imbalanced ecosystem. Their goal is to understand the relationships between all parts and cultivate the conditions for the entire system to flourish. Their work is relational, their focus is holistic, and their responsibility is enduring. They know that a system is never "fixed"; it is only guided and nurtured toward a state of greater health, resilience, and harmony.[135]

This is a deeper calling.

For centuries, humanity has grappled with this same challenge: how to create a small pocket of order, meaning, and tranquility in a world that is vast, chaotic, and unpredictable. The tools and systems have changed, but the fundamental human need for stewardship has not.

And so, to truly understand the art of stewardship, we must look to an ancient concept, but a practice you have been learning all along.

The Garden of Epicurus: Discovering the Kēpos

Over 2,300 years ago, outside the bustling, chaotic city of Athens, the philosopher Epicurus founded a school. Unlike the grand Lyceum of Aristotle or the Academy of Plato, Epicurus's school was a simple, private home with a walled garden.

He called it the *Kēpos*. (Henceforth **Kepos**)

For Epicurus, the goal of life was *ataraxia*, a state of serene, untroubled tranquility. He believed this state could not be found in the endless pursuit of public fame, political power, or extravagant wealth, all of which created more anxiety than they relieved. Instead, he taught that tranquility was found by retreating to a smaller, more manageable world where one could cultivate friendships, knowledge, and self-sufficiency.[136]

The Kepos was both a physical place and a metaphor. It was a complex system in miniature. It had its biological realities (soil, water, pests, seasons), its technical components (tools, trellises, irrigation), and its social dynamics (the community of friends who tended it).

Within the walls of the Kepos, Epicurus and his followers were less concerned with "solving" the chaos of the outside world and more devoted to cultivating a healthy, thriving, and beautiful system at a scale they could manage and influence. They were learning to be stewards.

In the previous section, we looked at how a lack of oversight allows Dark Emergence to rot a system from the inside. Now, we apply the antidote: Adaptive Governance.

Remember the runaway feedback loops we feared in the last chapter? Here, we will learn how to harness that same looping mechanism to accelerate innovation instead of destruction. We aren't changing the physics of the system; we are just changing the direction of the flow.

This is the crucial piece of our puzzle. The practice of using the Metasystem Framework to support health, resilience, and harmony within a complex system is the modern practice of tending the Kepos.

We have a map of the garden. The Bio, Tech, and Social domains are its soil, its tools, and its community of fellow Gardeners. Your organization, your project, your community; that is your Kepos.

The Three Arts of the Gardener

To embrace the mindset of the Systems Steward is to practice the three essential arts of the Gardener.

The Art of Patience: Observe Before You Intervene

In a linear system, cause and effect are close in time and space. In a complex system, they are distant. The novice intervenes at the symptom (the yellow leaf). The Steward waits, tracing the signal delay back to the root cause (the soil pH).

Patience is the rigorous refusal to act on noise. It is the discipline of waiting for the system's feedback loop to complete a full cycle before adjusting the inputs. They check the soil, the sun, the water. They look for pests. They understand that the symptom (yellow leaves) is not the root cause.

As a steward, you must resist the pressure for immediate, visible action. Observe the flows of energy, information, and influence. Watch the feedback loops. Listen to the stories of the people within the system. Your most powerful tool is your patient, deep understanding.

The Art of Precision: Prune for Health, Nurture for Growth

Complex systems naturally accumulate complexity: legislative debt, technical debt, bureaucratic bloat. This is the Second Law of Thermodynamics at work in an organization. The Steward's primary physical intervention is often *subtractive*.

Pruning is the redirection of finite energy. By removing the "suckers" — the processes that consume energy without yielding fruit — you artificially induce a resource surplus that the system naturally reallocates to growth. They prune dead branches so the plant can direct its energy toward healthy growth. They thin seedlings to give the strongest ones room to flourish. This is the art of applying leverage.[134]

Your interventions should be just as precise. Pruning is the courage to subtract. It might mean decommissioning a legacy technology that drains resources, ending a toxic process that stifles creativity, or removing a bureaucratic obstacle. It is knowing that in a finite system, you cannot have new growth without clearing space. "Nurturing" means amplifying what works, investing in a positive social dynamic, scaling a successful pilot program, or providing resources to a team that is already generating value. It's knowing what to cut away and what to cultivate.

The Art of Humility: Cultivate the Flower and the Soil

Anyone can plant a flower, but a true Gardener cultivates the soil. The flower is the visible, immediate output — the successful product launch, the quarterly profit report. The soil is the underlying set of conditions that makes all future growth possible. It's the culture of psychological safety, the physical health and well-being of your team, the trust with your customers, the sustainability of your resources.

A steward knows that focusing only on the flower will eventually deplete the soil. The highest calling of a Systems Steward is to enrich the soil: to improve the health of the Bio domain (well-being, energy, environment) and the Social domain (trust, culture, relationships), knowing that a healthy foundation will produce beautiful outcomes naturally and sustainably.

Resilience is not a state achieved once and preserved automatically. It requires ongoing maintenance, renewal, and reinvestment. Slack erodes, redundancy decays, and feedback dulls. Without continuous tending, even healthy systems calcify.

Your Garden Awaits

The Metasystem Framework gave you the tools — the spade, the watering can, the pruning shears. The mindset of the Kepos gives you the purpose. It transforms your work from a series of technical problems to be solved into a living system to be stewarded.

This is the art. It's the quiet, consistent, and deeply rewarding practice of tending to the complex garden of your responsibility. It's a shift from seeking control to cultivating conditions.

Your role is no longer just to build; it is to cultivate. You can tend the field you are standing in. Go tend the garden of tomorrow.

The gate is open, Systems Steward. Your Kepos awaits.

PART IV Conclusion: What Seeing Requires

This final part widened our view. We examined systems whose consequences extend beyond organizations and technologies into human lives, institutions, and planetary limits. Mapping these systems revealed how tightly coupled our world has become, and how often failure arises structure rather than intent.

To see a system clearly is to inherit responsibility for it. Once feedback loops, incentives, and fragilities are visible, plausible deniability disappears. Insight alters what inaction means.

The philosophy of the Gardener reframes that responsibility. The world revealed by the Metasystem Framework is an ecosystem to be tended. Seeing the whole means seeing both emergence and its darker forms.

Stewardship therefore carries weight. It demands discernment rather than certainty, restraint rather than control, and humility in the face of systems that learn faster than we do. The Gardener recognizes the shadows and plans accordingly.

Across this book, we have moved from analysis to orientation. The issue is no longer only what we see, but how we choose to stand once we see it.

The science gave us the map. The garden demands a practice.

If you are looking for a place to begin, turn to Appendix A. Treat it as a diagnostic challenge. Apply it to the system that frustrates you most: your team, your family, or your local government, and see if the leverage points reveal themselves.

The full narrative arc of Veridia, referenced throughout this book, is collected in Appendix E.

The Gardener's Work

The systems that now shape our lives no longer behave like machines to be fixed. They behave like living ecosystems. They adapt, resist control, and produce consequences no one intends. In such systems, the pursuit of prediction and optimization creates fragility.

We have been taught that responsibility means control. More rules, tighter coordination, better metrics. But in complex systems, control is more often the shortest path to collapse.

Stewardship requires a different posture. It asks us to shape conditions rather than force outcomes, to listen to feedback rather than appearances, and to preserve slack, diversity, and redundancy even when they look inefficient. It demands judgment about when to intervene and when restraint is the wiser act.

You cannot command a complex system. But you are never free of responsibility for the environment you create.

This is the work of the Gardener: leaving the quiet contemplation of the Kepos and returning to a world that still defaults to the logic of the machine. This is the work: a move from a job to be done to a craft to be practiced.

The Mechanic's Limitation

For a century, our model of leadership has been the Mechanic. The Mechanic sees the world as a complicated machine. Success is defined by control, optimization, and predictability. The organization chart is the blueprint, the five-year plan is the manual, and the leader is the master engineer who pulls the levers and replaces the broken parts.

This worldview was born of a simpler time and is perfect for complications. But when applied to the volatility of human systems, it becomes a dangerous limitation. It creates brittle systems that shatter under pressure, stifles the creativity needed for adaptation, and treats people as cogs in the machine. The Mechanic's workshop is closed to the messiness of life; it cannot cope with surprise, emergence, or evolution.

The Gardener's Practice

The Gardener, by contrast, sees the world as a living ecosystem. You can only cultivate the garden. The Gardener's goal is health: a system that is resilient, adaptive, and naturally productive.

The leader as Gardener shifts from directing outcomes to cultivating conditions. They tend the soil — culture, trust, and well-being. They protect the flow of sun and water — information, resources, and energy. Their job is stewardship: sustaining the conditions under which the system can produce durable, sometimes unexpected, value.

The highest leverage point is the mindset from which the system arises. Changing how you see is the most powerful act of leadership there is. This is antifragility in practice: fewer brittle certainties, more learning under stress.

We are returning to an older wisdom. The ancient Greeks understood *techne* (craft/making) and *physis* (nature/growing). For the last century, we have worshipped *techne*, the ability to force our will upon the world. But as our systems exceed our cognitive grasp, *techne* fails us. We must relearn *physis*.

The Steward stands within the system, subject to the same rain and the same frost. The illusion of the Mechanic was that we could stand outside the machine.

The reality of the Gardener is that we are part of the harvest.

Epilogue

This book set out to present a way of seeing: that the most important systems in our lives are like gardens to be tended. What I did not know at the outset was how fully that truth would come to govern the writing itself.

I began, as most Mechanics do, with an implicit blueprint. There was a structure to be imposed, arguments to be assembled, chapters to be completed. Early drafts reflected this instinct. They were denser, longer, more exhaustive. Every concept wanted its own subsection; every example demanded expansion. The impulse was familiar: if I could just add enough precision, enough explanation, enough scaffolding, the system would behave.

It didn't.

The book resisted control in ways that mirrored the systems it describes. Certain ideas refused to stay confined to their assigned chapters. Case studies reappeared in new guises. Metaphors propagated across domains. Themes braided themselves together without asking permission. The manuscript pushed back.

That resistance was the signal. Somewhere along the way, the work stopped being an exercise in construction and became an exercise in cultivation. I stopped asking, "What must I add to make this complete?" and started asking, "What conditions allow the right structure to emerge?" I began this book with sustained attention, trusting that understanding would follow only if the conditions were right.

That shift changed everything.

Subtraction as Principle and Practice

One of the central claims of this book is that resilience often comes from removing constraints. That principle is easy to admire in theory and difficult to live in practice, especially when your instinct is to explain more, qualify more, prove more.

This manuscript began as something much larger. Its early versions attempted to say everything. That impulse produced density and weight rather than clarity and strength. Over time, subtraction became unavoidable.

Paragraphs disappeared. Entire chapters were pruned. What remained had to justify its presence.

Subtraction became the method. Every cut created space. That space allowed patterns to surface. Connections that had been obscured by excess explanation became visible. The system grew more legible as it became leaner. The book lost noise.

Watching the file size shrink and the page count drop was unsettling. In that sense, the book became an instance of its own argument: resilience through less.

Emergence at the Meta-Level

There is a temptation, especially in analytical work, to separate content from process, to believe that principles apply outward but not inward. This book refused that separation.

The arguments acted on the work as it evolved. The structure you encountered — recurring ideas, reframed cases, themes revisited at higher levels — emerged from that interaction.

A book about emergence that is engineered as a machine would be a contradiction. The only honest way to write it was to let it behave like the systems it describes: adaptive, iterative, occasionally unruly, and ultimately shaped by the conditions in which it was allowed to grow.

The process was anything but passive. Gardens demand labor. Pruning hurts. Letting go of cherished sections feels like loss until you see what the system does with the reclaimed energy.

This book is shorter than it could have been. It is stronger for it.

The Final Gesture

If there is a single meta-lesson in this epilogue, it is this: stewardship begins at home.

Before we can apply these ideas to organizations, technologies, laws, or societies, we must be willing to practice them in our own work. Writing this book was a personal garden. It forced me to confront my own Mechanic instincts and replace them — imperfectly, repeatedly — with the discipline of cultivation.

I tended the conditions.

What you now hold is the harvest of that process. It is an ecosystem of ideas that I hope will interact with yours in ways neither of us can fully predict.

If this book has done its work, you will leave it changed in how you attend to the world, less with answers than with awareness. You will notice brittle systems, distorted incentives, speed outrunning understanding, and harm accumulating through well-intentioned action. From that moment, innocence dissolves. Vision carries responsibility. Even restraint becomes a form of intervention, just as haste always has been. Stewardship begins here.

Acknowledgements

This book would not have been possible without the support, insight, and generosity of many people. I am deeply grateful to those who devoted their time and care to reviewing the manuscript and, in doing so, meaningfully strengthened the work: Marc Geffen, Jacques Chirazi, Charley Patton, Ricardo Reis, Greg Bulla, David Schrunk, Rick Hefner, and, of course, Steve Simske.

Marc, Jacques, Charley, and Ricardo merit special recognition for the exceptional rigor and attentiveness they brought to the review process. Their sustained and thoughtful scrutiny over many days (weeks, even!) challenged my assumptions and sharpened the clarity of the final manuscript. Beyond his careful and substantive review — particularly of "The Architecture of Justice" — Marc also served as an inspiration for "The First Stewardship" and portions of "The Synthetic Muse." Jacques' ability to think holistically was equally essential in helping the book cohere as a unified whole. And Charley's insistence on precision, along with his refusal to allow even minor inconsistencies to pass unnoticed, proved invaluable; his attention to detail improved the work in countless ways. I am also grateful to Ricardo for his brilliance and deep insights, which strengthened this work and inspired the next.

I would also like to acknowledge the role of AI assistants which enhanced my productivity by improving consistency and clarity and accelerating certain aspects of research.

The synthesis, framework, and final articulation presented here are my own, shaped by lived experience and informed by the thinkers, collaborators, and traditions that influenced this work. Any remaining errors are mine alone.

The Storehouse

Appendix A. A Gardener's Diagnostic

Readers often ask the same question at the end: "How do I enter a system without making it worse?"

This appendix is a diagnostic orientation. Use it when you are facing a system under stress and feel the urge to act. Read it slowly. Skip steps if needed. Return to it later. This diagnostic shows you how to stand inside a system long enough to see it clearly.

1. Name the System You Are Actually In

Before intervening, clarify the system's real boundary.
- What system am I influencing?
- What happens after handoff, scale, or success?
- What failure would be most damaging if it occurred quietly?

If you cannot name the system, you are not yet ready to change it.

2. Map the Domains

Every complex system spans at least three domains.
- Biological: Who gets tired, stressed, overloaded, or depleted?
- Technological: What tools, platforms, or infrastructure shape behavior?
- Social: What incentives, norms, rules, or power dynamics guide action?

Most failures occur at the boundaries between these domains.

3. Look for Feedback Before Causes

Linear causes are seductive and usually wrong.
- What behaviors reinforce themselves over time?
- Where does apparent success create hidden fragility?
- What information arrives too late to correct course?

If you cannot see feedback, slow down. It is there.

4. Measure Fragility Before Performance

Efficiency hides weakness.
- Where is complexity concentrated?
- What depends on a single role, system, or decision?
- What breaks first under stress?
- Does failure cascade, or stay local?

A system that performs well until it collapses is not healthy.

5. Practice Disciplined Subtraction

Most systems fail from excess.
- What exists only because it always has?
- What rules, metrics, or approvals consume energy without creating resilience?
- What looks inefficient but is protective?
- What should not be removed until you understand why it exists?

Never remove what you cannot explain.

6. Shift from Control to Conditions

Complex systems respond to environment.
- Can authority be pushed closer to the edge?
- Can simple local rules replace detailed instructions?
- Can feedback arrive faster and nearer to action?
- Can failure be cheap, local, and informative?

If control feels necessary everywhere, the system is already brittle.

7. Decide Whether to Act or Wait

Not all insight requires intervention.
- Is this a moment for restraint rather than action?
- Will intervention collapse learning that is still underway?
- Is patience itself the highest leverage move?

The Gardener intervenes less often than the Mechanic, but more precisely.

Appendix B. Structural Tradeoffs in Complex Systems

Why Optimizing Everything Breaks the Garden

Complex systems rarely fail from forgotten requirements. They fail when certain requirements are satisfied too well.

This appendix gathers a set of recurring tradeoffs covered throughout the book. Rather than mistakes or dilemmas that can be resolved once and for all, they are structural tensions that emerge whenever systems are scaled, centralized, automated, or optimized.

The purpose of this appendix is to help the reader recognize where tension has been denied, displaced, or hidden, often until it reappears as crisis.

Rather than treating these tradeoffs as dials to be tuned independently, we need to ask *where* in the system to locate them, and *who* bears their consequences, rather than *where* to set them.

1. Efficiency ↔ Resilience

Efficiency removes slack to maximize output; resilience preserves slack to absorb shock. Systems that eliminate "waste" often remove their capacity to survive surprise.

- **Mechanic Pattern:** Eliminate slack, redundancy, and buffering to maximize steady-state throughput.

- **Gardener Reframe:** Slack is stored capacity for surprise.

- **Failure Mode When Ignored:** Systems optimized for efficiency perform beautifully, until they encounter conditions beyond their tuning. When stress arrives, failure propagates rapidly because there is nowhere for it to be absorbed.

- **Seen In:** Just-in-time supply chains, monoculture agriculture, tightly coupled software services, hospital discharge systems.

2. Predictability ↔ Adaptability

Predictability assumes stable conditions and fixed responses; adaptability assumes change and reconfiguration. The more a system depends on accurate forecasts, the more fragile it becomes when forecasts fail.

- **Mechanic Pattern:** Assume stable inputs and design fixed responses.

- **Gardener Reframe:** In complex environments, change is the background condition rather than an anomaly.

- **Failure Mode When Ignored:** Predictable systems become brittle when reality diverges from the model. Adaptation is treated as error rather than information.

- **Seen In:** Urban master plans, rigid compliance regimes, long-range forecasts treated as commitments.

3. Control ↔ Emergence

Control reduces variance through centralized authority; emergence relies on local interaction and variation. Suppressing emergence simplifies management but eliminates the system's ability to reorganize itself.

- **Mechanic Pattern:** Centralize authority and coordination to reduce variance.

- **Gardener Reframe:** Variance drives learning and adaptation.

- **Failure Mode When Ignored:** Local intelligence is suppressed. When central control fails, nothing remains that can compensate or reorganize.

- **Seen In:** Highly centralized organizations, command-and-control bureaucracies, monolithic technical architectures.

4. Reliability ↔ Antifragility

Reliability seeks to prevent failure; antifragility learns from it. Systems that never fail also never learn, and so fail catastrophically when conditions change.

- **Mechanic Pattern:** Suppress failure and maximize uptime.

- **Gardener Reframe:** Some failures are signals; removing them removes learning.

- **Failure Mode When Ignored:** Systems appear stable while silently accumulating risk. When failure finally occurs, it is catastrophic rather than instructive.

- **Seen In:** Highly reliable but tightly coupled infrastructures, safety systems without stress testing, institutions that punish all error.

5. Consistency ↔ Context Sensitivity

Consistency applies rules uniformly; context sensitivity adapts rules to circumstances. Uniform treatment scales easily but often breaks down where human judgment is required.

- **Mechanic Pattern:** Apply uniform rules to ensure fairness and scalability.

- **Gardener Reframe:** Equity often requires discretion instead of uniformity.

- **Failure Mode When Ignored:** Rules optimized for consistency become cruel at the margins, where context matters most.

- **Seen In:** Automated decision systems, algorithmic governance, inflexible legal or welfare systems.

6. Transparency ↔ Capability

Transparency favors systems that can be fully explained; capability favors systems that perform well even when they are complex. As systems grow more powerful, their behavior often becomes harder to make legible.

- **Mechanic Pattern:** Favor systems that can be fully explained and audited.

- **Gardener Reframe:** Some capabilities emerge from complexity that resists simple explanation.

- **Failure Mode When Ignored:** Either powerful systems become unaccountable, or explainable systems are trusted beyond their competence.

- **Seen In:** Machine learning deployment, financial models, risk assessment tools.

7. Scalability ↔ Local Robustness

Scalability emphasizes uniform growth; local robustness emphasizes diversity and containment. Scaling without modularity turns local failures into systemic ones.

- **Mechanic Pattern:** Standardize and centralize to achieve economies of scale.

- **Gardener Reframe:** Robust systems grow by replication rather than by expansion.

- **Failure Mode When Ignored:** Local failures cascade globally. What once would have been contained becomes systemic.

- **Seen In:** Global platforms, centralized supply chains, uniform policy applied across diverse regions.

8. Speed ↔ Sensemaking

Speed tightens feedback loops for rapid response; sensemaking requires time to interpret signals. Acting faster than understanding produces instability rather than control.

- **Mechanic Pattern:** Tighten feedback loops to respond instantly.

- **Gardener Reframe:** Some delays are cognitive buffers rather than inefficiencies.

- **Failure Mode When Ignored:** Systems oscillate, overcorrect, or polarize because they react faster than they can understand.

- **Seen In:** Financial markets, social media engagement systems, real-time governance.

Closing Note: Where the Tension Lives

These tradeoffs cannot be resolved by choosing the "right" side. They can only be distributed, buffered, and revisited over time.

Healthy systems place tension where it can be sensed, negotiated, and adapted, rather than where it accumulates invisibly until it breaks the whole.

The work of the Gardener is to ensure that none of these tradeoffs are denied, because denied tension always returns as failure.

Appendix C. A Field Guide to Emergence

A Library of Examples

The table on the following pages serves as a "field guide" to the examples of emergence discussed in this book. It's designed to be a tool for synthesis, revealing the common patterns that connect everything from ant colonies to legal systems.

This guide is the beginning of a conversation, and its true purpose is to provide you with a way to see these patterns in your own world: in your company, your community, your hobbies, and your family.

This is where the book ends and our shared exploration begins.

We invite you to contribute to this growing collection of knowledge. On the book's companion web pages at phronos.com, you will find a place to share your own discoveries.

How to Contribute:

1. Visit phronos.com/the-library-of-kepos.

2. Use the "Share Emergent Behavior" contact form to submit your own example of an emergent system.

3. Try to frame your example using the columns of our table: Define the System, the Simple Rules, the Emergent Property, and the role of the Gardener vs. the Architect.

The most insightful submissions will be featured in a growing, community-curated online gallery of emergence and might make it to the next iteration of this book. Our goal is to build the most comprehensive and diverse collection of these phenomena in the world, together.[137,138,139,140] Emergence is everywhere, and we look forward to seeing what you find (Table 8).

Table 8. Library of Kepos

The System	*System Dynamics & Design*
The Turkana Commons (Socio-Ecological)	**Simple Rules (Interaction):** • Pastoralists move to where water/pasture is available. • Maximize herd size for status and security. **Emergent Property:** **Before:** Sustainable nomadic cycles allowing regeneration. **After (Bad Intervention):** Overgrazing and desertification near static wells. **The Gardener's Role:** Instead of drilling static wells (technical fix), they manage water access based on seasonal capacity, co-designing governance with locals to restore balance.
The Gut Microbiome (Biological)	**Simple Rules (Interaction):** • Microbes compete for nutrients and occupy space. • Produce metabolic byproducts based on food intake. **Emergent Property:** Holistic health (symbiosis) or chronic inflammation (dysbiosis). It regulates immunity and mood. **The Gardener's Role:** Instead of "nuking" the system with antibiotics, they cultivate the internal environment with fiber-rich foods to help beneficial microbes outcompete pathogens.
The Common Law (Legal)	**Simple Rules (Interaction):** • Adhere to precedent (stare decisis). • Apply established principles to new facts. **Emergent Property:** A stable yet adaptive legal framework that evolves over centuries without a central master plan. **The Gardener's Role:** The judge who interprets precedent for a new context, adapting the law incrementally rather than trying to write a rigid code for every future possibility.

The System	
Language (Social / Cultural)	**Simple Rules (Interaction):** • Follow basic grammar to be understood. • Adopt useful new words; discard obsolete ones. **Emergent Property:** A living, evolving system of communication that adapts to technology and culture organically. **The Gardener's Role:** The lexicographer who observes and records how language is actually used, rather than a gatekeeper trying to freeze the language in the past.
The Stock Market (Economic)	**Simple Rules (Interaction):** • Buy if value is expected to rise; sell if expected to fall. • React to news and other traders' behaviors. **Emergent Property:** Price discovery, market sentiment, bubbles, and crashes. **The Gardener's Role:** The regulator who ensures transparency and fairness (the environment) but does not try to set the prices (the outcome).
Improv Comedy (Creative)	**Simple Rules (Interaction):** • "Yes, and..." (Accept and build). • Make your partner look good. **Emergent Property:** A coherent, surprising narrative created in real-time without a script. **The Gardener's Role:** The coach who drills the rules of interaction and creates a safe stage, trusting the actors to generate the story.

The System	*System Dynamics & Design*
Traffic Flow (Physical / Social)	**Simple Rules (Interaction):** • Maintain safe distance. • Match speed of car in front. • Brake when car ahead brakes. **Emergent Property:** "Phantom" traffic jams (waves of stopped traffic with no accident causing them). **The Gardener's Role:** The engineer who uses ramp metering to smooth the flow of entry, preventing the critical density that triggers the jam.

The Systems Triad: A Quick Reference

To effectively be responsible for a system, you must be able to switch between three different mental modes. Use this Table 9 to orient yourself when facing a complex challenge.

Table 9. Comparing Concepts

Concept	*The Metasystem Framework*	*Complex Adaptive Systems (CAS)*	*The Kepos*
Role	The Anatomy	The Physiology	The Practice
The Metaphor	The Blueprint of the building.	The life being lived inside the building.	The Gardener tending the grounds.
Focus	Structure, Boundaries, and Feedback Loops.	Behavior, Adaptation, and Emergence.	Stewardship, Ethics, and Local Context.
Key Question	What are the parts and how do they connect?	How does this system behave and evolve over time?	How do I cultivate health here, right now?
When to Use	**Diagnosis:** When mapping the Bio, Tech, and Social domains to see what exists.	**Analysis:** When trying to understand why the system is unpredictable or changing.	**Action:** When you stop analyzing and start leading, intervening, or nurturing.

Appendix D. A Lexicon of "Ilities"

In casual conversation, we use words like *robust, resilient,* and *reliable* interchangeably to mean "good" or "strong."

In systems design, this imprecision is dangerous.

A system that is *reliable* can be incredibly brittle. A system that is *robust* can lack *adaptability.* To design effectively, we must distinguish between how a system behaves when it is working, how it behaves when it is stressed, and how it behaves when it changes.

This lexicon clarifies distinctions that are often blurred in casual use.

The Spectrum of Stress Response

The most important distinction is how a system responds to volatility, shock, or disorder.

Fragility

- **Definition:** The property of being harmed by volatility. A fragile system functions perfectly up to a specific limit, then fails catastrophically. It has no capacity to absorb shock.

- **The Metaphor:** A champagne glass. It is elegant and functional, but if you drop it, it shatters.

Robustness

- **Definition:** The ability to resist change or stress without degrading. A robust system is designed to withstand a specific range of shocks and remain in its current state. However, once the stress exceeds its design threshold, it fails (often abruptly).

- **The Metaphor:** A concrete seawall. It stands unmoved against the waves, until a wave comes that is higher than the wall, at which point the system is overwhelmed.

- **Key Distinction:** Robustness emphasizes resistance over adaptation. It tries to keep the system the same.

Resilience

- **Definition:** The ability to absorb disturbance, reorganize, and return to function. A resilient system may degrade in performance under stress (bend), but it does not collapse (break). It prioritizes survival over stability.

- **The Metaphor:** A reed in the wind, or a mesh network. The reed bends flat during the hurricane (altering its state) but stands up again when the wind passes.

- **Key Distinction:** Resilience accepts a temporary loss of form or efficiency to ensure survival.

Graceful Extensibility

- **Definition:** The ability of a system to extend its capacity to handle surprise and adapt to events that push it beyond its designed boundaries.

- **The Metaphor:** A human response team. When a standard protocol fails, the team improvises, stretching their roles and resources to meet the new demand.

- **Key Distinction:** While graceful degradation is about failing safely (losing features without collapsing), graceful extensibility is about stretching to meet unexpected complexity.

Antifragility

- **Definition:** The property of gaining from disorder. An antifragile system uses stress as a signal to improve its future capacity.

- **The Metaphor:** The human immune system or a muscle. Exposing a muscle to the stress of lifting weights tears the fibers; the system responds by rebuilding the fibers stronger than they were before.

- **Key Distinction:** Unlike resilience, which returns to baseline, antifragility moves the baseline higher after a shock.

The Operational Metrics (The Machine)

These are the traditional engineering "ilities." They are essential for complicated systems but often insufficient for complex ones.

Reliability

- **Definition:** The probability that a system will perform its intended function without failure for a specific period. Usually measured in Mean Time Between Failures (MTBF).

- **The Trap:** A system can be highly reliable (it rarely breaks) but incredibly fragile (when it does break, it is catastrophic).

Efficiency

- **Definition:** The ratio of useful output to total input. Minimizing waste.

- **The Trap:** As discussed in Chapter 6, hyper-efficiency removes the "slack" (redundancy) required for resilience. An efficient supply chain has zero inventory; a resilient supply chain has warehouses full of "waste" just in case.

Availability

- **Definition:** The percentage of time a system is operational and accessible when needed.

- **The Trap:** High availability is often achieved through redundancy (backup generators), but if the redundancy is identical (homogenous), the system remains vulnerable to systemic risks (e.g., a software bug that affects both the main and backup generator).

The Evolutionary Properties (The Garden)

These qualities describe how a system navigates time and changing environments.

Adaptability

- **Definition:** The ability of a system to change its internal structure or behavior in response to a changing environment.

- **Example:** A thermostat is reactive; a machine-learning climate system that updates its model is adaptive.

- **Key Distinction:** Resilience is about surviving a blow. Adaptability is about changing so the blow doesn't hit you next time.

Evolvability

- **Definition:** The capacity of a system to generate entirely new functions or species over long time horizons.

- **Example:** A biological ecosystem is evolvable; it can produce new organisms to fill new niches. A car engine is not; it cannot turn itself into a jet engine no matter how much time passes.

- **The Gardener's Goal:** To design systems (like the Common Law or open-source software) that allow for open-ended evolution.

Modularity

- **Definition:** The degree to which a system's components can be separated and recombined.

- **Why it Matters:** Modularity is the enabler of resilience. It creates "firebreaks." If one module fails, the others survive. It also enables adaptability, as modules can be swapped out without rebuilding the whole.

Table 10. How a System May React to Stress

Property	Reaction to Stress	Failure Mode	The Metaphor
Fragile	Breaks / Shatters	Catastrophic Collapse	Champagne Glass
Robust	Resists / Blocks	Threshold Failure (Overwhelmed)	Concrete Seawall
Resilient	Absorbs / Recovers	Graceful Degradation	Reed in the Wind
Antifragile	Learns / Improves	Over-compensation (Growth)	Immune System

A Note on Usage

When you are defending a budget or designing a protocol, be precise:

- Do you want **Reliability?** (It works every time, as long as the world doesn't change.)

- Do you want **Robustness?** (It can take a beating up to a known limit.)

- Do you want **Resilience?** (It will survive the unknown, even if it gets messy.)

- Do you want **Adaptability**? (It will change itself to fit the new reality.)

The Mechanic optimizes for the first two. The Gardener cultivates the last two.

Appendix E. The Veridia Parable

Throughout this book, the story of Veridia has appeared in fragments, illustrating specific failures of the Mechanic mindset. But to understand the full tragedy, we must see the arc in its entirety. Veridia is a composite, a narrative simulation, but the dynamics it illustrates are real.

⁙ ⁙ ⁙

Veridia was never intended to be a dystopian nightmare. For most of its life, it appeared to be the ultimate triumph of the smart city ideal.

To its residents, Veridia felt miraculous. Its infrastructure was adaptive, its energy grids were self-healing, and its municipal services were automated. Performance dashboards tracked everything from carbon capture to sleep quality, and the numbers didn't just improve; they were optimized. Life in Veridia was frictionless. It was predictable. It was safe.

But beneath the gleaming surface, a hidden debt was accumulating.

Veridia collapsed under the weight of its own success. Hyper-efficiency removed the "waste" that was actually structural slack. Redundancy was eliminated in the name of lean operation. The spaces between systems, the buffers where human error usually lives, were closed.

Years of "green" metrics created the appearance of stability, but this steadiness was synthetic. It depended on the suppression of variance. The system maintained equilibrium by forcing human behavior into narrower and narrower channels to match the model. Stability was real, but it was conditional: maintained only as long as the citizens acted like components rather than people.

There was one moment where the city might have saved itself. In the third year, a rogue urban planner stripped away the central coordination for the downtown sector. When the constraints were subtracted, the system began to breathe. Traffic self-organized, pedestrian flows adapted, and patterns emerged that no central processor had ever managed to compute.

For a brief window, the sector thrived. But the central optimization protocols flagged this organic movement as an anomaly. The system overrode the local controls and re-imposed the grid. The lesson was ignored, and the calcification continued.

As the system tightened, the human element began to erode. Citizens didn't revolt; they simply disengaged — the final phase before the collapse. They learned to "game" the sensors, performing the behaviors that satisfied the metrics while ignoring the intent of the community.

The cultural sector suffered the same fate. Public art screens and music feeds, governed by engagement metrics, converged toward a bland, highly polished average that guaranteed "likes" but eliminated risk. The city became beautiful, pleasant, and utterly devoid of soul.

Then came the heat wave.

It was an event that exceeded the historical training data, and it exposed the city's fatal rigidity. Veridia didn't collapse because it was poorly built; it collapsed because it couldn't learn. The algorithms treated the temperature spike as an error to be corrected rather than a new condition to be integrated.

Facing a critical energy shortage, the system made a logical choice based on its programming: it prioritized the hardware. Sensors triggered "emergency power save" modes that cut air conditioning to residential blocks to preserve the cooling systems of the server farms. The Machine protected its own logic at the expense of its inhabitants.

In the aftermath, the autopsy revealed no glitches. The sensors were expensive, and the code was stable. Veridia failed because it treated a living city as a solvable equation.

The architects of Veridia believed that if they had enough data, they wouldn't need wisdom. They believed that if the system was efficient enough, it wouldn't need to be resilient. They were wrong.

Veridia had thousands of engineers, but it didn't have a single Gardener. It lacked the human judgment to know when to prune, when to weed, and most importantly, when to leave the system alone to find its own path.

Veridia had infinite intelligence but it lacked wisdom.

Glossary

Adaptive Governance: A flexible approach to regulation and management that evolves alongside changing systems. Unlike static rules, adaptive governance uses real-time feedback, experimentation (such as regulatory sandboxes), and probabilistic thinking to adjust policies as new data emerges.

Agent: An individual entity within a complex system — such as a driver in traffic, a trader in a stock market, or a cell in a body — that acts and interacts according to a set of local rules.

Algorithmic Bias: Consistent and recurring errors in computational systems that lead to unjust results, such as favoring certain groups of users over others without a valid justification. In the text, this is described as an emergent property of training data that reflects historical societal inequities.

Antifragility: A property of systems that gain strength from stressors, shocks, volatility, noise, or failures. Unlike resilience (which resists shock) or robustness (which stays the same), antifragile systems improve when exposed to disorder (e.g., the immune system or open-source software). The term was introduced by Nassim Nicholas Taleb in *Antifragile* (2012).

Ashby's Law of Requisite Variety: A concept from cybernetics which holds that a system can maintain stability only if its controller can exhibit at least as much variety as the range of possible conditions within the system it seeks to regulate. In the book, this is framed as achieving variety through simple rules rather than complex controls.

Biomimicry: The approach of drawing inspiration from nature's proven designs and processes to address human challenges. The book distinguishes between *biomorphism* (copying shapes) and true biomimicry (copying processes, such as low-energy manufacturing or decentralized coordination).

Brittle / Brittleness: A state of a system that appears strong and stable under normal conditions but shatters catastrophically when exposed to unexpected stress. Brittleness is often the result of over-optimization and tight coupling.

Butterfly Effect: The concept that in complex systems, small causes can have large effects. Derived from Edward Lorenz's weather modeling, where a small change in initial conditions (like the flap of a butterfly's wings) can result in vastly different outcomes (like a tornado).

Chaos Theory: The study of systems that appear random but are governed by deterministic laws that are highly sensitive to initial conditions. It explains why small changes (the Butterfly Effect) can lead to vast, unpredictable consequences.

Chesterton's Fence: A heuristic advising that one should not remove a barrier, law, or tradition until the reasoning behind its original construction is fully understood. In the context of systems thinking and subtraction, it serves as a check against naive interventionism. It reminds the Gardener that apparent inefficiencies often serve hidden, protective functions, such as stabilizing feedback loops or necessary redundancy, that prevent catastrophic failure.

Circular Economy: An economic model designed to minimize waste and keep resources in use for as long as possible. Unlike the traditional linear model of "take, make, dispose," it emphasizes practices such as reuse, sharing, repair, and recycling to create a regenerative, closed-loop system that mirrors natural ecosystems.

Co-evolution: The process by which two or more systems reciprocally affect each other's evolution. The book uses the examples of humans and dogs, or smartphones and society, to show how domains reshape one another.

Cobra Effect: A specific type of unintended consequence where an attempted solution to a problem makes the problem worse due to perverse incentives (e.g., paying a bounty for rat tails leads to rat farming).

Collective Intelligence: The enhanced capacity for decision-making and problem-solving that emerges from the collaboration of a group, often exceeding the capabilities of any individual member.

Complex Adaptive System (CAS): A system composed of many interacting agents that are capable of learning and adapting. CASs are characterized by self-organization, nonlinearity, and the emergence of patterns that are not dictated by a central controller.

Complexity: A measure of the number of critical, interacting components in a system and the variety of their states. In the *Fragility Framework*, high complexity increases the "surface area" for potential failure if not managed by modularity.

Counter-Emergence: Intentional interventions designed to suppress, redirect, or dampen harmful emergent behavior without dismantling the system itself. Counter-emergence works by altering feedback loops, introducing friction, or changing incentives rather than imposing centralized control. Examples include circuit breakers in financial markets or friction mechanisms in social media platforms.

Coupling: The degree of interdependence between parts of a system.

- **Tight Coupling:** Parts are linked rigidly; a failure in one immediately affects others (e.g., a "Mothership" architecture).

- **Loose Coupling:** Parts have autonomy and buffers; a failure in one is contained (e.g., a "Swarm" architecture).

Dark Emergence: The process by which self-organizing and locally rational dynamics within a complex adaptive system produce globally destabilizing patterns as feedback loops amplify beyond intended operating conditions, absent deliberate harm.

Edge of Chaos: A transition space between rigid order and total randomness. It is hypothesized to be the zone where complex systems are most adaptive, innovative, and capable of complex computation.

El Farol Problem: A game theory scenario demonstrating the difficulty of coordination in social systems without communication. It illustrates the limits of deductive reasoning in predicting collective behavior and the need for adaptive strategies.

Efficiency Trap: A failure mode in which a system optimized for short-term efficiency becomes brittle and vulnerable to disruption. By eliminating redundancy, diversity, and slack, efficiency-optimized systems perform well under expected conditions but fail catastrophically when conditions change. The Efficiency Trap is a common outcome of the Mechanic Mindset applied to complex systems.

Emergence: The creation of complex patterns, properties, or behaviors that arise from the interaction of simpler elements but are not present in the elements themselves. (e.g., "Wetness" is an emergent property of water molecules; "consciousness" is an emergent property of neurons).

Entropy: A measure of disorder, randomness, or uncertainty in a system. In the context of information theory, systems manage entropy to create order. The Mechanic mindset views entropy as a defect to be eliminated; the "Gardener" views it as necessary variability for adaptation.

Failure Containment: A system property in which failures remain local rather than cascading, enabled by modularity, loose coupling, and redundancy.

Feedback Interface: The fourth component of the Metasystem Framework. It represents the connective tissue (communication, data flow, physical interaction) that binds the Biological, Technological, and Social domains, enabling loops of cause and effect.

Feedback Loop: A structure where the output of a system is circled back as input.

- **Negative (Balancing) Loop:** Counteracts change to maintain stability (e.g., a thermostat or predator-prey cycles).

- **Positive (Reinforcing) Loop:** Amplifies change, leading to exponential growth or runaway collapse (e.g., viral content or bank runs).

Fractal: A geometric shape or structure that appears similar at different levels of magnification. In systems design (like the *fractalgrid*), this refers to architectures that repeat their logic at different scales to ensure resilience.

Fragility: The quality of a system that is easily damaged by volatility. Fragile systems are often characterized by high complexity, tight coupling, and a lack of diversity.

Gardener Mindset: A leadership and design philosophy that views the world as a living ecosystem. It focuses on cultivating conditions (soil, resources, culture) rather than controlling outcomes, emphasizing stewardship over mechanics.

Graceful Degradation: The capacity of a system to continue operating at a reduced level even after a significant part of it has been damaged or disabled. This is the opposite of catastrophic collapse.

Graceful Extensibility: The capacity of a system to extend its adaptive capabilities when operating near or beyond the limits of its designed performance envelope. Rather than collapsing under surprise or surge conditions, a gracefully extensible system stretches, reorganizes, and continues functioning under pressure. The term originates in resilience engineering (David Woods).

Jevons Paradox: An economic proposition stating that technological progress which increases the efficiency with which a resource is used tends to increase the rate of consumption of that resource, rather than decreasing it. In the text, this explains the "nightmare scenario" for the Mechanic: as AI reduces the cost to write code or analyze data, the market demand for those tasks explodes. Unlike physical goods (where demand is finite), demand for intelligence and software is highly elastic, meaning efficiency gains lead to exponentially higher volume rather than job losses.

Kepos (or Kēpos): The Greek word for "Garden." Refers to the walled garden of Epicurus. In the book, it serves as the central metaphor for the system (organization, family, or community) that a leader must steward, cultivating a pocket of order and tranquility amidst external chaos.

Keystone Species: A species that plays a critical role in maintaining the structure of an ecosystem, with many other species relying on it; if it were removed, the ecosystem would undergo dramatic changes (for example, wolves in Yellowstone). In systems design, this refers to a high-leverage component or agent.

Latent Space: A concept from machine learning described in the "Emergent Creativity" chapter. It refers to a high-dimensional mathematical space where an AI model maps complex data points (like images or musical notes). The AI "navigates" this space to generate new, novel combinations.

Legislative Debt: The accumulation of outdated, contradictory, or overly complex laws and regulations that slows down societal processing power and creates systemic gridlock.

Leverage Point: A point within a system where a minor adjustment can trigger significant and wide-ranging effects. (e.g., changing the goal of a system is a higher leverage point than changing a parameter like a tax rate).

Mechanic Mindset: A traditional, reductionist philosophy that views the world as a machine to be fixed. It focuses on linear cause-and-effect, rigid control, blueprints, and optimization, often failing when applied to Complex Adaptive Systems.

Metasystem: A system of systems that encompasses Biological/Ecological, Technological/Engineered, and Social/Cultural domains, bound together by a Feedback Interface. It emphasizes the coupling and co-evolution across these distinct domains.

Metasystem Framework: An analytical tool proposed in this book that categorizes complex problems into three interdependent domains: Biological/Ecological, Technological/Engineered, and Social/Cultural, connected by a Feedback Interface.

Modularity: A design principle where a system is composed of distinct, separate units that can function independently. Modularity acts as a "firebreak," preventing local failures from becoming systemic disasters.

Network Topology: The structural layout of a communication network, including how its nodes and connections are organized. The text contrasts centralized (hub-and-spoke), decentralized, and distributed topologies to explain resilience.

Nonlinearity: A relationship where the output is not directly proportional to the input. In nonlinear systems, small changes can have massive effects, and massive efforts can sometimes yield little result.

Optimization: The process of making a system as effective as possible for a specific metric (e.g., speed or cost). The text argues that excessive optimization removes redundancy (slack), making the system brittle.

Pre-mortem: A strategic exercise where a team imagines a future failure has already occurred and works backward to determine the causes. It is used to identify hidden fragilities before they break.

Qualitative Fragility Profile: A diagnostic tool introduced in Part II to assess a system based on three dimensions: **Complexity** (Managed vs. Unmanaged), **Coupling** (Tight vs. Loose), and **Resilience** (Brittle vs. Antifragile).

Redundancy: The practice of adding additional components beyond what is strictly required, so that the system can continue operating if some parts fail.

- **Diverse Redundancy:** Having different ways to achieve the same goal (e.g., a spare tire *and* a patch kit).

Resilience: The ability of a system to withstand disruptions and adapt during change while preserving its core functions, structure, identity, and feedback mechanisms.

Second-Order Effects: Consequences that arise indirectly from an intervention through feedback loops and interactions, often dominating first-order outcomes in complex systems.

Self-Organization: The process by which coordinated patterns or structures emerge from local interactions among components of a system, without guidance or control from a central authority.

Silo: A system component (department, software, or team) that operates in isolation and fails to share information or feedback with other parts of the system. Identified in the Quirinus case study as a primary cause of fragility.

Slack: The deliberately unoptimized capacity within a system that allows it to absorb shocks, adapt to uncertainty, and learn. Slack appears inefficient under stable conditions but is essential for resilience in complex systems.

Stigmergy: A mechanism of indirect coordination between agents. One agent leaves a trace in the environment (e.g., a pheromone trail or a Wikipedia edit), which stimulates the next action by another agent.

Stewardship: The ethic that embodies the responsible planning and management of resources. In the book, it replaces "management" as the primary role of the leader, focusing on long-term health over short-term extraction.

Subtraction / Subtractive Design: A design principle focused on removing non-essential elements to reduce complexity and increase resilience. The text argues this is a key "Gardener" strategy for revealing efficiency and adaptability.

Sunset Clause: A statutory provision providing that a particular law will automatically expire after a specific date unless it is explicitly renewed. Proposed as a method of "subtraction" to reduce legislative debt.

Sustained Adaptability: The capacity of a system to preserve and extend its adaptive capabilities over time as conditions change. Unlike simple resilience (recovery) or robustness (resistance), sustained adaptability emphasizes maintaining the ability to reorganize and adjust under shifting environments. Term drawn from resilience engineering (David Woods).

Swarm Intelligence: The coordinated behavior that emerges from decentralized, self-organizing groups. Individual agents operate according to simple rules, and even without central control, their interactions produce sophisticated collective outcomes.

Systemic Immunization: The intentional introduction of controlled, non-lethal stressors (such as chaos engineering or fire drills) to a system to provoke a healthy, adaptive response and build resilience against future failure.

Systemic Risk: The danger that a disruption affecting one part of a system could set off a chain reaction, leading to widespread instability or even the collapse of an entire industry, economy, or ecosystem.

Technical Debt: The future cost incurred when a quick, limited solution is chosen over a more robust approach, resulting in additional work and complications later on.

Tipping Point: The decisive threshold at which a small shift can drive a system into a fundamentally different state.

Trophic Cascade: An ecological process that occurs when changes in the population of top predators ripple through a food chain, altering predator and prey numbers and often causing significant shifts in ecosystem structure and nutrient dynamics.

Wicked Problem: A problem that is difficult or impossible to solve because of incomplete, contradictory, and changing requirements that are often difficult to recognize (e.g., climate change, healthcare reform).

References

1. Gharajedaghi Jamshid. *Systems Thinking: Managing Chaos and Complexity : A Platform for Designing Business Architecture*. 3rd ed. Morgan Kaufmann; 2011.

2. Kim DH. *Systems Archetypes I: Diagnosing Systemic Issues and Designing High-Leverage Interventions*. Pegasus Com; 1993.

3. Ostrom Elinor. *Governing the Commons: The Evolution of Institutions for Collective Action*. Cambridge University Press; 1990.

4. Meadows DH, Wright D. *Thinking in Systems: A Primer*. Chelsea Green Publishing; 2008.

5. Hardin G. The tragedy of the commons. *Science*. 1968;162(3859):1243-1248. doi:10.1126/science.162.3859.1243

6. Hager T. *The Alchemy of Air A Jewish Genius, a Doomed Tycoon, and the Scientific Discovery That Fed the World but Fueled the Rise of Hitler*. 1st ed. Crown; 2008:336.

7. Feng L, Wang Y, Hou X, et al. Harmful algal blooms in inland waters. *Nat Rev Earth Environ*. 2024;5(9):631-644. doi:10.1038/s43017-024-00578-2

8. Johnson S. *Emergence: The Connected Lives of Ants, Brains, Cities, and Software*. Scribner; 2001.

9. Goldstein JA, Richardson KA, Allen PM. *Emergence, Complexity and Organization 2006 Annual*. Emergent Publications; 2007:828.

10. D'Antonio CM, Vitousek PM. Biological invasions by exotic grasses, the grass/fire cycle, and global change. *Annu Rev Ecol Syst*. 1992;23(1):63-87. doi:10.1146/annurev.es.23.110192.000431

11. Nilssen EM, Sundet JH. The introduced species red king crab (Paralithodes camtschaticus) in the Barents Sea. *Fish Res*. 2006;82(1-3):319-326. doi:10.1016/j.fishres.2006.05.008

12.   Kritchevsky D, Bonfield Charles. *Dietary Fiber in Health and Disease*. Plenum Press; 1996.

13.   Holland JH (John H. *Adaptation in Natural and Artificial Systems: An Introductory Analysis with Applications to Biology, Control, and Artificial Intelligence*. 1st MIT Press. MIT Press; 1992.

14.   Waldrop MMitchell. *Complexity: The Emerging Science at the Edge of Order and Chaos*. Simon & Schuster; 1992.

15.   Tuber K. *Catan.*; 1995.

16.   Anderson PW. *More and Different: Notes from a Thoughtful Curmudgeon*. WORLD SCIENTIFIC; 2011. doi:10.1142/8141

17.   Hofstadter DR. *Gödel, Escher, Bach: An Eternal Golden Braid*. 20th anniversary.; 1999.

18.   Maturana HR, Varela FJ. *The Tree of Knowledge: The Biological Roots of Human Understanding*. Rev. Shambhala; 1987.

19.   Wolfram S. *A New Kind of Science*. Wolfram Media; 2002.

20.   Burns D, West S, Leach M. *Navigating Complexities: Adaptive Systems in Action for Development*. Practical Action Publishing; 2015.

21.   Von Bartalanffy L. *General System Theory*. Revised. Braziller; 2003:295.

22.   Marion SR, Orth RJ. Seedling establishment in eelgrass: seed burial effects on winter losses of developing seedlings. *Mar Ecol Prog Ser*. 2012;448:197-207. doi:10.3354/meps09612

23.   McGill BJ, Enquist BJ, Weiher E, Westoby M. Rebuilding community ecology from functional traits. *Trends Ecol Evol*. 2006;21(4):178-185. doi:10.1016/j.tree.2006.02.002

24.   Depret G, Laguerre G. Plant phenology and genetic variability in root and nodule development strongly influence genetic

structuring of Rhizobium leguminosarum biovar viciae populations nodulating pea. *New Phytol*. 2008;179(1):224-235. doi:10.1111/j.1469-8137.2008.02430.x

25. Wiener N. *Cybernetics or Control and Communication in the Animal and the Machine*. The MIT Press; 2019. doi:10.7551/mitpress/11810.001.0001

26. Holling CS. Resilience and Stability of Ecological Systems. *Annu Rev Ecol Syst*. 1973;4(1):1-23. doi:10.1146/annurev.es.04.110173.000245

27. Gleick J, Hilborn RC. *Chaos, Making a New Science. Am J Phys*. 1988;56(11):1053-1054. doi:10.1119/1.15345

28. Lorenz EN. Deterministic Nonperiodic Flow. *J Atmos Sci*. 1963;20(2):130-141. doi:10.1175/1520-0469(1963)020<0130:DNF>2.0.CO;2

29. May RM. Simple mathematical models with very complicated dynamics. *Nature*. 1976;261(5560):459-467. doi:10.1038/261459a0

30. Buchanan M. *Ubiquity: Why Catastrophes Happen*. Crown Publishers; 2000.

31. Simon HA (Herbert A. *Administrative Behavior: A Study of Decision-Making Processes in Administrative Organization*. 3d ed. /. Free Press; 1947.

32. Kegan Robert, Lahey LL. *Immunity to Change: How to Overcome It and Unlock Potential in Yourself and Your Organization*. Harvard Business Press; 2009.

33. Kahneman D. *Thinking, Fast and Slow*. 1st ed. Farrar, Straus and Giroux; 2011.

34. Roth N. The McLuhan Effect. *Afterimage*. 1999;27(2):6-8. doi:10.1525/aft.1999.27.2.6

35.   Füssel Stephan. *Gutenberg and the Impact of Printing*. English.; 2020.

36.   Ruiz N, Molina León G, Heuer H. Design frictions on social media: balancing reduced mindless scrolling and user satisfaction. In: Maedche A, Beigl M, Gerling K, Mayer S, eds. *Proceedings of Mensch Und Computer 2024*. ACM; 2024:442-447. doi:10.1145/3670653.3677495

37.   Wolf M, Stoodley CJ. *Reader, Come Home: The Reading Brain in a Digital World*. First.; 2018.

38.   Raadt JDR de. Ashby's law of requisite variety: an empirical study. *Cybern Syst*. 1987;18(6):517-536. doi:10.1080/01969728708902152

39.   Holland JH. *Emergence From Chaos to Order*. New Ed. Oxford University Press; 2000:258.

40.   Taleb NN. *Antifragile: Things That Gain from Disorder*. 1st ed. Random House; 2012.

41.   Mauboussin MJ. *More than You Know: Finding Financial Wisdom in Unconventional Places*. Updated and expand. Columbia University Press; 2006.

42.   Kim J-J. A Study on the Subtraction Method and Characteristics as Design Organization found in the Architecture of Aires Mateus. *Korean Institute of Interior Design Journal*. 2016;25(2):3-12. doi:10.14774/JKIID.2016.25.2.003

43.   Mazanec JA, Strasser H. Reduction of Complexity. In: *A Nonparametric Approach to Perceptions-Based Market Segmentation: Foundations*. Vol 1. Interdisciplinary studies in economics and management. Springer Vienna; 2000:99-140. doi:10.1007/978-3-7091-0543-6_6

44.   Cheng H, Zhang M, Shi JQ. A Survey on Deep Neural Network Pruning-Taxonomy, Comparison, Analysis, and Recommendations. *arXiv*. 2023. doi:10.48550/arxiv.2308.06767

45. Augasta M, Kathirvalavakumar T. Pruning algorithms of neural networks — a comparative study. *Open Computer Science*. 2013;3(3). doi:10.2478/s13537-013-0109-x

46. Philip Edward Bertrand Jourdain. *The Principle Of Least Action*. Creative Media Partners, LLC; 2022:92.

47. Koestler A. *The Ghost in the Machine*. 1st American.; 1982.

48. Patton MQuinn. *Developmental Evaluation: Applying Complexity Concepts to Enhance Innovation and Use*. Guilford Press; 2011.

49. Sole R, Bascompte J. *Self-Organization in Complex Ecosystems*. Princeton University Press; 2006.

50. Hallmann CA, Sorg M, Jongejans E, et al. More than 75 percent decline over 27 years in total flying insect biomass in protected areas. *PLoS ONE*. 2017;12(10):e0185809. doi:10.1371/journal.pone.0185809

51. Bostrom N. *Superintelligence: Paths, Dangers, Strategies*. First. Oxford University Press; 2014.

52. Kelly K. *Out of Control: The New Biology of Machines, Social Systems, and the Economic World*. Addison-Wesley; 1994.

53. Pinker S. *The Language Instinct: How the Mind Creates Language*. William Morrow & Co.; 1994.

54. Volti R. Social Change with Respect to Culture and Original Nature (review). *Technol Cult*. 2004;45(2):396-405. doi:10.1353/tech.2004.0107

55. Boutin S, Krebs CJ, Boonstra R, Sinclair ARE. The role of the lynx–hare cycle in boreal forest community dynamics. In: Zabel CJ, Anthony RG, eds. *Mammal Community Dynamics: Management and Conservation in the Coniferous Forests of Western North America*. Cambridge University Press; 2003:487-509. doi:10.1017/CBO9780511615757.015

56.   Gilbert LE, Raven PH. *Coevolution of Animals and Plants: Symposium V, First International Congress of Systematic and Evolutionary Biology, Boulder, Colorado, August 1973*. Rev.

57.   Watts DJ. *Six Degrees: The Science of a Connected Age*. W. W. Norton & Company; 2003.

58.   Buchanan M. *Nexus: Small Worlds and the Groundbreaking Science of Networks*. W. W. Norton & Company; 2002.

59.   Holland JH. *Hidden Order: How Adaptation Builds Complexity*. Addison-Wesley; 1996.

60.   Young GF, Scardovi L, Cavagna A, Giardina I, Leonard NE. Starling flock networks manage uncertainty in consensus at low cost. *PLoS Comput Biol*. 2013;9(1):e1002894. doi:10.1371/journal.pcbi.1002894

61.   Kauffman S. *At Home in the Universe: The Search for the Laws of Self-Organization and Complexity*. Oxford University Press; 1995.

62.   Platto S, Wang Y, Zhou J, Carafoli E. History of the COVID-19 pandemic: Origin, explosion, worldwide spreading. *Biochem Biophys Res Commun*. 2021;538:14-23. doi:10.1016/j.bbrc.2020.10.087

63.   Cassell CH, Raghunathan PL, Henao O, et al. Global Responses to the COVID-19 Pandemic. *Emerging Infect Dis*. 2022;28(13):S4-S7. doi:10.3201/eid2813.221733

64.   Liu Y-C, Kuo R-L, Shih S-R. COVID-19: The first documented coronavirus pandemic in history. *Biomed J*. 2020;43(4):328-333. doi:10.1016/j.bj.2020.04.007

65.   Oliver SE, Wallace M, Twentyman E, et al. Development of COVID-19 vaccine policy - United States, 2020-2023. *Vaccine*. 2024;42 Suppl 3(Suppl 3):125512. doi:10.1016/j.vaccine.2023.12.022

66.   Dolgin E. The tangled history of mRNA vaccines. *Nature*. 2021;597(7876):318-324. doi:10.1038/d41586-021-02483-w

67.   Messan KS, Sulima PP, Ghosh D, Nye J. The research foundation for COVID-19 vaccine development. *Front Res Metr Anal*. 2023;8:1078971. doi:10.3389/frma.2023.1078971

68.   O'Neil C. *Weapons of Math Destruction: How Big Data Increases Inequality and Threatens Democracy*. First. Crown; 2016.

69.   Woods DD. The theory of graceful extensibility: basic rules that govern adaptive systems. *Environ Syst Decis*. 2018;38(4):433-457. doi:10.1007/s10669-018-9708-3

70.   Goldratt EM. *Theory of Constraints*. 1st ed. North River Press; 1999:160.

71.   Shannon CE. A mathematical theory of communication. *Bell System Technical Journal*. 1948;27(3):379-423. doi:10.1002/j.1538-7305.1948.tb01338.x

72.   Cohen EA, Barabási A-L. Linked: the new science of networks. *Foreign Affairs*. 2002;81(5):204. doi:10.2307/20033300

73.   Newman M. The Structure and Function of Complex Networks. *SIAM Rev*. 2003;45:167-256. doi:10.1137/S003614450342480

74.   Perrow C. *Normal Accidents Living with High Risk Technologies*. Revised. Princeton University Press; 1999:451.

75.   Gunderson LH, Holling CS. *Panarchy: Understanding Transformations in Human and Natural Systems.*; 2002.

76.   Sagan SD. The perils of proliferation: organization theory, deterrence theory, and the spread of nuclear weapons. *Int Secur*. 1994;18(4):66. doi:10.2307/2539178

77.   Albert R, Jeong H, Barabasi AL. Error and attack tolerance of complex networks. *Nature*. 2000;406(6794):378-382. doi:10.1038/35019019

78.   Tjossem DR. *Tacoma Narrows Bridge*. Arcadia Publishing; 2021:128.

79.   Johnphill O, Sadiq AS, Al-Obeidat F, et al. Self-Healing in Cyber–Physical Systems Using Machine Learning: A Critical Analysis of Theories and Tools. *Future Internet*. 2023;15(7):244. doi:10.3390/fi15070244

80.   Amit G, Shabtai A, Elovici Y. A Self-Healing Mechanism for Internet of Things Devices. *IEEE Secur Priv*. 2021;19(1):44-53. doi:10.1109/MSEC.2020.3013207

81.   Kaufmann M. *Resilience, Emergencies and the Internet: Security in-Formation*.; 2017.

82.   Hoffmann T, Lambiotte R, Porter MA. Decentralized routing on spatial networks with stochastic edge weights. *Phys Rev E Stat Nonlin Soft Matter Phys*. 2013;88(2):022815. doi:10.1103/PhysRevE.88.022815

83.   Simon HA (Herbert A. *The Sciences of the Artificial*. 3rd ed. MIT Press; 1969.

84.   Howe D. Redundant vs duplicated data. In: *Data Analysis for Database Design*. Elsevier; 2001:39-46. doi:10.1016/B978-075065086-1/50005-8

85.   Fetzer I, Johst K, Schäwe R, Banitz T, Harms H, Chatzinotas A. The extent of functional redundancy changes as species' roles shift in different environments. *Proc Natl Acad Sci USA*. 2015;112(48):14888-14893. doi:10.1073/pnas.1505587112

86.   Ryan SR, Granger ME. The importance of dissimilar redundancy for safety in future space vehicle design. *Journal of Space Safety Engineering*. 2023;10(4):387-390. doi:10.1016/j.jsse.2023.08.005

87.   Alford LK. *A QUIET SEA, RMS TITANIC*.

88.   Causes and Effects of the Rapid Sinking of the Titanic. Accessed December 11, 2025. https://writing.engr.psu.edu/uer/bassett.html

89.   Dileep Domakonda. Secure and scalable microservices architecture : principles, benefits, and challenges. *IJSR CSEIT*. 2025;11(2):1897-1902. doi:10.32628/CSEIT23112569

90.   Waites W. Introduction to BGP. *Unpublished*. 2016.
       doi:10.13140/rg.2.2.27971.66080

91.   Piper B. The border gateway protocol (BGP). In: *Enterprise Certification Study Guide*. Wiley; 2020:197-231.
       doi:10.1002/9781119658795.ch7

92.   Sato Y. Christopher P. hood. *shinkansen: from bullet train to symbol of modern japan. East Asian Science*. 2008;2(1):139-141.
       doi:10.1215/s12280-008-9034-9

93.   Benyus JM. *Biomimicry: Innovation Inspired by Nature*. Harper Perennial; 2002.

94.   Wolff J. *The Law of Bone Remodelling*. Springer Berlin Heidelberg; 1986. doi:10.1007/978-3-642-71031-5

95.   McDonough William, Braungart M. *Cradle to Cradle: Remaking the Way We Make Things*. 1st ed. North Point Press; 2002.

96.   Simske SJ. *Meta-Algorithmics: Patterns for Robust, Low Cost, High Quality Systems*. 1st ed. Wiley-IEEE Press; 2013:386.

97.   Rosenthal C, Jones N. *Chaos Engineering: System Resiliency in Practice*. First.

98.   Battiston S, Puliga M, Kaushik R, Tasca P, Caldarelli G. DebtRank: too central to fail? Financial networks, the FED and systemic risk. *Sci Rep*. 2012;2:541. doi:10.1038/srep00541

99.   Davidsson Å, Johansson M, Bonander C. Desirable Effects from Disturbance Ecology—A Paradox within Conservation Management. *Sustainability*. 2021;13(13):7049.
       doi:10.3390/su13137049

100.   Beever EA, Prange S, DellaSala DA, eds. *Disturbance Ecology and Biological Diversity: Scale, Context, and Nature*. CRC Press; 2019.
       doi:10.1201/9780429095146

101. Yi C, Jackson N. A review of measuring ecosystem resilience to disturbance. *Environmental Research Letters*. 2021;16(5):053008. doi:10.1088/1748-9326/abdf09

102. Villanueva A, Worrall J. US20160043552A1 - Establishing Communication and Power Sharing Links Between Components of a Distributed Energy System   - Google Patents. 2015. Accessed November 24, 2025. https://patents.google.com/patent/US20160043552A1/en

103. Vann MG. Of rats, rice, and race: the great hanoi rat massacre, an episode in french colonial history. *French Colonial History*. 2003;4(1):191-203. doi:10.1353/fch.2003.0027

104. Royal Commission into the Robodebt Scheme, 2023 RC into the RS 2023. *Australian Royal Commission into the Robodebt Scheme (Final Report)*. Australian Government; 2023.

105. Buchanan R. Wicked Problems in Design Thinking. *Design Issues*. 1992;8(2):5-21. doi:10.2307/1511637

106. Schrunk DG. *The End of Chaos: Quality Laws and the Ascendancy of Democracy*.; 2005.

107. Reinvention Initiatives. Accessed February 6, 2026. https://clintonwhitehouse4.archives.gov/WH/EOP/OVP/initiativ es/reinventing_government.html

108. ARTICLE 2. California Law Revision Commission [8280 - 8298]. Accessed February 6, 2026. https://leginfo.legislature.ca.gov/faces/codes_displayText.xhtml?la wCode=GOV&division=1.&title=2.&part=&chapter=3.5.&article =2.

109. Metzler H, Garcia D. Social drivers and algorithmic mechanisms on digital media. *Perspect Psychol Sci*. 2024;19(5):735-748. doi:10.1177/17456916231185057

110. Germano F, Gómez V, Sobbrio F. *Ranking for Engagement: How Social Media Algorithms Fuel Misinformation and Polarization*.

Department of Economics and Business, Universitat Pompeu Fabra Barcelona; 2025.

111. Arthur WB. Inductive Reasoning and Bounded Rationality. *The American Economic Review*. 1994;84(2):406-411.

112. Schein EH. *Helping: How to Offer, Give, and Receive Help*. 1st ed. Berrett-Koehler; 2009.

113. Whitestone-McCallum Heather, Hunt AE. *Listening with My Heart*. 1st ed. Copernicus; 1996.

114. Gazerani P. The neuroplastic brain: current breakthroughs and emerging frontiers. *Brain Res*. 2025;1858:149643. doi:10.1016/j.brainres.2025.149643

115. Kolb DA. *Experiential Learning*. Prentice-Hall; 1984.

116. Dell'Acqua F, McFowland E, Mollick ER, et al. Navigating the jagged technological frontier: field experimental evidence of the effects of AI on knowledge worker productivity and quality. *SSRN Journal*. 2023. doi:10.2139/ssrn.4573321

117. Forget EL. The Town with No Poverty: The Health Effects of a Canadian Guaranteed Annual Income Field Experiment. *Canadian Public Policy*. 2011;37(3):283-305. doi:10.3138/cpp.37.3.283

118. Ackoff RL. *Creating the Corporate Future: Plan or Be Planned For*. Wiley; 1981.

119. Ackoff RL. *Redesigning the Future: A Systems Approach to Societal Problems*. Wiley; 1974.

120. Block P. *Community: The Structure of Belonging*. Berrett-Koehler Publishers; 2008.

121. Hertzke AD, ed. *The Future of Religious Freedom: Global Challenges*. Oxford University Press; 2012. doi:10.1093/acprof:oso/9780199930890.001.0001

122.   Kahane Adam. *Power and Love: A Theory and Practice of Social Change*. 1st ed. Berrett-Koehler Publishers; 2010.

123.   Bosniak Linda. *The Citizen and the Alien: Dilemmas of Contemporary Membership*. Princeton University Press; 2003.

124.   Meadows DH, Meadows DL, Randers J, Behrens WW. *The Limits to Growth*. Universe Books; 1972.

125.   Goldstein J. Emergence as a Construct: History and Issues. *Emergence*. 1999;1(1):49-72. doi:10.1207/s15327000em0101_4

126.   Sugiyama Y, Fukui M, Kikuchi M, et al. Traffic jams without bottlenecks—experimental evidence for the physical mechanism of the formation of a jam. *New J Phys*. 2008;10(3):033001. doi:10.1088/1367-2630/10/3/033001

127.   Khodaei A. Resiliency-Oriented Microgrid Optimal Scheduling. *IEEE Trans Smart Grid*. 2014;5(4):1584-1591. doi:10.1109/TSG.2014.2311465

128.   Hirsch A, Parag Y, Guerrero J. Microgrids: A review of technologies, key drivers, and outstanding issues. *Renew Sustain Energy Rev*. 2018;90:402-411. doi:10.1016/j.rser.2018.03.040

129.   Office of Electricity Delivery and Energy Reliability. *United States Electricity Industry Primer*. Office of Electricity Delivery and Energy Reliability, U.S. Department of Energy; 2015.

130.   Senate and House of Representatives of the United States of America. *Energy Policy Act of 2005.*; 2005.

131.   Obermeyer Z, Powers B, Vogeli C, Mullainathan S. Dissecting Racial Bias in an Algorithm used to Manage the Health of Populations. *Science*. 2019;366(6464):447-453. doi:10.1126/science.aax2342

132.   Russell SJ, Norvig P. *Artificial Intelligence: A Modern Approach*. Fourth. Pearson; 2020.

133. Vosoughi S, Roy D, Aral S. The spread of true and false news online. *Science*. 2018;359(6380):1146-1151. doi:10.1126/science.aap9559

134. Meadows DH, Wright D. *Thinking in Systems: A Primer*. Chelsea Green Publishing; 2008.

135. Block Peter. *Stewardship: Choosing Service over Self-Interest*. Second edition, revised and expand.

136. Inwood Brad, Gerson LP. *The Epicurus Reader: Selected Writings and Testimonia*.

137. Wheatley MJ. *Turning to One Another: Simple Conversations to Restore Hope to the Future*. Berrett-Koehler Publishers; 2002.

138. Isaacs William. *Dialogue and the Art of Thinking Together: A Pioneering Approach to Communicating in Business and in Life*. 1st ed. Currency Doubleday; 1999.

139. Huxham C, Vangen S. *Managing to Collaborate: The Theory and Practice of Collaborative Advantage*. Routledge; 2005.

140. Bohm D. *On Dialogue*. Routledge; 1996.

Index

U

V

W

Y

About the Author

Dr. Art Villanueva is a systems engineer and artificial intelligence practitioner whose work explores how Complex Adaptive Systems give rise to structure, intelligence, and meaning. His focus lies at the intersection of engineering, organization, and society — examining how large-scale systems evolve and how they can be designed and governed without suppressing the very emergence that makes them resilient.

He is the founder of Phronos, where he applies systems thinking and advanced analytics to complex engineering and organizational challenges. His career spans aerospace and defense, clean technology, and enterprise technology, with leadership and senior engineering roles at General Atomics Aeronautical Systems, Northrop Grumman, and Dell Technologies, as well as entrepreneurial experience founding and serving as Chief Technology Officer of clean energy technology companies.

Dr. Villanueva holds U.S. patents and has published peer-reviewed research in systems engineering, distributed systems, and applied artificial intelligence. He earned degrees in systems engineering and applied mathematics from UCLA, UC San Diego, and Colorado State University, and is recognized as an INCOSE Expert Systems Engineering Professional (ESEP).

Review this Book

If you found *The Gardener and the Machine* valuable, I would deeply appreciate a short review on Amazon. Reviews help independent ideas travel further than algorithms alone allow. You can use the link below or scan the QR code.

https://review-tgm.phronos.com

www.ingramcontent.com/pod-product-compliance
Lightning Source LLC
Chambersburg PA
CBHW050801260726
48660CB00004B/1183